# Pursuing the Horizon

**Also by Russell F. Canan**

*Tough Cases: Judges Tell the Stories of Some of the Hardest Decisions They've Ever Made* (Canan, Mize, Weisberg) (The New Press, 2018)

# Pursuing the Horizon

## Stories of Justice

◊ ◊ ◊ ◊ ◊

Russell F. Canan

Twelve Tables Press

ISBN: 978-1-946074-32-4



Twelve Tables Press
P.O. Box 568
Northport, New York 11768
www.twelvetablespress.com

Printed in the United States of America.

*To Lee, Lukas, and Ethan*

*For Jeff*

*I Saw a Man Pursuing the Horizon*

By Stephen Crane

I saw a man pursuing the horizon;
Round and round they sped.
I was disturbed at this;
I accosted the man.
"It is futile," I said,
"You can never—"
"You lie," he cried,
And ran on.

# Contents

Foreword ........ xi

Welcome to Smithfield ........ 1

Burning at the Wire: The Execution of John Evans ........ 33

Helter Skelter's Son ........ 61

Death on the Ho Chi Minh Trail ........ 129

Rough Justice ........ 175

The Right to Live; The Right to Die ........ 197

The Illusion of Delusion: The Murder of Viola Drath and the Strange Case of General Albrecht Gero Muth ........ 223

Acknowledgments ........ 321

# Foreword

◈ ◈ ◈ ◈ ◈

The pursuit of justice is a noble quest, but the particulars of how it is accomplished are often complicated, difficult and challenging. In this book, Judge Russell F. Canan describes struggles for justice in different contexts and from different perspectives. He examines the availability of justice for the powerless—migrant farm workers and poor people facing the death penalty. He confronts issues of life and death from different perspectives—as an attorney representing two people facing the death penalty, as a judge deciding whether to take a person off life support, and, in a particularly moving chapter, as a brother visiting Vietnam to answer questions about the death of his brother during the war and honor his service and his memory. We learn how as a lawyer he advocated for the condemned, and how as a judge he grappled with difficult issues of fact and law to answer the questions presented by the cases before him. Judge Canan's detailed descriptions of his experiences provide a rare and valuable look into how justice is dispensed in the courts.

Long before he became a lawyer and a judge, Judge Canan served as a health aide and saw the need for the rule of law and the consequences of its absence. In "Welcome to Smithfield" he describes what he aptly calls "twentieth century slavery"—the brutal abuse of migrant farmworkers in North Carolina in 1972. The workers were not allowed to leave the farms where they worked because of the debts they owed. This condition—called peonage—has been illegal since 1867 and is punishable by up to five years in prison. But no one enforced the law. In addition, some of the workers were brutally beaten with tire chains, leaving a pattern of scars across their backs. These were serious crimes—aggravated assaults—that should have been prosecuted, but were not. Judge Canan and a dynamic nun, Sister Joseph Beatrice, courageously recorded accounts of the abuse and turned them over to the governor and the Department of Justice, but no charges were filed. Justice required attorneys who would enforce the law, but local officials were unwilling and federal officials were indifferent. The best that could be done was getting some of the workers to their homes and out of harm's way.

As a criminal defense lawyer, Judge Canan took on the most challenging cases, including capital cases. He describes two cases at each end of the process of inflicting the death penalty—one at the start, "Helter Skelter's Son," when a Maryland jury decided whether to sentence a man convicted of murder to the death penalty or life imprisonment; the other is at the end, "Burning at the Wire: The Execution of John Evans," when Alabama electrocuted John Evans for killing a man in a pawnshop robbery.

John Evans was executed in 1983 as Alabama and the rest of the country were resuming the death penalty after a hiatus of ten years in the country and eighteen in Alabama. The Supreme Court ruled in 1972 that the death penalty was unconstitutional because it was imposed in an arbitrary and haphazard manner. The justices in the majority could discern no reason why some people were sentenced to death when many others who committed similar or even more heinous crimes were not. As one of the justices said, being sentenced to death was like being struck by lightning. Many people thought that was the end of the death penalty in America. But just four years later, the Court held that it could be carried out so long as states complied with certain procedures, including conducting a separate phase of the trial for sentencing and requiring the jury to consider factors to identify those deserving of the death penalty—the worst of the worst.

The first execution in each state following the Court's ruling attracted an immense political and media attention. It was a time when politicians were declaring a war on crime, calling for "law and order," and competing with each other to show that they were the toughest on crime. Alabama's attorney general, a demagogue, led the charge in demanding that Evans be executed. The media covered every aspect of the case.

What little hope Evans had of avoiding execution was a commutation from Governor George Wallace. The attorney general made it clear that there were no political benefits to commuting the sentence—the governor would be subject to blistering attacks if he commuted the sentence. But Wallace was near the end of his political career. He was in his fourth and final term as governor. He had apologized to African Americans for his past actions as a segregationist. He seemed to be interested in what Evans' family and pastor had to say about him and why his life should be spared. What does one say to a governor who has the power of life and death? Defense counsel Canan describes his plea for life along with the pleas by Mr. Evans, his family and his pastor, and the catastrophic botched execution in Alabama's electric chair that followed.

The question in the Maryland trial was what does one tell *a jury* that decides between life and death. Maryland had responded to the Supreme Court's concern about arbitrariness by requiring that the jury consider evidence in aggravation that supported the death penalty and any evidence in mitigation—circumstances about the defendant that might be a reason to reject the death penalty. Then the jury is to answer an unanswerable question—is this person so beyond redemption that he should be eliminated from the human community? How does a lawyer defending the person answer that question? What information about the crime and about the client does the lawyer give the jury to help it answer the question? It starts with an investigation into the life and background of the person and an attempt to understand how life experiences, intellectual development and brain function influence judgment and behavior.

Richard Mason was facing a jury for a second sentencing trial. The first jury sentenced him to death, but the Supreme Court set aside that sentence. Through the eyes of a defense counsel, Canan tells us about "two shattered men" who had suffered abuse and trauma throughout their lives and how they ended up in a cell together where one, Mason, stabbed the other to death. It was not hard to understand why the first jury sentenced him to death. Mason, who was just two years into a thirty-year sentence for another murder, stabbed the victim forty-five times, just as he promised to do in a letter to the warden, and wrote "Helter Skelter's Son" in the victim's blood on the wall of the cell. The death penalty is for the "worst of the worst" and Mason certainly seemed to fit that description. What could possibly explain what Mason did? What could a defense lawyer tell a jury to convince it to spare Mason's life?

It was an enormous task to examine every aspect of the life of Richard Mason and the murder that he committed. It would not have been done in many of the states that impose most of the death sentences in the United States. In those states, people who cannot afford a lawyer are often assigned lawyers who lack the competence to handle a capital case and the resources for investigation and experts. However, the Maryland Public Defender had a special death penalty unit that insured that any capital cases in that state were tried with the care appropriate for a decision of life and death. The unit made sure that Mason was represented by two experienced death penalty lawyers, Canan and Jerry Fisher, who also became a judge. The Public Defender also provided them with resources that enabled them to conduct an exhaustive investigation, and consult with and present leading experts in the fields of neurology, psychiatry, and social work. They found that even in a most difficult case of a man who had committed a murder while serving a sentence for murder, there was a compelling story to be told.

Judge Canan undertook a different investigation in "Death on the Ho Chi Minh Trail," to learn about the death of his brother, Jeff, who joined the Army at age seventeen and volunteered to serve in the infantry in Vietnam. He was killed in a combat operation eight months after arriving there. For many years, the circumstances of his death were a mystery to Judge Canan and his family. But thirty-four years later Judge Canan's sister discovered a picture of their brother and other information on the internet. This led to Judge Canan connecting with a soldier who had served with his brother. And a few years later Judge Canan visited Vietnam at the invitation of its judiciary to speak on the rule of law at programs in Hanoi and Ho Chi Minh City. This provided an opportunity for Judge Canan, his wife and two sons to visit the site of his brother's death to honor and respect his memory. In describing this remarkable journey, Judge Canan reflects on the war, the sacrifices, the protests, and questions of forgiveness, redemption and reconciliation.

It is not surprising that Judge Canan, who liked being the catcher when he played baseball growing up because he could call the pitches and direct the players on the field, would find fulfillment in being a judge presiding over cases in a courtroom. But, like catching, judging is not for the faint of heart. Judges must make very difficult decisions and there is no avoiding them. Unlike the attorney who can decide what cases to take, a judge must take whatever case is assigned and bring about a just resolution. Sometimes there is no good answer, and sometimes there is not as much information as one would like, but a decision is required. No case is more difficult than deciding issues of life and death for a person who is incapable of making that decision. In "Right to Live; Right to Die," Judge Canan was called upon to decide whether to remove life support from a person who had suffered massive brain damage and was left in a persistent vegetative state, lacking cognitive function. An additional layer of difficulty and complexity was added when family members disagreed –some wanted to remove life support and others wanted to maintain it. The judge must determine what the law requires and then follow it regardless of any personal preferences. Judge Canan describes how he determined the legal principles that applied, how he protected the interests of everyone involved, and how he applied those principles in deciding the question. It is a lesson in the application of the rule of law.

But what does a judge do when it looks like following the law may lead to an unjust outcome? Not all disputes are resolved by judges. Juries decide some cases and the overwhelming majority of cases are settled—plea bargains in criminal cases where the prosecution and defense agree, and settlements in civil cases where the parties agree to a resolution of the case. In "Rough Justice," Judge Canan tells us about a case committed to a deliberating jury that appeared to be headed toward a miscarriage of justice. It looked like the jury was going to find an innocent person guilty of a crime that required a minimum sentence of five years in prison. If it did, Judge Canan's hands would be tied—no matter what he thought about the crime or the fact that the person had no criminal record, he would be required to impose a sentence of at least five years in prison. What does a judge do in this situation? Judge Canan describes the ethical and legal issues he faced in dealing with the dilemma.

Another difficult case was presented in "The Illusion of Delusion: The Murder of Viola Drath and the Strange Case of General Albrect Gero Muth," by the bizarre and baffling behavior of a man who was accused of murdering his wife, a prominent writer, who was ninety-one years old and forty-four years older than him. He claimed to be a general in the Iraqi army and more than a few people believed that he was. The case presented a number of difficult issues: whether the man had genuine delusions because of a mental disorder or whether he was an accomplished con artist, psychopath, and master manipulator; whether he could understand the court proceedings and cooperate with his lawyers; whether he could discharge his lawyers and represent himself; and, not insignificantly, whether he was guilty of the crime. The mental health experts reached different opinions about his mental condition. Judge Canan conducted an eight-day hearing before deciding the questions about the man's mental conditions and his ability to understand the proceedings be tried. But not long after those rulings, the man complicated things further by going on a hunger strike. This presented yet another issue: how to conduct a trial when the man's starvation brought him so close to death that he could not be transported from the jail to the courtroom. These legal and practical challenges required Judge Canan's patience, creativity and perseverance. In this case and throughout the book, Judge Canan tells us about the role of the lawyers on each side. We see the importance of good lawyers on both sides of a case if justice is to be done.

We learn from these chapters that the pursuit of justice must be continuous and relentless; for we never reach justice as a final destination. It is a continuing and evolving process as lawyers, judges, jurors, law enforcement officers, investigators, experts and others involved in the legal system confront new controversies with complicated facts and complex issues. One case may require them to straddle the thin and precarious line between life and death. Another may ask them to fathom the working of the mind. Another may ask them to make sense of senseless violence. Yet another may present a new legal question that has not been previously answered. As we will see, there may be several issues of fact and law that must be resolved before reaching the main dispute in a case. Judge Canan tells us how he and others wrestle with what often seem like impossible questions in the pursuit of what justice can be obtained for each case.

Stephen B. Bright
August 26, 2020
Former Director of the Southern Center for Human Rights
and Professor at Yale and Georgetown law schools

# Pursuing the Horizon

# Welcome to Smithfield

Driving down U.S. 70 into a rural North Carolina town to start my first job after college, it could not be missed. The billboard sign was over a hundred feet in the air. Against a background of bright red, a Klansman in a white robe and conical hat sat on top of a white horse. The horse had its two front legs kicked up high in the air, ready to ride across the land. The Klansman held a burning cross in his left hand and the reins in his right.

Across the top of the sign in large capital letters read:

HELP FIGHT COMMUNISM & INTERGRATION

I couldn't help but notice that INTERGRATION was misspelled.

Next to the Klansman upon his horse, in even larger caps:

JOIN & SUPPORT
UNITED KLANS
of AMERICA Inc.

Finally, at the bottom of the sign:

KKKK WELCOMES YOU TO SMITHFIELD

I stared again at the Klansman atop the horse, legs kicking in the air. My mind drifted to early Saturday mornings of my childhood, watching TV with my older brother Jeff. Our favorite program was *The Lone Ranger*. The show opened with the masked man on his white stallion racing up a mountain to the stirring "William Tell Overture." Upon reaching the top, the Lone Ranger yanked the reins and the white horse kicked his two front legs, while he yelled, "Hi Ho Silver Away" and galloped down the mountain to do justice.

Now I watched a hooded Klansman in the summer of 1972 in Smithfield, North Carolina. Damn, this is serious. The late sixties and early seventies were tough and violent times. The senseless war in Vietnam still raged on. Four students were killed at a protest of the war at Kent State University in Ohio. The memories of the violence and sacrifices of the Civil Rights Movement were fresh and searing: the Selma and Montgomery marches; the Klan's murders of civil rights workers James Chaney, Andrew Goodman, and Michael Schwerner, with some of the Klansmen serving in the local police department;

and the assassinations of Dr. Martin Luther King Jr. and Bobby Kennedy.

I wanted to take a photograph of the sign but was afraid someone would see me. And I stood out. I drove an old, used car with New York tags. Just out of college, twenty-two years old and with long hair, I was there to work and not stir things up. I drove on and found my way to the Johnston County Health Department.

The East Coast Migrant Health Project was a grantee from the then United States Department of Health, Education, and Welfare. It was run by a consortium of Catholic nuns from a very small office in Washington, D.C., with teams of personnel spread up and down the East Coast. Most of the groups were nuns who had been nurses in their local schools and hospitals. Teams of two to four were assigned to the county health department to provide health care services to the seasonal migrant farmworkers who worked the fields and then moved on. My title was health education aide and I was to assist the nurse assigned to Johnston County.

On the East Coast many farms were cultivated by migrant farmworkers who spent the winter in small towns in central Florida and then traveled north in the spring to work the fields. They called it "working the season." The season was, in reality, twentieth century slavery. Mostly black farmworkers joined crews led by a crew boss. The crew boss used old buses and trucks to transport the migrants to local farms up north. They stayed in ramshackle huts and dorms on the farms, usually without running water or screens. The crew boss charged the workers for food, liquor, cigarettes, and lodging. Before long the workers were in debt and not free to leave. First of all, without money, there really was no place to go other than hitchhiking one's way out of town. Crew bosses were known to sic dogs after escapees and track them down. Once captured, they were often beaten. I heard that every now and then the U.S. Department of Justice would get involved, but they were very hard cases to investigate, as witnesses were either unwilling to cooperate or had moved on and were nearly impossible to locate.

As I walked into the health department building I was still in a bit of shock. I knew enough to know that I didn't really understand much about the Klan and what I was getting myself into. That would have to wait until later when I learned the ropes of my new town and new job. Luckily, everyone in the health department was very cordial and welcoming. The director was particularly interested in having help serving the migrant population since there was a great need and few resources. As we were chatting a woman in her early sixties or so walked in. She wore a nun's veil on her head, but was otherwise in layperson's clothes.

"So you're the young man they sent to help me?" she said. Her eyes twinkled and she had a great smile.

"I'm Sister Joseph Beatrice, but you can call me Jo B."

I smiled back, introduced myself and we shook hands. I didn't know it then, but I had just entered one of the great friendships of my life.

Sister Jo B was a woman to be reckoned with; an unstoppable force of energy, passion, and toughness. Friendly and compassionate most of the time, she also took no guff and was a real fighter. She was raised in Kentucky in a prosperous Catholic family. During high school she felt a calling to serve God and wanted to enter into a sisterhood community. Her parents prevailed upon her to get a college education first, saying that would only help her and the church in the future while giving her time to reflect on this momentous decision.

Sister Jo B told me a number of times that "My daddy really wanted the best for me, and if that was the path I felt I had to follow, he would respect that. But he also wanted grandbabies!"

A dutiful daughter, she went off to college to study nursing. By her senior year, while she was having too much innocent fun with the boys, she realized that her commitment to serve God was so deep that she would enter the sisterhood upon graduation.

She entered the novitiate with the Sisters of Charity of Nazareth in Bardstown, Kentucky. All aspects of religious life—prayer, study, and sisterhood—moved and inspired her. When taking her final vows as a Sister of Charity, she chose the name Joseph Beatrice, after the two Catholic Saints who spoke to her. Her career as a nurse took off at schools and clinics as she settled into a peaceful life at Nazareth. She then saw a documentary on TV about migrant farmworkers and their horrible work and health conditions. Sister Jo B knew there was more she could do—and she did. She did some research and found the East Coast Project, volunteered, and was first assigned to Apopka, Florida, and now Smithfield.

Sister Jo B, the director, and I sat down and were briefed on farming and farmworkers in Johnston County. Although soybeans, vegetables, and potatoes were plentiful, tobacco was king and ranked high in production in the county and the state.

Cropping tobacco was a hard, mean business. Tobacco ripened in the heart of the summer and was picked by starting at the bottom of the plant. Each following week a migrant would pull another section higher up in the plant. The farmworker would have to walk down tobacco rows in the early morning hours and again later in the afternoon during the hottest time of the day, stooping over to take the buds off the plant by hand to allow it to fully grow. Later in the season the farmworker would pull the plant from the bottom up to complete the cropping.

The worker also had to watch out for worms that ate the plant, which they were required to squish and kill. The pulled plant was then carried to a sled and—either by mule or tractor—taken to a barn to be cured. Although mechanization was gradually eliminating some of the need for harsh manual labor in the tobacco fields, much of modern farming had not yet come to Smithfield.

Health care for the migrants was almost non-existent. Every now and then a migrant would be dropped off at the emergency room after suffering a serious accident or illness.

Our job was to go out to the camps and provide basic services such as dispensing over-the-counter medicine, cleaning wounds, and transporting workers to a doctor's office or a hospital, if necessary. We were also asked to do some preventative medicine such as taking tuberculosis ("TB") tests, as well as checking up on basic sanitation in the camps. Finally, we were to try and recruit some local doctors and ask them to be available to treat farmworkers if we took them to their offices. Because of federal money there would be compensation, not much, but not insignificant either. The director said that would probably be the hardest part of the job, as the local doctors would likely not be responsive. Left unsaid was that the migrant farmworkers were poor and black and not desired patients.

Sister Jo B had been in Smithfield for a few weeks and offered to show me around some of the camps. Although I was listed as a health aide, I had very little training and I was there to assist her. Luckily for me, when we drove to the camps I was usually behind the wheel of my car. When she drove it was hang-on-to-your-hats time as she would fly down empty rural roads, curves and all. Soon I was calling her the Flying Nun, a reference to a popular TV show, featuring a young Sally Field. Sister Jo B loved her new name.

The camps were located on farms that were, for the most part, miles away from Smithfield. When we arrived at the first camp it was mostly empty, as the workers were in the fields.

We met with the crew boss's wife, Sheila, who was cooking dinner. She was friendly enough and Sister Jo B appeared to have a good relationship with her. Sheila said one of the workers was in the bunkhouse and not feeling well, but she was sure it was nothing.

Sister Jo B said, "Well, let me take a look anyway."

Sheila said, "It's not necessary. It's nothing, and I can take care of him."

Sister Jo B said, "That's okay. No bother. I'll take a look just in case."

"Sister, I told you I take care of the men, and he's going to be fine," Sheila said.

"Ma'am," said Sister Jo B, "I'm getting paid to nurse these men, and it's my job." With that she walked away at a brisk pace toward the dormitory. I froze until she turned around and looked at me. "Well come along, then. Don't just stand there. I need your help."

We walked into a windowless, cement-block dormitory, flies buzzing, insufferably hot and moist, reeking of feces and urine from the outhouse in back. The dorm slept about thirty and had old cots with single sheets and no pillows. The farmworker laid on a cot, softly moaning. He wore shorts, and a sleeveless, red T-shirt with a picture of a bottle of Coca-Cola and the words "Drink Coke." He looked to be around twenty or so.

Sister Jo B knelt down beside him and put a gentle hand on his head.

"You're burning up son," she said. "What's your name?"

He muttered, "Joey." He moaned some more, tried to stifle a cough, and looked up at her. He tried to talk but his soft words just drifted off. He coughed again.

Sister Jo B looked at me. "We're taking this man to the hospital. He's probably got pneumonia. Here, take my keys and pull the car around. The quicker, the better."

I grabbed the keys and went for her car. As I was getting in the car, Sheila approached.

"Where's the Sister?" she asked.

"She's with Joey. We're taking him to the hospital."

Sheila put her hand on my shoulder, her eyes narrowed, her fists clenched. I was worried she was going to come after me. Instead, she lowered her voice in a threatening way and said, "I told her I was taking care of him!" She stormed off to the dormitory.

I got in the car and drove around to the rear of the bunkhouse. As I entered the dormitory, Sister Jo B sat on the cot with Joey, who slumped on her shoulder, looking faint. She motioned for me to go around the other side.

"Put your arm underneath his shoulder. When I say three, we'll both lift him up."

Sheila entered the bunkhouse. She was still hot.

"Sister—I told you I was taking care of this man, and you got no business taking him off my husband's property."

Sister Jo B scrunched her nose and looked Sheila in the eyes. "Ma'am, this man may be dying of pneumonia, and you don't think I'm just going to let him lie here, do you? We're taking him to the hospital, and when he's better we'll take him back."

Sheila stormed off.

Looking over at me, Sister Jo B commanded, "Okay, one, two, three. Lift."

Gradually pulling Joey up, we steadied him on his feet and slowly walked him to the car.

"Hold him with both arms under the shoulders. I'll open the door."

I held him as Sister Jo B opened the door. She then directed me to gently put him in the car.

"Watch his head."

She helped me lay him down on the back seat. Sister Jo B removed her sweater and tenderly placed it underneath Joey's head. He closed his eyes and went to sleep.

We drove along country roads to the nearest hospital, about fifteen miles away.

Sister Jo B was quiet for most of the ride. Finally, she turned to me.

"They treat their own people like slaves, you know."

She shook her head in disgust.

I didn't know what to say. The image of the Klan sign still haunted me.

When we got to the hospital she said, "Look for the emergency room entrance."

I pulled up to a circular driveway that had an ambulance parked outside.

"Stay here with Joey," she said. "I'll get him admitted. It might take some doing."

Joey hadn't said a word the whole time. He had coughed a few times the first few minutes, but then nothing the entire ride.

"Joey, are you okay?" I asked.

He didn't say anything. I was afraid he might be dead, but then he coughed again. *What's taking so long*, I wondered.

It must have been a half hour, maybe longer until two orderlies walked up with a stretcher. They took Joey into the hospital. I followed them inside.

At a distance, I saw Sister Jo B in a lively discussion with two guys in suits who looked like hospital officials. Their faces had the look of tired resignation, as one of them raised his hands outward in a "what do you want me to do, lady?" gesture. Sister Jo B cracked a winsome smile and nodded her head in their direction.

"Bless you," she said and turned to leave.

She walked straight over to me and motioned for me to turn around and head out of the door. As we walked outside, she whispered to me, "Let's skedaddle before they change their minds."

The rest of the week was a blur. While I looked for a short-term lease on an apartment, I stayed in a rundown local motel with a wall air conditioner that made a lot of noise but very little cool air. The small swimming pool had no water. "Out for repairs," a sign said.

Some nights Sister Jo B and I would go to the local Howard Johnson's right off Highway 95. She would regale me with stories from her days at the convent.

She loved the times the community had "music night" when the young novitiates would sing songs for the entire sisterhood.

Sister Jo B said, "Well, me and Sister Joan and Sister Cecilia rehearsed and rehearsed. Cecilia was a darn good piano player, and Joan and I can carry a tune. When music night came along we belted out "The Surrey with the Fringe on Top," from the Broadway play *Oklahoma*.

All of a sudden, Sister Jo B snuck a look around and saw that Ho Jo's was pretty empty and started singing the Broadway tune:

*Chicks and ducks and geese better scurry*
*When I take you out in the surrey,*
*When I take you out in the surrey with the fringe on top!*
*Watch that fringe and see how it flutters*
*When I drive them high steppin' strutters.*
*Nosey pokes'll peek thru' their shutters, and their eyes will pop!*
*The wheels are yeller. The upholstery's brown,*
*The dashboard's genuine leather,*
*With isinglass curtains y' can roll right down*
*In case there's a change in the weather.*
*Two bright sidelights winkin' and blinkin',*
*Ain't no finer rig, I'm a-thinkin'.*

*You can keep your rig if you're thinkin' 'at I'd keep to swap*
*Fer that shiny, little surrey with the fringe on the top!*

She broke out in laughter when she finished and I clapped loudly. "Wellsiree," she said and giggled some more. "Mother took us to the side afterwards and told us we had just sung 'a courtin' song and didn't think it was appropriate. Mother wasn't really too mad at us and even smiled some, but we were embarrassed. That was the last 'a courtin' song we sang for the sisters!"

She nodded her head emphatically with a twinkle in her eyes and smiled while she dug into her peppermint twizzle-stick ice cream as I slurped my chocolate shake.

I grew up in the New York City area and suburbs, roughly divided between Jews, Italians, and Irish, and had seen many priests and nuns at various events, but I had never met or talked to a nun before.

The days were full. Sister Jo B and I would drive out to the camps around lunchtime and in the early evenings, when the workers were likely to be there and not in the fields. Our main job was to test for tuberculosis, which was a severe threat in the camps. As she examined workers, Sister Jo B would swab their inner forearms with alcohol and then inject the area with a solution. If the worker had been exposed to TB bacteria, the skin would develop a red bump in a few days. We would return later and measure the bump with a ruler. If the test proved positive, we would take the worker to a hospital for further tests.

Taking the test in the first place, however, was no mean feat. Many of the workers were afraid of needles, and could not remember when, or if, they had ever been injected. Although these were tough men and had taken much abuse in their lives, their fear of the needle was intense.

One worker, Jonah, was in his forties, strong, and well-muscled. He wanted no part of any needle.

"Sir, this little test can save your life. It will just pinch for a little second, and it will be over. Won't even hurt, I promise," Sister Jo B said, her face beaming.

"Ma'am, thanks all the same, but I've been doing just fine without no needles," he replied.

"Now, Sir, I'm a registered nurse and know what I'm doing. Living here in this place can get not just you but all the folks sick with TB. It's contagious you know. You don't want TB, and we don't want it to spread. I promise it won't hurt. Just a little pinch." She grinned and nodded her head.

"Now, Ma'am, I don't want to be rude, but thanks all the same," he said.

Sister Jo B did not give up.

"Now look, Sir, I've tried to tell you this ain't gonna hurt but one little pinch and I'll leave you alone." She grabbed his forearm and pinched it hard.

"Now come on honey," she said gently. "Did that hurt?"

He looked at me for some male support, I guess.

I shrugged my shoulders as if to say, listen to the woman and we'll be done already.

"Okay, already," he said. Turning his face away from Sister Jo B and closing his eyes, he stood still as she swabbed and poked him before he knew what happened.

On the weekends I would walk over to the local library, a small, red-brick building, to learn more about Smithfield and the Klan. As I scanned through local newspapers, books, and pamphlets, I read several articles about Smithfield's favorite daughter—glamorous actress Ava Gardner, who grew up on a tobacco farm. The Gardner family was still active in the tobacco business.

Smithfield was the seat of Johnston County, a very rural area where tobacco farms were the main cash crop. During the Civil War, the Smithfield area stood in the way of General William Tecumseh Sherman's march through the South. The Battle of Bentonville, twenty miles to the south of Smithfield, was the last major battle of the Civil War, where the Confederates vainly attempted to halt Sherman's drive. Standing on the steps of Smithfield's county courthouse, Sherman announced Lee's surrender at Appomattox.

I didn't think the library would have much, if any, information on the Klan. But it did. The Klan had been formed by former Confederate soldiers after the Civil War, during the Reconstruction Era, as a secret society bent on suppressing the newly freed slaves. They relied on terror, intimidation, and lynchings. The white supremacy movement initially focused mainly on the newly freed blacks, some of whom were trying to enter Republican Party politics. Thousands were killed and injured throughout the South, oftentimes in the lead-up to elections. The Klan later went on to spew its hatred and violence against Jews, Catholics, and immigrants. It seemed like the Klan pretty much faded away after World War II but made a comeback as an attempt to counter the desegregation of the South in the 1950s and 1960s.

The name Ku Klux Klan itself was mysterious. The most common theory was that the name came from a Greek word, "Kuklos" or circle, coupled with clan. Apparently, some Klansmen themselves said it meant "White Racial Brotherhood." They wore white robes, masks, and conical hats, not only to hide their faces to attend public demonstrations without risk, but also to give the illusion of ghosts from a glorious past. The burning cross was used to proclaim their faith and intimidate, especially at night.

The folks that worked at Smithfield's Health Department were not shy about talking about the local Klan billboard. The sign was a clear embarrassment to them, and they stressed that the Klan did not represent the people of Johnston County. I learned the sign had been built about five years earlier and had originally been placed at street level. After a number of protests from several groups and individuals, one night someone or some group tore down the sign and vandalized it. The Klan replaced the original sign, this time up 100 feet in the air, where it now stood.

I asked around and rented a small, two-room cottage behind a large, white clapboard house in town. The rent was cheap, and the landlady was happy to lease it for three months.

My life in Smithfield was quiet. After work I would usually read on the cottage's porch, maybe play some guitar, and ended the night with a short walk around the two main streets in town. Every now and then I might meet Sister Jo B at Ho Jo's for peppermint twizzlestick ice cream and chocolate shakes.

One day after work I saw an old Cutlass Oldsmobile with New York tags parked outside the house with a Syracuse University sticker on the bumper. I had just graduated from SU and was amazed at the coincidence. A few days later, arriving home from work, I pulled up to my cottage and saw a young man with a ponytail and woman roughly my age, get out of the Syracuse University bumper-stickered car. I walked over and introduced myself.

They told me they lived on the top floor of the white house in front of my cottage. Very quickly we learned that we all had just graduated Syracuse University, comparing notes on where we had lived on campus, and who we knew in common. Richard was an architect and working in a very small firm in town. Susan was doing bookkeeping for a local business. We laughed and shook our heads at the chances of the three of us ending up in Smithfield just after college, let alone living on the same property.

They graciously invited me to their apartment many nights for dinner and we became fast friends. Richard and Susan liked to cook together and shared smoking cigarettes, taking a drag or two a piece, passing it back and forth in an effort to cut down. Their wonderful home cooking was a delight, since my usual diet of pasta with Ragu sauce or junk food was getting old.

It was the summer of Bobby Fischer playing Boris Spasky for the world chess championship in Reykjavik, Iceland. Many nights Richard and I would play chess, sometimes replaying the last Fischer/Spasky match. We did more laughing than playing and loved listening to scratchy Bob Dylan records. Richard called himself a "lo-fi" guy rather than a "hi-fi" guy, since he didn't like the clean, pristine sound of a recently purchased LP. He liked his sound rough and choppy, like you were listening to live music with creaky speakers.

Some nights we'd walk over to the only bar in town, sip a beer, listen to the juke box, and play some pool. It was a small, friendly place with a red, neon sign. They played their music loud, and when "Long Cool Woman in a Red Dress" by the Hollies came on, Susan got us up dancing together.

At work, Sister Jo B and I spent a good deal of time trying to recruit general practice doctors to care for the farmworkers. It was a short season, and there were not many doctors in this rural town, so we had to move fast. Federal funds were available to pay for medical services so we were not asking for free labor. We would try and set up an appointment in advance and visit the doctors in their offices.

We were told some doctors did not treat Blacks at all, so not to bother. The remaining doctors treated both races, but, for the most part, old customs were still alive. There were several offices with a "Colored Waiting Room" sign. In some offices no sign was necessary, but the waiting rooms were

segregated nonetheless. Even with money to offer, it was a hard sell, and we weren't very successful. The best we could do was to secure promises from some doctors to meet patients at the health department or the hospital. It was third-class treatment, to be sure, but it was certainly better than nothing.

Sister Jo B taught me how to properly clean and change bandages, read TB tests, take basic medical histories, and recognize signs of serious illnesses. This basic training allowed us to split up and go to many more camps. If I saw someone who I thought needed more attention, I would join up with Sister Jo B at the health department, and we would go back out to the camp together. The crew bosses did not like our coming around as much as we did, but for the most part did not prevent us from doing our work. It was on one of these routine visits, however, that I met Luther Brown.

The camp seemed quiet and deserted the day I drove in on a red dirt road. As usual, I stopped by to see Clarence, the crew boss, in his cabin, but no one was there. A courtesy call was expected and I didn't want to ruffle any feathers.

I walked around the camp, and in one of the side tin huts that slept four or five men, I saw a small white guy with large black glasses, wearing only a white T-shirt and underpants, lying still in bed. His eyes were open and he was staring at the ceiling. Our eyes locked in and he took a slow, deep breath.

"Are you with that Catholic nun?" he asked, his voice low, breath shallow.

I nodded. "Are you okay?"

"They busted my ribs the other night and won't take me in. I can't hardly move. I'm really hurting, mister."

"Who busted your ribs?"

"Clarence and Doc. I was walking down to the store and they came up on me and pulled out them chains. Said I was trying to get away. I told them I just trying to get to the store and get some cigarettes. They said, 'Ain't no store around, and you can get your damn cigarettes from Miss Pearl.'"

He stopped speaking, appearing to let the pain settle down before going on.

"They brung out them tire chains and started whipping me in the chest and carried me back here. I can't barely move, mister."

My first thought was to tell him to hang in there, and I would go get Sister Jo B, and we would be back later to bring him to a hospital. But that might take hours, and he was in pain. I also wasn't sure if moving him with injured ribs was the right thing to do, but I didn't like the idea of having to negotiate with Clarence and his people when they returned several hours later.

"What's your name, sir?" I asked.

"I'm Luther."

"Luther, if I help you, can you make it to the car?"

"Yes, sir. I'll sure try."

I pulled the car as close as I could and helped Luther into the back seat where he lay down. I drove away slowly, not wanting to hit any bumps on the dirt road. Having gotten Luther safely out of camp, I quickly realized I was in over my head, and had no clue how to deal with hospital administrators. This was a job for Sister Jo B. Stopping along the road at a grocery store, I called the health department and breathed a sigh of relief when I heard her voice. We agreed to meet at the hospital. By the time we got there, Sister Jo B had worked her magic and admission to the ER was easy.

The next day we went to visit Luther at the hospital. Three of his ribs had indeed been broken. The doctors taped his ribs and gave him some medication to ease the pain. The ribs would heal, but Luther understood nothing would ease going back to Clarence's camp.

Sister Jo B took charge. "Sir, you don't have to go back if you don't want to. It's that simple."

"Sister," he said, "you don't understand. I owe Clarence money. I'm surprised he ain't here right now."

"Luther, Clarence can't hold you like a slave. We'll send you on a bus to wherever you want to go."

"You can do that?" he said.

"You bet your business we can," Sister Jo B said to him and winked at me.

I didn't know we could do that, either.

Luther had a niece in Dauphin Island, Alabama, and thought she would help him out. He said Dauphin Island was near Mobile, and once he got there he could take a ferry to the island. Sister Jo B asked me to go down to the bus station and investigate how to get Luther to Mobile.

Before I left, Sister Jo B turned to Luther.

"Luther, would you be willing to speak into a tape recorder and tell your story? I don't know what we would do with the tape exactly, but maybe give it to the Sheriff's department or even to the FBI."

Luther paused and scratched his bald head.

"Dang it," he said, "I'll do it. But please wait till I'm outta here before you give it to someone."

I drove down to the Greyhound station and found out that getting to Mobile was easier than I thought. A bus to Raleigh left at 4:00 p.m., and after a few hours layover, an overnight bus got you to Mobile. On the way back to the hospital I stopped by my apartment and grabbed my cassette tape recorder. Within an hour I was back at the hospital. Luther slept in a chair, eyes closed and resting. Sister Jo B sat next to him.

"Sister, we can get him on the four o'clock to Raleigh; he changes buses in Raleigh and catches a direct bus to Mobile. From there, I guess he's on his own."

Sister Jo B smiled. "The Lord works in mysterious ways! I also have a few dollars for the bus and some walking money."

"Luther, honey," she said, "are you ready?"

He opened his eyes and smiled.

"Shoot, let's go." He spoke into the tape recorder.

"I used to work for as big a company as is, E.D. Saul and Sons Construction in Columbia, South Carolina. Making dern good money. I decided I wanted to go down to Florida and went to driving a tractor for Naples Fruit and Vegetable Company. I worked for them three years. Me and one of the foremans had a disagreement, and I went to Immokalee to work day labor. That's where I met Clarence. He asked me to work the season with him and promised me big things."

"He told me we were going in cucumbers and peppers. He didn't mention nothin' about potatoes, but after we got here, we got to pulling potato draws. He told me, 'I'm giving $1.50 a box.' I asked him how big a box, and he said about the size of an orange crate. Well, that's true, but when I got here he had cut them to $1.00 a box. Well, it don't make any difference how many you pick, you weren't ever going to pick enough to pay for your bill. When I first come up here, they did, they fed us good, but they got to where they don't feed worth a dern. Charge $1.25 for half pint of bootleg whiskey. Worst camp I ever been on. No paperwork, no Social Security, no nothing."

We asked him about other beatings in the camp. He told us if we could catch up with them, we should talk to Big Shorty, Diane, and Russell. Also Benjamin. They had all been beaten with chains because they either complained or wanted to leave. They were still at Clarence's camp.

After we finished the taping, Sister Jo B looked Luther in the eye.

"Luther, honey, we're going to put you on the four o'clock bus. You change the bus in Raleigh, and it takes you all the way to Mobile. Please write down your niece's address. I don't know what's going to happen with your tape, but we may go to the police or the FBI. You sure that's okay with you?"

"Sister, that's just fine. I ain't ever going to work the season if I can help it. Too much pain. Can't live like that."

Luther took a two-hour nap, and then it was time to leave. Sister Jo B helped with the discharge, an orderly put him in a wheelchair, and we were good to go.

As we walked down the hospital hallways, I started to get nervous. What would we do if we saw Clarence and Doc outside? I looked around but didn't see any security.

As if she read my mind, when we reached the front entrance, Sister Jo B turned to us and said.

"Why don't you wait inside here for a spell. I'm going outside and make sure there's no trouble out there."

She went through the front door and disappeared. Quickly, she returned.

"Coast is clear," she said with a grin. "Let's skedaddle."

Several weeks later we received a letter, postmarked Dauphin Island, Alabama. Inside the envelope was a postcard showing a picture of a motel with a sign reading "BAY SIDE Motor Court Apartments." In an uneven hand was a short note:

> *Dear frens i rite you to let you no I got home fine thanks to you all i am sending you a card showing you where I live an work i can not never thank you all a nuff Love Luther*

One morning a few days later, Sister Jo B came rushing into the health department out of breath.

"Whee, I gotta slow down," she said as she sat down in our little office.

"I was up at Willie Ray Singleton's camp last evening, and who do I meet? Big Shorty, Diane, and Russell. Somehow they all switched over to Willie Ray's camp and are really happy and feel they are being treated right. They're all willing to talk into the tape recorder."

"Sister, what are we going to do with the tapes if they do talk?" I asked.

"Go right to the Governor of the State of North Carolina. We can't just sit here and do nothing. They treat these simple people, white and black, just like slaves." She nodded her head.

"Do you think Willie Ray is okay with us doing this in his camp? He's a crew boss too, a good one, but just the same. Why would he want to help us?" I said.

"Willie Ray's wife, Bertha, is just mad as can be about all this violence. Says it doesn't have to be like this. She's a strong Christian woman and willing to go to the Governor herself. We'll go out this evening around five o'clock and speak to them all." She nodded her head. I nodded mine back.

That evening we drove eighteen miles out of town to Willie Ray's camp. Willie Ray and Bertha shared a house that had a large kitchen and space for the crew to eat. The rest of the camp was a series of tin huts, sleeping about six to a hut. We stopped by first to talk to Willie Ray and Bertha.

When Bertha saw Sister Jo B her face lit up and she gave her a big hug. "So good to see you again so soon," she said.

They chatted and laughed like old friends. Willie Ray, a tall, wiry man, wearing blue jeans and a blue T-shirt, didn't say much and took it all in. After a few minutes more, Sister Jo B got down to business.

"Willie Ray, thank you for taking care of your people the way you do. If everybody followed your example there wouldn't be so many problems and violence working the season. I really appreciate your kindness. Thank you."

Willie Ray nodded his head. "Bertha and I just trying to do things the Christian way. It's hard working the season, but we try and be fair to our people. You talk to anyone you want. Bertha tells me you want to talk with the Governor. Just fine with me if you can," he said

"Thank you, Willie Ray. We'll just go and talk with Diane, Russell, and Big Shorty."

"I'll take you to them," Willie Ray said.

He walked us to their hut and said his good-byes.

Inside the small, tin hut with a rough, wooden floor, Diane and Russell were playing cards across from each other on a cot. They were one of the few couples who worked the season together. Both in their forties, they looked beaten down, like they had lived twice that many years. They were an unlikely pair—Diane was heavy and lucky if she was five feet tall, without any front teeth. Russell was well over six feet, thin, and with a full beard. They set aside their cards and greeted us quietly. They sat next to each other on the cot, side by side, and held hands as they talked.

Sister Jo B gave them a big smile.

"Thank you both so much for sitting with us tonight. It's very brave of you," she said. "We won't use this tape without your permission, if that's okay with you."

They both nodded yes.

"Let me know when you're ready," I said, as I placed the tape recorder in front of them.

Russell gave me the thumbs up and said in a low voice:

"I worked from five to six days a week from morning to sundown. I was getting seventeen cents a box for sweet potatoes. I picked about forty to fifty boxes a day. The largest amount of money that I drawed was $13.50. He charges $3.00 a pint for moonshine and fifty-five cents for a pack of cigarettes.

"We told him we wanted to leave. Clarence has a 22 magna revolver, and he beat me with the butt over and over. He then had his man, Doc, whip me with chains."

"'You owe me money,' Clarence shouted at me. 'You go when I let you go.'"

"We waited for our chance. One day Harold Strickland came round in the evening driving his red Oldsmobile. He the only man driving his own car in the season. He says Willie Ray treats everyone right. Clarence and them are not in camp. Diane and I grab our things and holler to Big Shorty to come along. Big Shorty says, 'Yeah,' grabs his stuff, and off we go with Harold. Keep expecting to hear from Clarence, but nothing so far. That's our story."

Sister Jo B looked Russell straight in the eye.

"Anyone else beaten in that camp?" she asked.

"Well besides me, there was Luther, Big Shorty, Benjamin, and Sonny."

"Thank you, Russell," she said.

"No problem, Ma'am. I'll go fetch Big Shorty. I know he wants to talk to you all."

A few minutes later, Big Shorty walked in. I thought his name was perfect—he was both a big man and short. A wide smile crossed his face as he sat down.

"Russell been telling me he already talked into the tape. I'm ready myself," he said.

Sister Jo B came over and shook his hand and gave him a big grin.

"Thank you, sir, for coming forward. So good to see you again. Please have a seat. We won't use this tape without your permission."

Big Shorty sat down on a cot and clapped his hands.

"Ready to go," he said.

I turned on the tape recorder and Big Shorty told his story.

"My real name is Joseph Rich and I'm from Miami, Florida. They be calling me Big Shorty since I was a boy. I'm thirty-three now. A man saying he represent Clarence talked to me about cooking for Clarence's crew. I'm partly paralyzed in my left side and can't do field work. I've cooked in the season before in South Carolina, near Aiken, so I know I can do that. When I got to Smithfield, Doc, the truck driver, says they don't need a cook no more and I got to work the field. I told them I can't do that, and they just laughed. I said I wanted to go back to Miami, but Clarence said I owed him money for stuff.

"I tried at first working six days in the field from morning to sundown. I was supposed to be paid eighteen cents a box for sweet potatoes. I remember picking seventy-eight boxes over two days, but Doc said I was no damn good. He carries them tire chains, and he just whupped me in the back in front of everyone. You can still see the scars."

He stood up and unbuttoned his cotton shirt, took it off and turned around.

The scars were still raw and oozing. He couldn't have gotten them more than a few days ago. They formed a pattern running zig-zag across his back. Hearing a story told into a tape recorder is one thing. Seeing scars across a man's back is something else.

"Lucky for me, lucky for us, Harold come driving by a few days later, and I jumped at the chance to go with Diane and Russell. Miss Bertha lets me help her with the cooking for my keep and gives me some small money too, but I'm scared all the time thinking that Clarence and Doc will come looking for us. I really want to go home. I can find work there, I'm sure."

A couple of tears welled around his eyes. He just let them come.

Sister Jo B placed her hands on Big Shorty's hands.

"We can get you a bus ticket home if you want, not a problem. Bless you all."

Sister Jo B walked over and one by one gave Diane, Russell, and Big Shorty big hugs. I awkwardly shook their hands, and we left.

Outside, we walked to my car, and before we got in, Sister Jo B stopped and gazed into the clear, starlit sky. It was eerily quiet and peaceful. As she looked into the black night, she looked contented and walked in a circle, taking it all in.

"I've always loved the stars," she said. "When I look into this splendid night sky I feel I can touch the heavens. Did I ever tell you I studied astronomy in college? My favorite times were looking through a telescope."

She pointed to the western sky. "You can see Orion over there. See, there's Betelgeuse, the bright, reddish star. Orion is named for the Hunter. Can you see the bow to the right?" She nodded. "Time to go home. It's a long ride."

I gazed at the stars a new way.

On the drive through dark and empty country roads, Sister Jo B was uncharacteristically quiet.

"Sister, are you okay?"

"Just like slaves, Russ. Just like slaves. Growing up in Kentucky I'm sure there was lots of violence and racism going on, but I guess I was kind of blind to it. Going to the community taught me a lot and helped build my faith, but we led privileged lives. As a nurse I've seen a lot of human suffering, but that was part of God's way. To see Big Shorty's scars tonight was too much. Having folks whipped with tire chains is not God's way. I'm going to pray for our new friends tonight."

The next day when I was out at the camps, Sister Jo B worked the phones. Two days later we had an appointment to see Governor Robert Scott in the State Capitol in Raleigh. I didn't know how exactly she accomplished this, but I wasn't surprised.

"Sister Jo B," I asked, "just how did you go about making this happen?

She smiled. In an exaggerated southern accent, she mimicked:

"Well I'll tell you, honey. I'm just a nun from Kentucky, but what we've seen here is shocking, and I know the Governor would want to know all about it. I really got to see him because I got to go somewhere and share what I know. If the Governor won't see me, I don't know where I should go. Now whatdya say?"

She looked at me and laughed. "Now, you, young man, had better cut your hair a bit and buy some nice clothes and a tie." She nodded.

Two days later, Sister Jo B, Bertha, Willie Ray's wife, and me, with shorter hair and wearing a tie, waited in the lobby of the Governor's office. I was nervous and tried to read the sports page of the newspaper. Sister Jo B and Bertha quietly hummed a spiritual together. Finally, one of the Governor's aides escorted us into an office, and Governor Scott, a friendly man, shook our hands warmly and asked us to have a seat around a circular table.

The walls were full of photographs of the Governor with various people, mainly shaking hands at what appeared to be political events—picnics, rallies, and conventions.

Sister Jo B introduced us and quickly got down to business.

"Governor, I know you're a busy man with a lot to do, so I'll get right to the point. I've only been here in the state about six weeks, but what we've seen is shocking and needs to be investigated."

Sister Jo B told the stories that Luther, Diane, Russell, and Big Shorty shared with us. "They are brave souls and were willing to speak into a tape recorder." Transcripts of their interviews in hand, she gave them to the Governor. "You can read about the violence in their own words."

Governor Scott quietly read through a few pages.

"Thank you, Sister. I'll read their statements in detail later."

Bertha talked about how the crew system worked out of Florida and how Willie Ray always tried to do right by his men.

Sister Jo B turned to Governor Scott and looked him square in the face.

"Governor, only someone in your position can do something about this outrage. We simply can't let this go on. We've come to ask you to help these folks."

The Governor watched her closely as she was talking.

"You know, Sister, I was a dairy farmer in Haw River before I got into politics, though my Daddy was governor way back in the early fifties. We didn't need migrants on our farm, but I've heard stories like you've told me today. I'll see what we can do about Johnston County."

He started to stand up to end the meeting, but Sister Jo B remained seated.

"Governor, we can't take no for an answer. Just come out to Johnston County soon. We're only an hour away, and we will take you for a ride around the camps. And bring the press along with you. That would be a first step in right direction."

Governor Scott and his aide were both standing now.

"Sister, my thanks for coming to see me. I'll do the best we can."

Sister Jo B stood up. I knew her well enough by now to know she wasn't happy.

He extended his hand, and we all shook it, one by one.

"Bless you. I look forward to seeing you again soon," said Sister Jo B, and we left.

In the car on the way back home, Sister Jo B asked me to write him a letter from all of us inviting him to Smithfield to tour the camps.

"I don't take much stock in him, but we can't give up."

Several weeks later he personally replied to my letter, saying he was too busy at this time to come to Johnston County and thanked us for bringing this situation to his attention.

The season in Smithfield was winding down. The crews would be heading north to Virginia, New Jersey, New York, and Connecticut. It was time for us to go back to Clarence's camp to read some TB tests. We hadn't been back there since we took Luther to the hospital. On the surface, Sister Jo B and Clarence got along fine, but taking away one of his men was bound to cause trouble. The fact that Diane, Russell, and Big Shorty also left would likely be blamed on us as well.

The day we were supposed to go to Clarence's camp, I meekly suggested to Sister Jo B that since everyone—Clarence, his crew, and us—were all moving on in a couple of weeks, maybe we should just skip the camp.

She would hear none of it.

"There's no way we're going to let Clarence, Doc, or any of them intimidate us. We got to stand up to them if anything is ever going to change. Let's get a move on."

Of course, she was right, but the thought of a confrontation with Clarence and Doc and their tire chains was frightening. Sister Jo B was fearless, but I was scared. She saw the look on my face.

"Not to worry. I said some special prayers last night. We'll be fine."

"Okay, Sister, but if things get hot up there, we're skedaddling," I said.

She laughed. "Now you're starting to sound all Kentucky to me."

I laughed too, and we got in the car and drove up to Clarence's camp. As we walked up to Clarence's hut, he and Doc were sitting outside playing cards on a makeshift table.

"Good evening, Clarence. Good to see you," Sister Jo B said.

He barely looked up. "Where's Luther?" he grunted.

"I believe he went on back to his family," Sister Jo B replied.

"That drunk owes me money. You're not wanted here, lady. Get off the camp."

"Clarence, we have some TB tests to read and some checking up to do. We won't be long."

Clarence nodded to Doc. Doc threw his cards on the table and stood up.

*Oh shit*, I thought. *It's going to happen*. I put my hand on Sister's Jo B's arm. She didn't budge.

Doc glared at Sister Jo B, walked right by us without saying a word, and got into his pickup truck and drove off. I breathed in and out slowly.

Sister Jo B turned on her heels and walked off into the camp. I followed right behind her. About ten to fifteen minutes later, as we were finishing our exams in one of the huts, we saw two pickup trucks roar into camp.

Doc got out of his truck, and a tall white man got out of the other. He was wearing blue jeans, work boots, white cowboy shirt, and an Atlanta Braves baseball hat. Clarence joined them and they all walked over to us.

Sister Jo B motioned to me to go with her. We walked directly to the three approaching men.

The tall white man's face was clenched up and mean. He looked directly at Sister Jo B. Clarence and Doc stood on either side of him, like wingmen at a Western shootout.

"This here is my farm, and you're fuckin' trespassing," the tall white man said. "Git out now. And you better not be messing with my niggers anymore. Git out now."

Sister Jo B, hands on her hips, stared right back.

"Mister, don't you dare talk to me like that. What kind of Christian allows slavery to take place under his nose? You think you scare us with your dirty talk, well, mister, you got another thing coming. Next time we come back, we're coming with the FBI!" She nodded, turned around, and headed for our car. I followed behind.

As we were walking away, the tall man yelled out, "Git out now. Next time y'all come back, I'll have my boys ready for you and your fuckin' FBI!"

The next morning we met with the director of the health department and told her about our encounter with the farmer, Clarence, and Doc. Sister Jo B related the whole story, curse words and all.

The director was deeply offended by it all. "I'm embarrassed to say there are still some ignorant people in this county, and times haven't changed for them at all. I can't say for sure, but that farmer is rumored to be high up in the Klan. Now I don't have any proof, but that's what people have been saying, and I believe it. His daddy was a leader in the Klan many years ago. When he's talking about his boys, I think he's talking about his Klan boys.

"Since the crews are leaving soon, I don't want you getting hurt up there. By all means go back to the Governor or the FBI. I wouldn't waste time with the local sheriff, though. Some of his people are rumored to be Klan boys."

Sister Jo B nodded. "I understand. I can't disagree with you. Thanks for being so supportive. You've been a blessing."

The next few days we wrote long, detailed letters to the Governor, the Department of Justice, the FBI, and the press. We included the transcripts from our interviews with Luther, Diane, Russell, and Big Shorty and wrote our own affidavits.

Several weeks later, I received a call from a lawyer from the Department of Justice. He had read all the transcripts and was planning to track down Luther, Diane, Russell, and Big Shorty, and start an investigation.

The season slowly came to an end. The crews headed up north. Sister Jo B left for Apopka, Florida, to set up a clinic for the workers when they returned.

I was sent to Edgefield, South Carolina, for the peach season.

On my way out of Smithfield, I took a photo of the Klan sign.

After my time in South Carolina was finished, I went to work with Sister Jo B in Florida for a few months.

A few months later, when we were together in Florida, I heard from the attorney at the Department of Justice. He called to say that Luther had left Dauphin Island. Some folks thought he was going home to Mississippi, but no one knew exactly where. Big Shorty was cooking in Miami but didn't want to cooperate with law enforcement. Big Shorty said that he wasn't going to work the season anymore and was afraid he might run into Clarence again in Miami. As best as the lawyer could find out, Diane and Russell left Willie Ray's crew in New York and joined another crew, but no one knew which one.

◊ ◊ ◊ ◊ ◊

I started law school shortly thereafter, but Sister Jo B and I remained close friends. I visited her at various workplaces—Holly Springs, Mississippi, and upstate New York. She came to visit my family in the New York City area every year. My dad, Eli, and she hit it off. Both were big personalities who told great stories and laughed loudly. One night we went out to dinner, and after Dad ordered his usual vodka, Sister Jo B stunned me by ordering a Manhattan—just one, mind you. She said she'd get silly if she had more than that. After she retired, I would regularly visit her at the convent in Nazereth.

Twenty-one years after we worked together in Smithfield, I was being sworn in as a Judge of the Superior Court of the District of Columbia. My mom had passed away. Dad's health was bad, and he was housebound and could not come to D.C. for the ceremony. Sitting in the front row in the courthouse was Sister Jo B, smiling and nodding.

About five years after we left Smithfield, someone from the health department sent me an article from the local paper. A Jimmy R. Flowers from nearby Clayton had bought the property on which the Klan sign stood and wanted to tear it down but did not know who actually owned it. Mr. Flowers was quoted as saying, "I don't want to take a dozer and tear down something and get sued for it. I'm sure it belongs to the Klan." Apparently, the Klan was no longer that active in the Smithfield area, and Flowers did not know whom to call about removing it.

The Town Manager, Hugh Talton, said he would "be glad to see the sign go."

Jimmy R. Flowers wanted to replace the sign with an advertisement for his realty company or maybe just a sign that said, "Welcome to Smithfield."

# Burning at the Wire: The Execution of John Evans

◈ ◈ ◈ ◈ ◈

I stared at my client, John Evans, sitting on Alabama's electric chair. They call the chair "Yellow Mama." John's head was shaved; he had declined the State's offer to let him wear his own clothes and wore prison garb. His hands and legs were strapped to the chair. The witnesses were now in place in the observation room, separated by a glass partition from the execution chamber. John sat no more than fifteen feet away. The warden was about to begin the ritual of the execution.

My mind flashed to a conversation I had had with attorney Millard Farmer in Atlanta several days before. Millard had been on the front lines of the death penalty fight longer than just about anyone. Mentor and friend to all death penalty lawyers, he often spoke with great wisdom on matters far beyond the legal strategy of a case. John Evans's appeal had seemed hopeless, and there was some talk that perhaps it would be futile to go to Alabama and make a last-ditch fight. Millard said that we must never make it easy for them to kill our clients and that we should go. He also said, "Be careful, don't get dirty at no damn killing."

The State was seconds away from killing John Evans. John was to die a long and terrifying death. The State would have blood on its hands. Those chosen to bear witness would indeed get dirty.

◊ ◊ ◊ ◊ ◊

John Evans killed Edwin Nassar during a pawn shop robbery. Although it was clear the shooting was not planned and committed when Evans felt that Mr. Nassar was going to grab a weapon and fire upon him, it was unquestioned that John Evans shot and killed Mr. Nassar. John never denied his role in the crime and in fact told the jury that he had done so.

John Evans was born into a steady middle-class family in Texas. He had loving and concerned parents as well as fine brothers and sisters. For reasons that could never be fully explained or understood, John had drifted from the family and entered a life of crime. Starting with minor, juvenile-delinquent offenses, he moved his way up to armed robbery. He lost contact with his family and ended up in prison. Shortly after his release, he and another former prisoner ended up in Mobile, Alabama, where they committed the capital offense.

The legal battle to save his life was hard and complex. John insisted on representing himself at critical times during the proceedings. At one point in 1979, the extremely harsh and cruel conditions on death row drove him to waive his appeals and even volunteer for execution. His attorney throughout these proceedings, John Carroll of the Southern Poverty Law Center, had been brilliant in keeping John alive. His family, and especially his mother, Betty, had rallied around John's life and given him a reason to live.

By 1983, John Evans had decided to represent himself. The conditions on death row had so depressed him that he felt that his only choice was between immediate execution and a commutation to life imprisonment by Governor George

Wallace. When an execution date had been set for April 22, 1983, his family prevailed upon him to contact the Southern Prisoners' Defense Committee in Atlanta to seek legal advice.

The Southern Prisoners' Defense Committee was a small, non-profit project that represented death row prisoners and challenged unconstitutional prison and jail conditions throughout the South. It is now called the Southern Center for Human Rights. Despite its rather powerful name, in 1983 the Committee consisted of only four lawyers: Steve Bright, Bob Morin, Christy Freeman, and myself. Bryan Stevenson joined us in the summer of 1983. We often found ourselves traveling from state to state to handle last-minute crises.

At that time, only six men had been executed in the United States since the Supreme Court had upheld the death penalty. Four of those men—Gary Gilmore of Utah, Jesse Bishop of Nevada, Steven Judy of Indiana, and Frank Coppola of Virginia—had withdrawn their appeals and volunteered for execution. John Spenkelink of Florida and Charles Brooks of Texas were unsuccessful in challenging their convictions and sentences and were put to death against their will.

Alabama had not executed a prisoner in over eighteen years. Public opinion and the media clamored for a killing in Alabama. The Attorney General of the State, Charles Graddick, was particularly in high gear. He had been the local county prosecutor who had brought the case against John and had exploited the prosecution for all it was worth in his later run for statewide office. Graddick now had his eye on the Governor's mansion and was pounding the drums in the media that if there was to be respect for law and order in the State, John Evans had to be executed, and executed now.

John was ready to give up the fight. Years on death row had worn him down. Life in the death house is the most dehumanizing and spiritually devastating form of existence that our society has chosen to inflict on its prisoners. Physically, the conditions of confinement are severe and harsh. The prisoner is locked in a small cell for twenty-three and a half hours a day. Imagine being locked up in your bathroom all day, year after year, John would say.

The prisoner is allowed a half-hour a day of solitary recreation in an isolated outside cage where he can do no more than walk in circles. And a death row inmate is always manacled in chains, hand and foot, whenever he is let out of his cell. John compared the recreation to a guard walking his dog. He often refused the walk as too demeaning. He'd rather exercise in his cell and try to maintain his dignity. For life on death row was a constant and never-ending battle for integrity. The barrenness, cruelty, and boredom of life on the row was designed to break down a man's will.

John, I think, could have endured the physical deprivation. But like so many others, the despair of life on the row, the life of the "living dead," as they all called it, seeped into his very soul. For John was a proud man and life on death row was intended to reduce him to an animal state. He rebelled against this attempt to crush his spirit.

He did not have any faith in the legal system, and he knew the political reality all too well. He did not expect freedom, though he craved it. He knew that his crime deserved punishment and that by his actions he had surrendered his liberty. He only sought an inner peace with the hope of redemption. He had come to terms with his crime; his remorse for the death of Edwin Nassar was genuine and deeply felt. He knew that his actions had senselessly taken away a husband and father. He prayed that the Nassar family would someday forgive him.

Father Kevin was John's best friend and supporter. John's mother, Betty, had written to Father Kevin and asked him to look in on her son. Father Kevin, a boisterous and good-humored Irishman, was pastor of a small Catholic parish near the prison. He never thought that he would minister to a man on death row, and he very personally took John in as his son.

John had always been cynical about the Catholic religion, but his relationship with Father Kevin gave him faith and a newfound sense of maturity.

And yet John was still a character. He had a ready grin and a sarcastic sense of humor. He made a show for his friends of his strength and would fight fear with a certain brashness. He liked me, but made it quite clear that he would make the decision on his legal case. It was, after all, his life, and he wanted to make his own statement.

Further legal appeals appeared hopeless. If Governor Wallace would grant him clemency, then he would accept a lifetime in prison. At least he would be off the "row," and he could study and participate in programs. The freedom to walk outside a cell without handcuffs on his wrists and chains on his legs meant everything to him.

I thought that John was rolling loaded dice by placing all his faith in the compassion of George Wallace. After an assassination attempt in 1972 rendered Governor Wallace paralyzed from the waist down, he appeared to soften some of his virulent racist and tough law and order views while embracing Christianity. Nonetheless, I could not believe that Wallace would commit political suicide and grant clemency. There were no established procedures for a clemency hearing, but it was clear that those who sought John's death were determined to bring public pressure to bear on George Wallace.

Attorney General Graddick set the tone with a press release issued four days before the scheduled execution, calling on Governor Wallace to deny clemency. In typically overblown language Graddick stated that "if you commute his sentence to life imprisonment your action will probably result in the de facto abolition of the death penalty in this State.... It is important that capital punishment exist and that it be applied in this case. Capital punishment reaffirms the moral sanctity of innocent life and it is a legitimate weapon in society's arsenal against crime."

Not content with challenging the Governor to be tough on crime. Graddick then took on the Alabama Parole Board, warning that "if you commute his sentence all that will stand between Evans and the law-abiding citizens of this State is the Parole Board and past experience has shown that the Parole Board is quite capable of and willing to release any criminal, no matter how dangerous he is." As for John Evans's character, Graddick said: "You take a gun out of his hands and he's a gutless wonder."

Graddick had certainly pushed all the right buttons, and he was only too happy to parade before the media and take credit for bringing John Evans to the electric chair. In April 1983 there was talk of little else in Alabama; letters to the editor, radio call-in shows, man-in-the-street television interviews, were all joining in the debate. Should John Louis Evans live or die?

Many people supported John. Family, friends, religious leaders, and numerous others all over the state and the country wrote compassionate and pleading letters for Wallace's consideration.

John himself wrote to the Governor. His letter was a direct and sensitive plea for his life:

> *There hasn't been a day since Edwin Nassar's death that I haven't thought about him, his wife, and his two little girls. Only God can know the extent of the hurt and shame that I feel.*
>
> *Because of my relationship with God, He has taught me how to love and care about others and He has blessed me with fantastic desire to do something constructive and productive with my life.... I believe with all my heart that God wouldn't have reached so far down to lift me up and change my whole life around from being something ugly to being something worthwhile. I am a living example of the unlimited*

*Love and Mercy of God and that fact never ceases to amaze me....*

*I've read several things that you have had to say about your physical tragedy and one thing is obvious—because of your faith in God, you were touched with a sense of mercy and the capacity for forgiveness. None of us can go through the things we do in life without at some time needing God's Mercy but we in turn have to be able to show mercy....*

*I pray that after reviewing all that I have said, you will find it in your heart to commute by death sentence.*

*May God Bless and keep you.*

*John Louis Evans III*

The buildup for the meeting with the Governor was intense. Betty, Mark, John's brother, Father Kevin, and I drove up to the Alabama State Capitol in Montgomery and used a side entrance in the hope of avoiding the media. We were unsuccessful. TV cameras, sound mikes, pushing and shoving, and general chaos followed us until we got inside the Capitol. The Governor's press aide ushered us into Wallace's office. John's life was in the balance.

The clemency hearing was a farce. Wallace was sitting somewhat imperiously behind a large desk. His legal aide and a PR person sat beside him on either side. Two security types stood erect in the back of the room.

Wallace greeted Betty and Mark warmly. He commented on Mark's military uniform and made small talk about the place and duty of station. Father Kevin and the Governor talked briefly about common friends and seemed at ease with each other. The Governor shook my hand and nodded.

"Speak from your heart," he said. And Betty, Mark, and Father Kevin did just that. He looked at us intently with a kindly and paternal face. His presence was commanding, and he showed warmth. He really did. Betty talked about John and how he had grown and matured, and about how he had returned to the family after such a long absence. Mark said he had never known his older brother until John got locked up and they wrote to and confided in each other. Father Kevin talked about John's life in prison and how he learned to truly know Christ and how a young and angry man had learned to love others and care for those around him.

It was odd, but I felt that Wallace was moved and concerned. You could see it on his face, in his expression, and in his voice. And yet, as I sat there and watched him, I felt taken in. The guy's a great politician, he has charm, sincerity, and the right moves.

Perhaps in some way he was for real. Who knows with these guys? How could anyone not see the grief and agony of this wonderful family? The sickness and the evil of the death penalty is never more apparent than when another mother is reduced to tears in a futile attempt to save a son.

Wallace saw those tears. He heard their pleas. He pulled out a copy of the Bible. "This is a matter that weighs heavily with me. I'm going to pray over John. Ma'am, you have a wonderful family and I thank you for coming to see me."

After leaving Wallace's office, we were ushered into the office of the Governor's press spokesman. While he was talking to the family, another aide, a young lawyer, motioned for me to come into the hallway.

"I just thought that you should know that although nothing is official, the Governor's position is that he does not feel that it is appropriate to interfere in this case at this time. The Governor thought that you as counsel would like to know that as soon as possible." He looked at me somewhat sheepishly. Showtime was over. The execution would go forward as scheduled.

◈ ◈ ◈ ◈ ◈

I waited until we were in the car before I told them the news. We drove in silence to John Carroll's office in Montgomery. All hope was lost and tears were shed. The execution was scheduled for Friday morning at 12:01 a.m.

That night John Evans and I talked in the visitors' room. We still had some legal options left, but John did not want to talk about them. "I'll let you know. I know that Mom wants me to fight but I'm so tired. Even if we win a new trial, Charley Graddick will never let me alone. He needs me dead.

"Russ, I do have one request. But I want you to know that you can say no and I'll understand completely. I've asked a friend of mine, Rick Dent, to witness my execution. He's a young kid and wants to write. I'm glad that he'll be there. I want to know if you could go with him. He might need some help.

"I know that this is asking a lot, and please believe me, I will understand. This is not part of your job. Do it, if you can, as my friend."

I told John that I would be with him and that I would go as his friend.

◈ ◈ ◈ ◈ ◈

Albert Camus wrote in *Reflections on the Guillotine* that "[t]he man who enjoys his coffee while reading that justice has been done would spit it out at the least detail." This country has never used the guillotine, but has tried almost every method of killing known to the Middle Ages. Burning at the stake, decapitation with the axe, gibbeting (a man is hung in a cage with the body exposed until decomposition), breaking at the wheel, hanging, and the firing squad are part of our history.

Daniel Frank of Jamestown, Virginia, was probably the first man executed in this country. He was hanged in 1622 for stealing a hog and a cow. In March 1988, Willie Darden was electrocuted by the State of Florida. Watt Espy, a historian

living in Alabama, has so far documented and confirmed over 16,000 executions in the United States and expects the final tally to exceed 22,000 when his work is completed.

The electric chair was authorized by the New York State legislature in 1888. It was considered then to be the state-of-the-art technology for humane and practical executions. It was promoted by its supporters for its certainty in producing an instantaneous death.

Under the law, any method of execution that causes unnecessary pain, violence, or mutilation to the body is supposed to be barred by the Constitution. The "mere extinguishment of life" is acceptable; torture or a lingering death are not.

In 1890 William Kemmler became the first person to die in the electric chair. He was killed in Auburn Prison in New York State. By all accounts, it was a gruesome death. The generator supplied by the Westinghouse Electric Company used alternating current. George Westinghouse, the company's president, is reported to have said that he "thought that the job could have been done better with an axe." The *New York Press* stated that the "age of burning at the stake is past; the age of burning at the wire will pass also."

But it did not pass. Instead, electrocution became the most popular mode of slaying in the twentieth century in this country. The reports of numerous witnesses to these executions have much in common. The electrodes that make contact with the shaved human head and leg reach temperatures over 1,900 degrees Fahrenheit and can melt copper. The awesome power of 2,000 volts of electricity shoots through a human being and makes the body leap and cringe. The condemned's eyeballs can literally pop out of the sockets. The face, as well as the fingers, legs, and toes, become hideously contorted and disfigured.

It is not unusual for the prisoner to defecate and urinate during the surge of current. The vomiting of blood and saliva is common. The prisoner actually smolders under the force of the current, and the temperature of the brain approaches the boiling point of water. Doctors who have performed autopsies on electrocuted men report that the liver is so hot that it cannot be touched by a human hand.

Nicola Tesla reported after studying the effects of electrocution: "The current flows along a restricted path.... in the meantime the vital organs may be preserved, and pain, too great for us to imagine, is induced.... For the sufferer, time stands still; and this excruciating torture seems to last for an eternity."

This pain is often prolonged and repeated. In many cases it is necessary to refasten the power lines to the chair after the first surge of electricity sears the flesh but does not kill the prisoner. In May of 1946, Willie Francis of Louisiana, a seventeen-year-old teenager, survived two separate jolts of current.

Sheriff Harold Resweber described the attempt to execute Willie Francis: "Then the electrocutioner turned on the switch and when he did Will Francis' lips puffed out and he groaned and jumped so that the chair came off the floor. Apparently the switch was turned on twice and then the condemned man yelled, 'Take it off. Let me breathe.'"

The Sheriff finally unstrapped Mr. Francis, and the execution was halted. The State was unrelenting in its attempt to kill Mr. Francis. His attorneys argued before the Supreme Court that to subject a man to such an electrocution two separate times constituted cruel and unusual punishment. The Court rejected the plea. In a decision split by a 5-4 vote, the Court asserted that although the first attempt on Willie Francis's life caused "mental anguish and physical pain," it was "an unforeseeable accident" and not deliberate. That being the case, the Constitution was not offended.

In his dissent, Justice Burton called the Francis execution "a form of torture [that] would rival that of burning at the stake." A short time thereafter, Willie Francis was again strapped into Louisiana's electric chair. This time it worked and he was killed.

◈ ◈ ◈ ◈ ◈

On the morning of April 21, 1983, I drove from Atmore to the federal courthouse in Mobile. The execution was set for 12:01 a.m. on the twenty-second. Executions are often set at that time on the theory that if there are no stays of execution in effect, the killing should proceed at once. A midnight execution prevents the legal team from having another twenty-four hours to go to another court and try to stop it.

We were waiting for the Supreme Court to rule on our petition to stay the execution. We were ready to act as soon as the Court turned us down. Because the case was in a complex and unusual legal posture, we had the right to file another motion to stay the execution along with a writ of habeas corpus in the lower federal court. Steve Bright and I had drawn up the legal papers the past weekend. Although we had raised some new and substantial issues in our court papers—issues that, if given serious and reflective consideration, would have merited a reversal of John's death sentence—the timing was not right. John had tied his case in legal knots and had frustrated the system for too long. Besides, his case had become a *cause célèbre*. The public clearly wanted an execution, and legal delays were not going to save the day this time.

A Mobile attorney, Arthur Madsen, had graciously let me use his office to wait and take phone calls. Bright was in Atlanta, ready to file pleadings in the Eleventh Circuit Court of Appeals if necessary. Two other attorneys, Jerry Fisher and Brad Stetler, were in Washington, D.C., monitoring the Supreme Court. The waiting was on. The local federal magistrate had found out that I was in Mobile and called to ask my intentions. I had to put him off. I didn't really know at that time. It depended on the Supreme Court.

Word had filtered through that the Governor was open to seeing us again in less formal circumstances. Our source was a member of the press who had gotten to know John and wanted to do all that was possible to save him. He apparently had open lines to Wallace's staff. The execution was weighing on Wallace's conscience. The Governor might ask to see us again. There might be an opening. The Governor's aide would get back to us.

John's sister Susan called around noon. She was excited. The Governor wanted to see us. Could we be there by 4:00 p.m.? Was it really possible? A private plane could pick us up at Atmore at 1:00 p.m. and take us to Montgomery. We could be there by 3:00 p.m. I got on the phone to Betty and we talked it over. She wanted to be near John this day. Susan and I would take the plane.

I rushed to the Atmore airport. George Kendall of the ACLU hurried from Atlanta to Mobile in case the pleadings had to be filed while I was in Montgomery. I met Susan and we were in the air. I don't mind flying, but small, private planes I can do without. I think Susan felt the same. We talked about John and how much he had grown over the past few years. About how he had come back to the family, and that no matter what, the family had been brought back together. She had feelings of guilt that she had let her brother down and that's why he had gone the way he did. Indeed, the whole family felt that way.

We started talking about my family. I also had a brother, Jeff, who somehow had gotten lost. Committing petty crimes, dropping out of high school, he ran around with other juveniles in trouble with the law. My parents finally enlisted him in the army with a guaranteed posting in Western Europe. Vietnam heated up and he volunteered for duty there and was killed in action.

And so we talked of families and guilt and responsibility. I think Susan was grateful for the opportunity to plead for her brother's life. We arrived in Montgomery and went straight to the Governor's Mansion.

Governor George Wallace sat in his wheelchair in his upstairs bedroom. He was dressed informally in casual slacks and a sport shirt. Next to him was a legal aide. Susan was next to me; she was all strength and grace. She was there to plead for her brother's life, but she would retain her dignity.

We sat in a small circle, all of us leaning forward as if sharing secrets. Wallace had impaired hearing, and one had to talk very, very loudly in order to be understood. The effect was strange; the four of us were sharing something very intense, the power of life and death in the balance, huddling together and almost shouting to be heard. The execution was seven hours away. This was our second meeting with the Governor. We had been through the formal clemency hearing, such as it was. John's mother, Betty, had been eloquent in her plea for her son. Why were we going through this again? To what point?

The Governor looked at Susan. "I heard that you all wanted to talk again, and I am always willing to talk to you folks so please talk from your heart."

Susan's hand slowly clenched. "Governor, you heard my mother the other day. You heard that John is really a different person today than he was years ago. That he has found the Lord and that he gives the family so much. We love him so much and need him so much.

"My mother has been through so much, this will just hurt her and grieve her so. After all this time John has come back to the family and we all need him.

"I know that you believe that people change. I have heard so much that you have changed and that your feelings towards blacks have changed, you even said so in your inauguration speech. So John has changed and has become a good person. Just like you, he has seen the light, and we need him and love him so much. Please spare his life, Governor. Only you can do that now."

Wallace seemed a little startled. The reference to blacks and his well-publicized inauguration speech clearly surprised him. "I do believe that people can change. But you may have misunderstood some of the things about my feelings about black people. I grew up among black folk. In fact, black folks raised me. I love black people and always have. What I said recently is that we lived in a different time back then when things were done differently and the way of life was different. Times have changed for the better, and I wanted everyone to know that I, for one, am glad that times have changed. But I have always loved the black people. Always.

"I'm glad to know that John has found Christ. I have found him too and I pray for him and have prayed for him every day. I was deeply moved with what your mother said and with what you have said today about John. I am glad that he has found peace."

This all sounded like a canned speech to me. What were we doing here, wasting our time and listening to a politician give a speech? And yet something about the Governor was truly sincere. He did appear to be troubled about the execution. I certainly did not know the man, but my sense was that he was listening.

Wallace was in bad health. He had been in and out of hospitals the last few months. He looked terrible. His speech was slow and exaggerated, his face puffy. He seemed heavily medicated. It was clear that he had run for his last election. His political career was over. There was even talk that he might resign from office because of his health. Maybe he really didn't care about public opinion. I knew that such hope was perhaps naive, but we had no choice. George Wallace and George Wallace alone could save John Evans's life. If there was any chance to persuade him, it had to be now.

I had gone through a number of clemency pleas, and had even secured the minutes of appeals that had been made years ago. Those words didn't seem to fit. But I had also heard that Wallace had once defended a death row inmate many years ago.

"Governor, I heard that years ago when you were a young lawyer, you sat in my chair before another governor and that you saved a man's life. And now, years later, I am trying to search for those very same words that you used when you pled for clemency, the same feelings and thoughts that crossed your mind, and came from within when you reached out and found that common bond of mercy that is within us all.

"You already know John's fine family. Betty told you about John's upbringing in Texas and how he got away from the family; of how he was lost at an early age. And you know the change in him, the real change that has been attested to by so many people, by his mother, sister, and brother. By Father Kevin, who has been with John for all these years on death row. And by John himself, you have read his words and I know taken them to heart. This is a human being worth saving—and only you can save him, Governor. This is a fine, good, decent family worth protecting—and only you can protect them from the pain and grief that is sure to follow."

Wallace sat there with his eyes locked into mine. He leaned back. "I remember that case very, very well," he said in a soft voice. "It was a case where a young colored fellow was as stubborn as he could be. Well, he just about cut his girlfriend's head off in a fight. Before the trial the State offered him a life sentence, and this fella was as stubborn as he could be and so he refused. The jury gave him the chair.

"I told the Governor two things, as I recall." He said this with just a slight smile, as every trial lawyer does when recounting a well-played move. "I told him that we shouldn't give this fella the chair just because he was stubborn and that the State didn't really want to see the man die."

Wallace then paused, thought something for a few seconds, and then went on. "I also told him that in the county where the killing took place, there had never been an execution for a colored man who killed his girlfriend over a fight. It had never been done and I didn't think it fair that this fella should have been the first, just because he was stubborn—especially when the State was going to let him off with a life sentence.

"You know, in my other terms as Governor I never had to go this far. I was always glad when the term ended and I didn't have to make the decision." He gently tapped his Bible and said he would pray some more. He then looked at Susan. "The Lord came to me late in life, and I'm glad that John has found him too. When I was young and vigorous I didn't really think of such things. But now...

"John has found some peace and he has a fine, fine family. If the Lord takes him tonight, then he will be home."

◈ ◈ ◈ ◈ ◈

John spent the day saying good-bye to his family and friends. He saw Kathy Ansheles and Jenny Johnston of the Alabama Prison Project. Kathy and Jenny had supported John through his many years on death row and were very close to him. Their efforts for John and other prisoners in seeking to make the conditions on death row more humane were remarkable. Outside on the prison grounds, other supporters maintained a vigil in protest against John's execution.

Betty and Mark had their last few minutes with John. The loss of a loved one is hard enough; that the State will deliberately kill a son and brother in the name of justice is much too hard to bear.

Later that night, Mark drove me to the prison. He would wait for me while I went in to see John. It was 8:30 p.m.—three and a half hours before the execution. I stopped in to see Warden J.D. White. The Warden had been courteous and considerate to the entire family. There was none of the harassment of the condemned that seems to be part of the killing ritual. The guards had been respectful of John's situation and had not taunted him. Some were even sympathetic.

One guard in particular, Joe, was friendly with John and had been asking me what I thought of his chances. He seemed very nervous. "Russ, I'm damned glad that I'm not part of the execution squad. I've grown to think that John's all right. I never wanted this part of the job. Never really thought we'd have this back, if you want to know the truth."

Joe let me in to see Warden White. The Warden let me know the details. He talked about the last meal, steak and shrimp. No beer allowed—it was against regulations. John's head would be shaved an hour before the execution. Father Kevin would be allowed to administer the last rites. At 11:30 p.m. the witnesses would assemble at a guard station and would be escorted into the witness room.

Later, the prison chaplain, Martin Weber, would be allowed to see John. I didn't like Weber at all. He was all too much the company man. After all the years John had spent on death row, he hardly knew Weber. Now, with John's death hours away, Weber all of a sudden had a deep reverence for his soul. Weber also owned and operated the only motel in town, where we were all staying. He had made a deal with John that in exchange for free lodging for the family, John would make a video for Weber's church group on lessons for youth. After the execution, Weber hawked the video to the highest bidder in Hollywood, where it was used in a docudrama. Weber later had to plead guilty in criminal court to conflict-of-interest charges for profiting from his state employment.

The execution squad had practiced their roles every day for the past seven days. Under Alabama law, the Warden is the one who pulls the switch. No blank bullets in the rifle here. Everyone was a professional. The Yellow Mama had been tested every day for the past week, and it was all set.

"John seems ready. He seems at peace. In some way I think he's relieved. Joe will bring you to John's cell. I hope you understand that regulations require stricter security, and he'll have to strip-search you. I appreciate your professional attitude through all this."

I thanked him too. I thanked him for his professional attitude and his courtesy. I thanked him for making it easier for John and his family. We shook hands.

I had to wonder at our roles. We were professionals. He was the executioner and I was the defense lawyer. Here we were thanking each other for being so professional. One pro to another. For doing what? Making a hard job more bearable? For helping reduce tensions all around? For making it go down easier?

*Damn*, I thought. *This man is going to kill John in about three hours. He is going to pull the switch and shoot electricity through John's head and fry his brains out. That's exactly what he's going to do.*

*And here I am thanking him for being a pro. What was I doing in all this? Another pro. A respectable cog in this grotesque machinery of butchery. My job was to help provide a clean execution. I should be screaming and shouting. I should make them drag me out of there—create a scene. I should make it as hard and tough and as sick and inhumane as it was. I should be making my voice heard in the ritual of cruelty. I should make these bastards hear my voice and know what the hell they are doing.*

And yet my rage gave way to thinking about John and his suffering. I had to serve him. And serving him meant taking my role as set out in the rites of the execution.

I tried to focus on the ceremony. Byron Eshelman, a former death row chaplain at San Quentin Prison, once wrote:

> *Only the ritual of an execution makes it possible to endure. Without it the condemned could not give the expected measure of cooperation to the etiquette of dying. Without it, we who must preside at their deaths could not face the morning of each new execution day.*
>
> *Nor could you.*
>
> *No matter how you think you feel about capital punishment, no matter how you imagine you would face the legal giving or taking of life, you would meet the reality of it by holding tightly to the crutch of ritual.*

I had to be strong for John. If it was easier for him to accept his death and make peace within himself, then I would do all I could do to help him.

Joe escorted me to a side office, where I was to be strip searched. Joe was apologetic and I told him that I understood and that it didn't matter. I then took off all my clothes and, spread-eagled against the wall, completely searched.

Joe told me that he thought John was holding up. I told him that if I didn't get the chance later on, I appreciated all he had done. I thought that his eyes were tearing up, although I'm not sure.

I walked past the execution chamber. I didn't look at the chair. John's cell was next to the chair. A number of officers were assigned to watch him. According to prison regulations, he had been observed twenty-four hours a day for the past three days. John would not be allowed to commit suicide. The sentence of the court had to be fulfilled.

His TV was on for the guards to watch. I remember that it was loud and that *Hill Street Blues* was on. Frank and Joyce in bed, or something.

They would not allow me into John's cell, but we embraced through the bars. He was being strong for me. I told him that the Eleventh Circuit Court of Appeals was still considering his case and that there was hope. He knew this sounded false and he smiled. I forced a smile too. Even if we got the court in Atlanta to go our way, the Supreme Court would have their shot, and we both knew what that meant.

"Russ, if we get the stay tonight, I want to be alone to wait out the Supreme Court. I don't want to have to say goodbye all over again. It's just too hard on my mom and the family. They shouldn't have to go through it all over. They really love me." He paused and got a little choked up. He paused and waited. We held hands. "And I really love them."

"Don't feel bad. You did all you could do. Thank all the people that I don't even know, in Atlanta and D.C. and those folks out there in the vigil. You know it's a great feeling to have all those people behind you. It makes it so much easier."

I looked at him and felt some trembling. "John, I really admire you. I wish that we could have done more. I—"

He interrupted me. "Hey, buddy, please. You guys were great. You really were. Have a Bud on me. I'll see you later. Thanks again."

We embraced one more time and I left.

◈ ◈ ◈ ◈ ◈

Later that night the Eleventh Circuit Court of Appeals in Atlanta granted a stay of execution. Back at the motel there was confusion. Some of John's friends were ecstatic and joyous. The family was more restrained. I had told them that the fight was not over, and that the State would undoubtedly take an emergency appeal to the Supreme Court.

The State did so first thing in the morning. We filed our legal opposition shortly thereafter. Under Alabama law, the warrant to carry out the execution expired at 11:59 p.m. that night. If the Court failed to rule on the State's appeal by midnight, we might make it. Word was out from the prison that if the Court lifted the stay, the execution would go forward promptly. I was told by Warden White to be available by phone all day. If the authorities could not locate me, the execution would go on as planned.

We waited in the motel all day. Outside, more and more people joined the vigil. We walked from room to room in fearful anticipation. Betty, Susan, and Mark told warm stories of family life in Texas. We all played with Jenny Johnston's two-year-old daughter, Sarah, who laughed and giggled at every chance. We created a game with Sarah's giant beach ball as she ran up and down the hallway kicking and punching it all over.

Rick Dent and I talked briefly about our fear, and wondered if we should actually watch the execution after they put the black hood on John's head. We had no idea what to do.

Around 7:00 p.m. Steve Bright called from Atlanta. I could tell from the tone of his voice that it was all over. The Supreme Court had dissolved the stay. There was nothing left to do.

As soon as I hung up, Warden J.D. White was on the phone. He was very formal this time. I was informed that a state police car would pick us up at the motel in forty-five minutes.

I went to tell Betty but she already knew. The news had flashed on the radio. There was confusion and fear. Jenny was hysterical. Rick and I looked at each other in desperation. I excused myself for a few minutes and called my parents and told them that I was all right.

I sat down and wrote out a statement for the press. A last appeal to George Wallace.

We all gathered in Betty's room. We stood in a circle and held hands as Father Kevin said a prayer. Betty hugged Rick and me as we went to the motel lobby.

I went in front of the cameras and read my plea to Governor Wallace. "The legal process is at an end. There are no more appeals to take. Yesterday we had a personal conference with Governor Wallace asking clemency for John. The Governor said he would keep an open mind and would pray on the matter.

"We are now attempting to call the Governor to ask for mercy. John Evans' life is now in Governor Wallace's hands. We ask him to save it." The state police car waited for us outside.

It was pouring rain with thunderstorms and lightning. We could barely see the countryside in the storm. The flashes of lightning brightened the land every so often and made it all the more surreal. There were two state troopers in the front, Rick and me in the back seat. Nobody said a word.

We arrived at the prison in a few minutes. Drenched by the gusts of wind and rain, we were directed to a small guard outpost. Inside were three reporters. The five of us stood there waiting. Mark Harris, from the United Press International, was shaking his head. He had just found out that day that his wife was pregnant, and now he was doing this job. The wind and the rain pounded the shed.

A guard came in and patted us down. We then followed him outside to the rear entrance to the prison. It was a short walk to the witness room.

As soon as I walked in, I saw John sitting on the electric chair. Our eyes locked immediately, and he nodded to me. I nodded back and kept eye contact with him. His head was shaved and his legs, chest, and arms were strapped to the chair. There was a slit cut open on the left leg of his pants where an electrode was attached.

Inside were two doctors, Chaplain Weber, and Commissioner Fred Smith. Weber operated a closed-circuit video camera, which was to show the execution to the rest of the press somewhere inside the prison. Smith was on an open telephone line to Governor Wallace and his aides. Warden White entered the witness room and announced that the civilian witnesses were now in place. Smith communicated that information to Wallace, and asked if there were any stays of execution now in effect. He announced to Warden White that there were not and that the sentence of the Court could now be executed.

We were separated from the execution chamber by a glass window. We were about fifteen feet away from John. Warden White went into the chamber and read the formal death warrant. It was supposed to take only a few minutes, but it seemed much longer. Two other uniformed guards were next to the chair.

John was calm. He kept staring at Rick and me. John was then allowed to his final statement. He said, "I have no malice for anyone, no hatred for anyone."

Warden White then left the chamber and went to a room behind the chair, where he would pull the switch. John looked at us one more time. The guards attached an electrode-filled headpiece to his shaved head. They put a black hood over his face.

The guard then took a three-foot-long stick that looked like a lollipop with the word "Ready" on it and raised it to the back window of the chamber as a signal to Warden White.

At 8:30 p.m. the first jolt of 1,900 volts of electricity shot through John's body. It lasted thirty seconds. Sparks and flames erupted from the electrode tied to his leg. John's body slammed against the straps holding him in the chair, and his fists clenched. The electrode burst from the strap holding it in place and caught on fire. A large puff of grayish smoke and sparks poured out from under the hood that covered his face. John's body straightened out and quivered. An overpowering stench of burnt flesh and clothing began pervading the witness room. When the current stopped, he fell back into the chair.

The two doctors went into the chamber to pronounce him dead. One doctor put the stethoscope on his heart. He turned and nodded to us, the usual sign that a person is dead. But he meant the opposite, that he had found a heartbeat. The other doctor examined John and confirmed it.

The doctors left the execution chamber. The guard reattached the electrode to John's leg and fixed the strap. He set up the power lines again.

John's chest rose evenly as he continued breathing. A gush of saliva oozed from his face and out from the black hood onto his white prison clothes. John's breathing was slow and regular.

Mark Harris, the reporter, said out loud, "He's survived."

At 8:34 the second jolt of 1,900 volts of current was sent into John's body. The stench of burning flesh was nauseating. More smoke came from his head and leg. John's hands gripped the arms of the chair. Again, the doctors examined John. Again, they reported that he was still alive.

It was all out of control. Commissioner Smith did not know what he was doing. Warden White was walking from the generator to the execution chamber.

I called out to Smith: "Commissioner, I ask for clemency. This is cruel and unusual punishment. Communicate that to the Governor."

Smith ignored me. Again, I made my plea.

"I'm his lawyer. I ask for clemency."

Smith's eyes appeared to be tearing. This time he spoke into the phone and informed Wallace of my request. Meanwhile, they prepared the chair for the third attempt. Warden White opened the door to the witness room, and Smith said: "Hold everything. They're asking for clemency."

Minutes later Smith announced: "The Governor will not interfere. Proceed."

They were ready for the third jolt. Once again another charge of electricity was sent through John's body. Once again, his head and leg boiled. There was more smoke and sparks. Rick and I held hands in horror. This jolt lasted thirty seconds.

At 8:44 the doctors pronounced him dead. His body was charred and smoldering. The execution of John Evans took fourteen minutes.

As Warden White escorted us out of the institution, a prisoner blew "Taps" on a trumpet. Outside the rain and thunder kept pounding.

Later that night Betty issued a statement for the press. It read: "I am proud of my son. He left this life as a true Christian."

◈ ◈ ◈ ◈ ◈

John's barbaric death was just another part of the ritual of killing. He had been burned alive and his body mutilated. The cruelty and suffering that John endured shocked many people around the country and the world. The *Times* of London called John's death "grotesque." The *Oakland Tribune* said that the "torture execution of John Louis Evans lifts the veil on official murder.... It is the law of the jungle brought indoors, carrying with it, inevitably, jungle sights and sounds."

◈ ◈ ◈ ◈ ◈

Several weeks later ten-year-old Stan Cox, a schoolboy in Valdosta, Georgia, decided to build a model electric chair as a school project. The press reported that he wanted to make the chair as realistic as possible. A photograph of young Stan and his electric chair made the papers. It did indeed look very realistic.

The boy got the idea following John Evans's execution in Alabama. According to Stan's teacher, the chair couldn't kill anyone, but you couldn't tell by looking at it. When you flip the switch, the chair lights up.

Stan got some help in building his electric chair from his Uncle Jack. The leg cuffs were made from an old belt. The headpiece was made from a baseball cap.

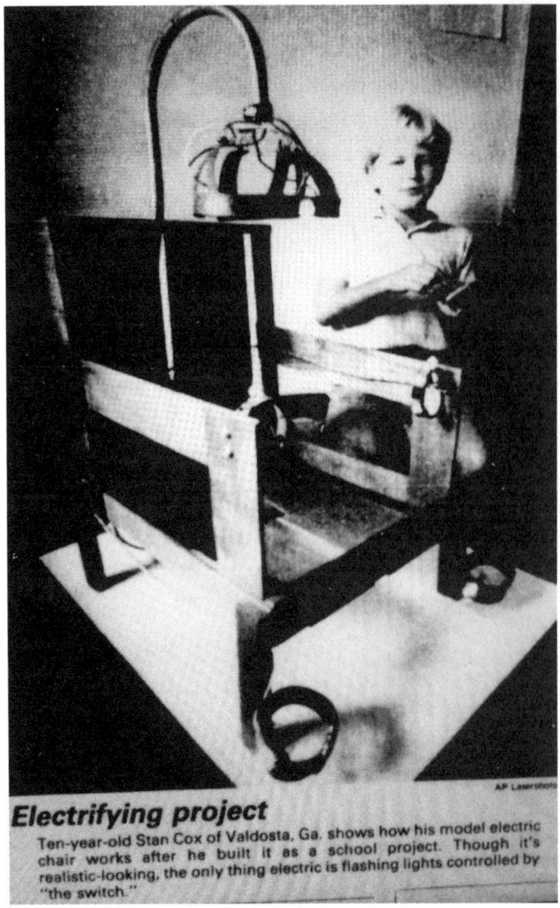

AP Laserphoto

**Electrifying project**

Ten-year-old Stan Cox of Valdosta, Ga. shows how his model electric chair works after he built it as a school project. Though it's realistic-looking, the only thing electric is flashing lights controlled by "the switch."

# Helter Skelter's Son

◈ ◈ ◈ ◈ ◈

## For Whom the Bell Tolls

I slowly walk down the jury box and separately look each juror in the eye.

"Ladies and Gentlemen of the jury, as I conclude my remarks, I ask each of you to consider the poet's words as you return to the jury room to begin your overwhelming and humbling deliberations to determine Richard Mason's* life or death.

> *No Man is an Island,*
> *Entire of Himself,*
> *Every Man is part of the Continent, a piece of the*
> *Main,*
> *Every Man's Death Diminishes me,*
> *For I am Involved in Mankind,*
> *Therefore, Never Send to Know,*
> *For Whom the Bell Tolls,*
> *It Tolls for Thee.*

---

* For reasons of privacy, the names of the non-professionals have been changed.

"Ladies and Gentlemen of the jury, the bell tolls for Richard Mason and the bell tolls for you.

"Richard is a life worth saving. Please save it.

"Thank you for listening."

I sit down on my chair next to Richard and my co-counsel Jerry Fisher. We have done all that we could do and I try to relax, but I cannot. It is now Richard's turn to address the jury. His hands are trembling a bit as he stands up and looks at the jury, getting ready to plead for his life. After he finishes it will be up to the jury, and all we can do is wait to learn his fate. It has been a tough case. This was not the first time Richard had committed murder.

## The Murder of Joe Wilson

Richard was a seventeen-year-old teenage prostitute hustling the streets of East Baltimore in 1982 when his eyes locked on to Joe Wilson, a fifty-two-year-old well-known artist and appraiser.

Joe took Richard to his house, and although all the facts leading up to the killing were never fully known, Joe was found lying nude on his bedroom floor, with an excess of twenty stab wounds to his face and torso. His eyeball had been cut out and was lying on the floor. The house had been ransacked and pieces of silver—serving pitcher, sugar bowl, and candlesticks—were missing. Joe's car was also missing and later found abandoned off the Pulaski Highway in Baltimore. To avoid spending the rest of his life in prison, Richard pleaded guilty to Second Degree Murder.

A Presentence Report prepared for the sentencing judge's consideration summarized Richard's social background and criminal history. The report also gave Richard's abbreviated account of the murder. According to Richard, he was only defending himself from Joe Wilson's aggressive sexual advances when he stabbed him numerous times.

The judge, not swayed by Richard's explanation, sentenced him to thirty years incarceration.

## The Murder of Pete Bunning, the First Trial, and Death Sentence

Two years later, Richard was in prison in the Maryland Correctional Institution in Hagerstown, Maryland, often just called MCIH.

On August 6, 1984, at 10:48 p.m., a prison guard, hearing a loud noise coming from the G-1-20 cell went to investigate. He found Richard, shirtless, standing by his cell door, his chest covered with blood.

"Get me out of here," Richard yelled. "I just killed this guy."

Pete Bunning was lying face down on the upper bunk bed with thirty-nine stab wounds to his back and six to his chest in the 6 x 9 cell he shared with Richard.

In Pete's own blood Richard had written HELTER SKELTER'S SON in large uppercase letters on the wall over the body. The writing covered a 4 x 5 foot area of the wall. Richard's visible fingerprints were all over the bloody words. Richard stood in the locked cell beside Pete, wearing a black glove and holding in his hand a crude seven-inch shank made from a metal meal tray. After a trial, the jury quickly found Richard guilty of First Degree Murder for the killing of Pete Bunning.

After his conviction, the State sought the death penalty.

Richard Mason was now nineteen years old, and had served only about a year of his thirty-year sentence for the stabbing murder of Joe Wilson.

A death penalty trial is brought in two phases. The first is the traditional trial, generally called the guilt/innocence phase, where the jury is called upon to find whether the State proved beyond a reasonable doubt that the accused is guilty of First Degree Murder.

Once the jury found Richard guilty of First Degree Murder, a separate trial was held before the same jury to sentence him to either Life Imprisonment or Death. In order to obtain a death sentence, the State would have to prove that "aggravating circumstances" outweighed any "mitigating circumstances." The State was limited by the death penalty statute to certain specific aggravating circumstances, and the only one that applied to Richard was the fact that the murder was committed while he was confined in prison. Other aggravating circumstances, such as where the victim was a law enforcement officer, or a child, or where the crime was a contract murder, committed during a rape, robbery or arson, simply did not apply.

The jury was then asked to weigh the aggravating circumstance against specific mitigating circumstances set forth in the sentencing statute. Some mitigating circumstances did not apply to Richard as well:

- the defendant did not have a criminal record for a crime of violence;
- the victim was a participant in the defendant's conduct or consented to the act that caused his death;
- the defendant was not the sole cause of the victim's death.

The other listed mitigating circumstances were to some greater or lesser degree possible justifications for the jury to spare Richard's life:

- defendant was of a youthful age at the time of the crime;
- defendant acted under substantial duress, domination, or provocation of another person, even though not so substantial as to constitute a complete defense to the prosecution;
- the murder was committed while the capacity of the defendant to appreciate the criminality of his conduct was substantially impaired as a result of mental incapacity, mental disorder, or emotional disturbance;
- it is unlikely that the defendant will engage in further criminal activity that would constitute a continuing threat to society.

Although the State was strictly limited to the aggravating circumstances set forth in the statute, the defense could go outside the specified mitigating circumstances and suggest others for the jury's consideration that would be relevant to Richard's background and the facts surrounding the crime. Essentially, the jury could write in mitigating circumstances on the verdict form as grounds for sparing a life.

The jury in 1985 found the obvious aggravating circumstance that the murder was committed while Richard was in prison. The jury found no mitigating circumstances and sentenced Richard to death. The trial judge issued a stay of execution to allow Richard to appeal his conviction and death sentence.

Under Maryland law, the trial judge was required to file a report to ensure the death sentence was appropriate. The trial judge noted that "The victim was stabbed 45 times (6 times in the chest and 39 times in the back) with a homemade knife. The evidence strongly suggests that he was asleep when he was attacked."

The trial judge was then called upon to indicate whether he or she agrees with the jury's verdict. The judge wrote:

"I agree with the jury's Findings and Determination. There was evidence from which the jury could have found the existence of mitigating circumstance No. 5 (youthful age); however, in my opinion that circumstance would not have outweighed the aggravating circumstance by a preponderance of the evidence."

Richard was sent to death row in the Maryland Penitentiary in Baltimore.

## Winning the Supreme Court Lottery

Lawyers from the Maryland Public Defender's Office represented Richard at trial. They also filed an appeal in the Maryland Court of Appeals, the highest appellate court in the state. The Court rejected his appeal and affirmed his conviction and death sentence. Richard's lawyers then appealed to the U.S. Supreme Court.

The Supreme Court only hears about two percent of the cases filed for review so Richard hit the Supreme Court lottery when his case was accepted. His lucky streak continued when in June of 1988 the Court, in a 5-4 decision, concluded the trial court's jury instructions regarding how to evaluate mitigating circumstances were unconstitutional.

The Court noted that in Maryland in order to prove an aggravating circumstance, all twelve jurors had to agree. The finding of an aggravating circumstance had to be unanimous.

Maryland law also required the jury to unanimously find a mitigating circumstance. The flaw in this law, the Supreme Court held, was that it created a scenario where all twelve jurors might believe the defendant should be sentenced to Life Imprisonment, but, because they might have different reasons for such a belief, the law prevented them from doing so.

For example, six jurors might believe that Richard's youth was such a mitigating circumstance that he deserved to live. On the other hand, the other six jurors might believe that Richard's difficult childhood was such a mitigating circumstance that he deserved to live. Under this very realistic situation, even though all twelve jurors wanted to sentence him to Life Imprisonment, the law prevented the jury from saving his life.

The Supreme Court ruled that this very possible scenario unduly restricted the jury's prerogative to issue a Life Imprisonment verdict and vacated Richard's death sentence. The Court upheld his conviction for First Degree Murder, but sent the case back to the trial court for a new sentencing trial before a new jury to determine either a life or death sentence.

## Helter Skelter

Gary Christopher, the Chief of the Maryland Public Defender's Capital Unit, called and asked if I would take on the resentencing trial for Richard. Although I was in private practice and not a member of his office, he thought a fresh pair of eyes could only help in warding off another death sentence.

"The good news," he said, "is that both the State's Attorney and the judge are good guys, and you shouldn't have problems with them."

"Also good, race will not be in play; all the key players—Richard, victim, witnesses, judge, and State, are white and the trial will be in Allegany County. The County is ninety-five percent white, and at the first trial the jury was all white."

Not having the ugly specter of race dominate the case was a relief. All too often racism, express or implied, played a major role in a death penalty trial.

"Okay, Gary," I said, "all good so far. And the bad news?"

"Russ," he said, "I got to be honest with you. This is a real tough one. Richard was doing time for a stabbing murder when a couple of years later he stabbed his cell buddy forty-five times. To top it off, he wrote in the cell buddy's own blood, "Helter Skelter's Son" on the wall over the body. I hope you can take the case, and of course you can select another lawyer for the trial team."

I knew all about "Helter Skelter." I am a Beatles fan and knew their 1968 song "Helter Skelter" was a loud, raunchy, sexy, screamer with a threat of violence ringing out through its screeching guitars and Paul McCartney's rough singing.

But it was more than just a rock n' roll song to Charles Manson. To the psychopathic cult leader of "The Family," "Helter Skelter" was a clarion call to the apocalyptic race war to come that would lead to his rise as King of the World. In the name of Helter Skelter, Manson and his cult followers carried out a series of nine brutal stabbing and shooting murders in the summer of 1969, including Hollywood actress Sharon Tate as one of his victims.

*Helter Skelter*
*When I get to the bottom I go back to the top of the slide*
*Where I stop and I turn and I go for a ride*

*Till I get to the bottom and I see you again*
*Do you, don't you want me to love you*
*I'm coming down fast but I'm miles above you*
*Tell me, tell me, tell me, come on tell me the answer*
*Well, you may be a lover but you ain't no dancer*
*Helter Skelter, Helter Skelter*
*Helter Skelter*
*Will you, won't you want me to make you?*
*I'm coming down fast but don't let me break you*
*Tell me, tell me, tell me the answer*
*You may be a lover but you ain't no dancer*
*Look out*
*Helter Skelter, Helter Skelter*
*Helter Skelter*
*Look out 'cause here she comes*

I put my lawyer's hat on and remembered "Helter Skelter" was on the 1968 Beatles record that came to be known as "The White Album," a record I played over and over in my college dorm. That was over twenty years from the time I was asked to handle the resentencing. I was a Beatles nut and also followed the Manson murders closely. While most folks would probably remember Charles Manson and his murder spree, how many would make the Helter Skelter connection? I was already thinking of jury selection, and the task of identifying and striking from the jury pool potential jurors who closely followed the Manson murders and would likely know the macabre history of Helter Skelter.

But I was getting ahead of myself. I needed to build a team and called my friend and experienced death penalty lawyer, Jerry Fisher. I gave him the basics, including Helter Skelter.

His response was short and to the point.

"Jesus."

"Tell me something I don't already know," I said.

"Okay, I'm in."

Several days later a number of boxes arrived at my office from the Public Defender. We were ready to hunker down and scour the files and transcripts for the strengths and weaknesses of the State's case for another death sentence and what evidence we could present in Richard's favor. The heart of our job was to develop a strategy to minimize the aggravating circumstance if possible, and develop credible mitigating circumstances that would touch the compassion of the jury.

We wrote a letter to Richard introducing ourselves and let him know we would be visiting him shortly after we reviewed the record and files.

The first step was to review the transcript of the guilt/innocence stage of the trial to make sure we fully understood all the facts leading up to Richard's conviction for First Degree Murder. The State would be allowed to introduce that evidence in the new trial to give the new jury a full flavor of the enormity of the murder.

The facts were clear-cut. What else was there to find? Richard butchered his sleeping cell buddy in cold blood and the jury found him guilty of First Degree Murder. The mystery was why? What drove Richard to such a state of violence?

We assumed the underlying beef between Richard and Pete Bunning that drove Richard to such a shocking murder would never be truly known.

We were wrong.

The prison institutional records were incomplete but apparently during a visiting session with Richard's girlfriend, she was accused of a lewd act and her visiting privileges were suspended. Richard appealed to the Warden writing on June 6, 1984, that "my girlfriend did not do such an act as officer Hardy says she did. She's all I have, and I wouldn't allow her to mess it up... she's a lady, not a slut; I'm a convict, but a civilized one!"

There days later Richard fought with the guards and was sent to segregation—solitary confinement—for 720 days. For reasons unknown, Richard was released from solitary shortly thereafter and placed in a cell with Pete Bunning. In a second letter dated July 4, 1984, Richard claimed he acted in self-defense while confessing that during the fight, "I began losing my mind . . . I was squirted with mace, kicked in the privates . . . bleeding from the beatings . . . and treated like some kind of fucking animal."

There is no record of a reply from the Warden.

At trial, the State introduced into evidence another letter Richard wrote to the Warden on July 20, 1984.

> *I think it is really fucked up that I can't get a reply from you. I asked you and even stooped up to your level concerning the bullshit with my visits and visitor.*
>
> *Man I'm fed up with this Bull-shit. I have a lot on my mind and now, and I'm telling you this sir, If I'm not sent to the penitentiary I will get an ice-pick, stab my cell buddy in the throat, lay him on the bed, take a razor blade and cut from his throat to his asshole. I'll take his insides and sling them all over the room. I'll pull his eyes out and put string through them, and wear as earrings. I'll have his guts on my clothes line, then when the little ones come to get me, I'll stick that steel in their faces until I get tired.*
>
> *This you shit head are my thoughts, and if I can't get help for them, I'll demonstrate them! So that's why I made a copy of this cause, when I lose my mind again, like I did when I cut that faggot's eyes out and run a turkey knife in and out of him 79 times, you'll be the blame for not taking immediate action against this letter and take my word, I mean what I say . . . The clock is running Sir!*

He drew a picture of the devil; underneath the drawing he wrote: "Fuck the World; Fight to Win." Another drawing had a man peeing into a cup with the words: "Live or Let Die Asshole; F.L.B./L.F.Y."

The Warden never wrote back.

Three weeks later on August 6, 1984, his cell buddy Pete Bunning was murdered, a death foretold.

Richard had written to the Warden and threatened to kill his cell buddy in bone-chilling detail. The prison did nothing. What the hell were the prison folks thinking? Were they thinking at all?

I took a deep breath. Our job became much harder.

Next, I reviewed the verdict form returned by the jury to see what they found at the first sentencing trial. That did not take long.

The jury found the obvious aggravating circumstance—that Richard committed the murder at a time when confined in a correctional institution.

The jury rejected each applicable mitigating circumstance. Every single one; even the fact that Richard was still a teenager at the time of the crime was not considered a reason to save his life. The jury verdict form did not disclose whether the defense even suggested a non-statutory mitigating circumstance for the jury's consideration. It was time to dig deep into the trial record and get to work to see if there was anything we could do.

Having easily obtained a death sentence at the first trial, there was little reason to suspect that the State would depart from the simple strategy used at the first trial. Defendant already serving time for murder butchers his cellmate just three weeks after threatening to do so. The photographs of Pete Bunning's mutilated body lying face down in his bed would shock the hell out of anyone. Richard's finger painting "HELTER SKELTER'S SON" in Pete Bunning's blood showed not only a depraved killer, but a boastful one as well. What could be more compelling than executing a murderer who kills while in prison and not only shows no remorse, but perversely gloats about his crime? How many murders does it take for the State to say that society, including the dangerous society of a prison, cannot be safe until Richard is walked into the gas chamber?

The State called only two witnesses at the sentencing trial. The chief of security at the prison simply verified the obvious—Richard was confined in a correctional institution. Aggravating circumstance proven.

As the keeper of Richard's institutional files, the chief of security also presented to the jury a two-page Psychological Evaluation that was completed on January 24, 1984, while Richard was locked up in the Maryland State Prison. There was no indication as to why it was prepared, who received it, or for what purpose it served.

The psychologist conducted intellectual tests and concluded that Richard was "presently functioning in the lower limit of low average range of intelligence."

The Evaluation continued: "The inter-test scatter is somewhat unusual and suspicious. It helps confirm previous findings of minimal brain damage... which may affect his intellectual functioning and contribute to his acting out behavior. RM also has strabismus of the right eye which also may be an indication of damage to the optic nerve or to the cortex."

This was the first morsel of information that might prove helpful. The Evaluation referred to previous "findings" to support the conclusion that Richard may have, at the very least, minimal brain damage to his cortex that might help explain his conduct. I knew enough basic anatomy of the brain to know that the cortex helps determine intelligence, personality, motor function, and other key cognitive qualities. I hadn't realized that strabismus, or what is commonly called "crossed-eyes," could be a sign of more complicated brain damage.

A defendant who is a sociopath or a psychopath is terrifying to a jury. Being brain damaged might be sympathetic. We had to follow up on this aspect of the Evaluation because the rest of report could easily spell another death sentence.

Okay. Maybe we had something to work with. I read on.

"He is an exceedingly dangerous individual who harbors much hostility within the personality structure. He is homicidal and could easily commit the crime again for which he was originally charged. There is no evidence of regret or remorse over his past criminal behavior and in particular the act of murder."

I had defended many accused murderers and read many psychological evaluations, but never had seen such a devastating opinion that the client was homicidal and would kill again without repentance.

I read on. It got worse.

"This appears to be an entrenched antisocial personality who is rather proud of his past criminal behavior. At the age of 19 he is going to have trouble with authority figures and be constantly involved in assaultive damaging behavior.

"If released into a free society he could again inflict the same bodily harm onto a victim.

"Prognosis for his future is extremely poor."

I went back to check on the date of the report. January 24, 1984. Less than seven months before the murder a psychologist predicted Richard would kill again; that he would be proud of it and that he could not change.

Three weeks before the murder Richard specifically threatened to kill his cell buddy.

Did anyone at the prison even read this stuff? Why would any rational prison authority give Richard a roommate in the first place? Why would they keep the cell buddy in a 6 x 9 foot cell with Richard after he threatened to kill him? Was this killing pre-ordained and bound to happen? Was the prison partly at fault?

We were desperate to find a theory that could reach the mercy of the jury. Maybe planting the seed that the prison was partly to blame and ignored a homicide-in-waiting could be used as well.

The next witness at the first trial was the probation officer who had prepared the Presentence Report for the Joe Wilson murder. She meticulously went through Richard's juvenile and adult criminal history. Thrown out of elementary school for fighting, Richard was arrested and released at thirteen, arrested and released again for fighting and then sent to German Children's Home. "It's like an orphanage kind of situation… They're taken in because they're ungovernable… or because they do not have parents." After numerous arrests for assaults, breaking and entering, and stealing, he was committed to the Maryland Training School for Boys, a juvenile prison with locked doors and confinement. The pattern of Richard's release from prison followed by his more serious arrests for robbery and other crimes was repeated again and again right up to the murder of Joe Wilson.

The probation officer testified that there had been attempts at rehabilitation through counseling but that Richard was resistant. Nothing worked with Richard. She didn't say it, but it was clear she thought he was a hopeless case.

But worse was to come.

She had interviewed Richard's mother after the Joe Wilson murder for background history on Richard's upbringing.

> *Q. You indicated… that Richard's mother expressed some concern to you?*
>
> *A. Yes, sir.*
>
> *Q. And some fears… would you tell the jury what those were about?*
>
> *A. Okay. She expressed the fear that Mr. Mason would commit a murder if given the opportunity again.… She did not want him in the community,*

> *but she felt that while confined he should be treated because at the end of a long sentence, if he was released even after a long sentence, he would do it again, it didn't matter how long he stayed inside an institution, that wouldn't change him; he needed some change internally or he would commit another murder.*

A psychologist said he was homicidal and would kill again. His mother said he would kill again. Richard even said he would kill again.

The State rested its case.

Richard's lawyer called only one witness: Richard's mother.

It made for hard reading. She painted a picture of a young boy out of control at a very young age and a juvenile treatment system that simply could not meet his needs. She testified that as Richard grew bigger and stronger he became even more violent and dangerous. She acknowledged upon cross-examination by the State's prosecutor that she had told the probation officer that Richard should remain locked up because if he was released, he would kill again.

Yikes! This was the defense case for a life sentence. Have Richard's mother testify as to how her son was a hopeless cause; that the juvenile system could not rehabilitate him; that he would murder again.

The closing argument to the jury by Andrew Norman, the Assistant State's Attorney, was concise and to the point:

"Ladies and gentlemen, it takes a special kind of person to do what the Defendant did to Pete Bunning on August the 6th, 1984. It takes the kind of person that has absolutely no value at all on the life of another fellow human being. That is the kind of person it takes. And if the death penalty exists with people like Richard Mason, if the death penalty is to mean anything in the State of Maryland other than two empty words, this is the proper case for it."

The law allows the family of a victim to write what is called a victim impact statement to express the impact the murder had on the family.

The prosecutor read to the jury a summary of an interview with the probation officer and Pete Bunning's brother, William, and sister in-law.

"Pete and William Bunning came from a family of six. At a very young age, they were removed from their parents' custody because of neglect and placed in separate foster homes. Removal by the Department of Social Services was prompted by Pete being hospitalized at age four for anemia and malnutrition.

"Pete was a hyperactive child and hard to handle, which resulted in a lot of beatings from his various guardians. He ran away constantly from the various homes in which he had been placed. After a while, Pete, at the age of fifteen, just started living on the streets. He was eventually sent to the Maryland Training School for Boys.

Mr. Norman, the prosecutor, then directly quoted a statement from Pete's brother. "Pete never really had a home or a family as such. I tried to keep in touch with Pete by writing and visiting whenever possible. I always had good homes and a good life, and I always felt guilty that there was nothing I could do to help Pete. After all, I was only one year older than he. Pete was a good person who had a tough life, a lot of bad breaks, no family, no home, nobody to really give him a chance. I sometimes think he felt more secure in prison, because he had no one on the outside. Sure he committed crimes. But he wasn't violent. He did what he had to do to survive, and he got involved with a lot of bad people."

Mr. Norman finished in his own words.

"Ladies and gentlemen, Pete Bunning had a right to live. So did the Defendant. But by murdering, by murdering Pete Bunning in the way that he did, as it's shown in the evidence in this case beyond all reasonable doubt as you found it to be... I put it to you that Richard Mason has forfeited his right to live. And ladies and gentlemen, I ask you to impose the ultimate penalty. And you know what it is. And I thank you for your kind attention and for being patient throughout this trial."

The defense closing argument was a rambling speech that contended the death penalty in Maryland was not applied fairly in that some counties regularly sought death sentences while others did not. Counsel criticized the juvenile justice system for not adequately treating Richard, and said Richard's age of nineteen was a reason to spare his life. Counsel stated, without anything to back it up, that it was unlikely that Richard would commit other crimes of violence.

The defense closing argument seemed perfunctory to me and could not have taken more than ten or fifteen minutes.

The jury only deliberated several hours before they returned their verdict of a sentence of Death. The trial judge set an execution date and then issued a stay of execution to allow Richard to appeal his conviction and sentence. Richard was transferred to death row in the Maryland State Penitentiary in Baltimore.

## Building the Defense Team

What struck us was the scarcity of information provided to the jury about Richard by both the State and defense at the sentencing trial. Because Richard had been in the juvenile justice system since he was thirteen, there were bound to be tons of psychological, probation, and court reports detailing his family, criminal, and institutional history. The probation officer who testified clearly had it in for Richard. It would not have surprised us if Richard had suffered severe abuse and neglect in his young life which contributed to his rebellious and violent conduct. If so, that never came out at trial.

We needed to get his complete files and take another look at Richard's life.

It appeared the juvenile system had failed Richard and we needed to pursue that angle. Counsel had argued that point at trial, but we felt we could do better. Jerry and I readily agreed to hire a top-flight social worker who had experience developing mitigation evidence in a capital case. We asked Jerry Miller of the National Center for Institutions and Alternatives, an organization dedicated to the rehabilitation of offenders, to provide a complete background of Richard's life, not just a recitation of his failures.

We had to try and face head-on the devastating psychological report predicting Richard's future homicidal intent. That cursory two-page report must have carried powerful weight in the jury's deliberations. The defense at trial never tried to counter the report's conclusion that Richard would kill again and even seemed to acquiesce to it. We had to see if we could fight back.

Dr. Neil Blumberg was a well-respected forensic psychiatrist who had been retained in the past by both the State and the defense in death penalty sentencing cases. We were confident that he could conduct a professional examination of Richard. If there were mitigating evidence to discover in Richard's mental health background, Dr. Blumberg would give us the straight scoop. He was also a very credible and convincing witness before the jury. If Dr. Blumberg could present mitigating evidence, it could go a long way to counter the one-sided narrative of Richard's violence and perhaps save his life. I gave him a call.

The fact that Richard had at the very least "minimal brain damage" also needed to be explored. But did we really know what "minimal" meant? And maybe it was "minimal" in one examiner's eye; this kind of determination can be as much art as it was science. The last report helped confirm previous findings of brain damage which might explain limited intellectual functioning and contributed to his "acting out" behavior. Relatedly, Richard's strabismus of the right eye also may be an indication of damage to the optic nerve or to the cortex.

There had been a great deal of recent scientific inquiry into the effects of brain damage and its relationship to violent individuals. We were aware that Dr. Jonathan Pincus, a professor of neurology at Georgetown University Medical School, had done ground-breaking research on what made killers kill. Dr. Pincus studied a number of death row inmates and published his findings on the relationship between murder and brain damage. Perhaps the viciousness of the murder itself could in some way be attributed to Richard's brain damage which might lessen his responsibility in the eyes of a jury. The defense at trial never sought to develop Richard's brain damage as mitigating evidence. Like insanity, brain damage is beyond the power of the accused; can the State really put to death someone who did not intentionally kill but was driven to violence by forces beyond his control? We asked Dr. Pincus to evaluate Richard.

To save Richard's life and truly reach the humanity of the jury, we had to present a sympathetic justification that Richard's was a life worth saving and that this broken man could be redeemed; that his plight in life was caused by damage to his brain at birth and a horrific upbringing that no child should ever have to suffer; that Richard had to struggle against dark forces far beyond his control; that Richard was not evil; that Richard should be saved.

Redemption in the Bible calls upon the grace of God to save a lost soul for his sins. In a court of law, however, it is the jury that plays God. They decide who lives and who dies.

If Richard approved of this strategy, we had the beginnings of a defense.

It was time to meet Richard.

## The Maryland Penitentiary

There had been a death penalty in Maryland since 1638, a punishment brought to the Maryland shores by British colonists. Since then over 300 people had been executed in Maryland, most by hanging. Carrying over another British custom, the hangings were public exhibitions in the county where the crime took place. In the 1920s the State moved the hangings inside the Maryland Penitentiary as the public spectacle of executions created unruly mobs.

In 1955, the law changed to provide the gas chamber as Maryland's killing machine, considered to be more humane than the rope. On June 9, 1961, Nathaniel Lipscomb was the last man to be executed in Maryland's gas chamber.

In 1972, the Supreme Court in *Furman v. Georgia* ruled that death penalty statutes around the country were applied in an arbitrary and capricious manner and found them all unconstitutional. Many hoped that the Court's action would signal the end of the death penalty. The States, however, including Maryland, responded by modifying their laws. In 1976, the Supreme Court in *Gregg v. Georgia* approved a statute that would be the model for most of the other states that wanted to continue using capital punishment.

Now that we had studied the trial transcripts and all the records pertaining to Richard, we felt we had enough information to meet our client and begin working together on his defense. Before we went any further with experts, such as a psychologist, social worker, or neurologist, we needed to run these possible approaches by Richard, hear what he had to say, and consider any suggestions that he had.

Jerry and I drove up I-95 from D.C. to Baltimore and the Maryland Penitentiary, one of the first prisons built in the country. It was an old-fashioned Gothic-style prison from the early 1800s that was built like a gray stone castle with a white pyramid roof and white turrets.

The Maryland Pen had an appalling history of torture, disease, and corruption and was widely known by the convicts as the worst place to do time in the State of Maryland. Intermittent riots and violence among the prisoners were rampant and the murder of a guard in the mid-1980s added to the perpetually tense atmosphere.

It was dirty and grimy as we waited in line with other lawyers and various family members. We showed our identification at the steel-barred gates. The gates opened with a buzzing sound as we walked through the halls with dull gray peeling paint to the visitors' room.

Attorneys were allowed "contact" visits with clients and we waited patiently in a large room with other lawyers talking to their clients. Eerily, the gas chamber was on the second floor, just above us. Twenty minutes later Richard slowly shuffled in with two security guards in tow, looking much older than his twenty-five years. He was shackled in handcuffs and leg irons and wore a white prison jumpsuit. He was thin and wiry, about 5′9″, and probably weighed no more than 160 pounds. He wore his long hair parted down the middle, like John Lennon from The White Album photographs. He had a thin, wispy, light brown beard, and mustache.

We asked Richard how things were going in the prison and if we could help in any way. Richard eyed us warily but eventually talked about his family and visits that he was receiving. He was having a hassle getting visiting privileges for his new girlfriend and we told him we would do what we could to help.

We briefed Richard on our work so far and our initial thoughts about asking him to sit for interviews with experts. We felt that we needed to radically change the defense from the last trial; we wanted to explore his possible brain damage as a child, and his rough family upbringing as possible mitigating factors.

As this was our first meeting with our client, we decided that it was best to hold off any discussion of Richard's relationship with his cell buddy and what led to the fatal encounter. If we had to have that difficult conversation, it was for another day when, hopefully, we would have earned his trust.

Although we never discussed it, Richard had to be keenly aware of the real possibility that he might be the first condemned inmate to actually be executed in the modern era in the State of Maryland.

After leaving the prison, we headed to East Lombard Street to meet Richard's mother and sister. They lived in a small and cramped row house in East Baltimore. Susan, his sister, had sandy, long brown hair, and was initially reserved. She looked as though living with the burden and guilt of a brother on death row and a fragile mother at home was overwhelming her. She told us her mother believed that her testimony had sent Richard to the gas chamber, and she couldn't bear to testify again. Despite agreeing to meet with us, the mother refused to leave her bedroom.

We told Susan that we understood, but asked her to relay to her mother that even if she didn't want to testify, she could give us, and our experts, some very useful background material that could help Richard. Susan said her mother was adamant and didn't want to meet us, but that she would pass along our request.

Waiting quietly as Susan went upstairs to the mother's bedroom, Jerry and I aimlessly looked at some files. Fifteen minutes later Susan returned.

"She's just not ready," she said. "Maybe never will be."

We told her that we had read Richard's entire file and had, at the very least, an understanding as to what the juvenile social services and court system thought about her brother. But we wanted to hear the family version, the real account.

She sighed as if she had told this story one too many times. Susan was intelligent and thoughtful and went on for the next two hours to tell a tale that was cold and dark; a young boy regularly beaten and sexually abused by an uncle; a house where fear dominated daily life; a life without joy or affection. Father had been locked up, and mother struggled with her drunken and abusive second husband. Richard rebelled early against the trauma that was his daily life. Richard's childhood became a daily hell that was only relieved when he was institutionalized at age thirteen, never to live full time at home again.

We thanked her for her time, and as difficult as it was, asked her to talk to our social worker, Jerry Miller. She said that she would, but could not promise what her mother would do.

Walking to our car, Jerry and I looked at each other, shook our heads, and headed home to D.C.

## The Experts

Several months later, we were not at all surprised when all three experts produced reports that painted a horrifying picture of abuse, neglect, and brain damage.

The reports from social worker Jerome Miller and Dr. Neil Blumberg showed that Richard was born prematurely at six months and weighed only three pounds. He was born with a "lazy eye," had jaundice, and was hospitalized thirty-four days before he was released. His mother was an alcoholic; his father incarcerated. His maternal grandmother was schizophrenic and his maternal grandfather was unknown. Family life was extremely chaotic. His mother divorced and remarried a violent man who abused not only her but also Richard and his siblings. Drug and alcohol abuse were rampant throughout the family. Richard suffered many head injuries causing loss of consciousness.

At eight years old Richard started having temper tantrums and began setting fires. Diagnosed at nine years old as hyperactive with attention deficit disorder, he was a discipline problem at school, frequently out of control with impulsive behavior, and showing signs of paranoia. Although failing at school, he was "socially" promoted from one grade to another until he dropped out at thirteen.

He had few friends.

Richard was institutionalized almost continuously at either an "orphanage" for ungovernable children, or a juvenile prison for various crimes such as vandalism, breaking and entering, and assaults.

He was released to the community at seventeen. Two weeks later he killed Joe Wilson.

Although there had been attempts to provide services and treatment to Richard—some half-hearted, some genuine—his institutional record screamed of a system that warehoused and pushed him along to the next stop, all the while washing its collective hands of a troublesome youth.

The extent and depth of Richard's sad, neglected, and unhappy childhood had not been presented to the jury in the first trial, and we felt we had the makings of a case to reach the compassion of a new jury.

Dr. Pincus's report and findings tied it all up. His evaluation of Richard tracked much of his past research.

Earlier psychological reports indicated that Richard suffered from brain damage either at birth or through blows to the head as a child, or maybe a combination of the two. Richard came from a very abusive family and suffered elements of paranoia and other mental illness. Dr. Pincus's theory, which Richard sadly exemplified, was that the interplay of family abuse, mental illness, and brain damage caused Richard to act violently. Richard's mind had been damaged through a childhood of horrors and cruelty, while his frontal lobes had been damaged at birth and through childhood blows to the head. As Pincus later wrote in his book, *Base Instincts*, "Abuse generates the violent urge. Neurologic and psychiatric diseases of the brain damage the capacity to check that urge."

## Trashing the Victim

And just who was Pete Bunning? The victim impact statement from his brother at trial certainly painted a very sympathetic picture of a young man abandoned by his parents and left to the mercy of an indifferent and even evil foster care system. But was there more to Pete Bunning that we did not know? One stark fact of the murder got our attention. Under Pete Bunning's mutilated body, near his head, was a blade from a disposable razor.

Jerry and I batted around the problem of Richard's brutal letter to the Warden threatening to kill his cell buddy. Was that the real reason he killed Pete Bunning. Was there something more to it? The letter seemed like a braggart strutting his toughness, while screaming out for attention. If he really intended to kill his cell buddy if he didn't get his visiting privileges restored, why would he place in the hands of the police and prosecution the keys to his conviction for First Degree Murder? Perhaps there was a history with Pete Bunning that had never come out at trial that could help explain the fury with which Richard killed him. Richard's co-defendant in his first case claimed that Richard had been a teenage prostitute in East Baltimore when he was picked up by his first victim, Joe Wilson. Although Richard eventually pled guilty to the murder, he justified his actions by saying that Wilson had sexually come on to him.

Might sex be at the heart of the death of Pete Bunning? Even at this late date, could we point the finger at least in part at Bunning? Could it be possible that there was some form of self-defense?

When I was working with the Southern Center for Human Rights in Atlanta, I was shooting the breeze in the hallways of a Georgia county courthouse with a fabled defense lawyer who dressed in the style of Colonel Sanders of Kentucky Fried Chicken fame. We were talking about murder cases and the defenses for homicide.

He smiled, and with a deep Southern drawl said, "Son, there are only two defenses to a murder. Did the son of a bitch need killing, and did the right son of a bitch kill him?"

We laughed long and hard, but the point was well taken.

There was no question that Richard was the person who did the killing. But did Pete Bunning need killing? Or, at the very least, was his killing somewhat justified or understandable?

It is a sad fact of life for a criminal lawyer defending a murder charge that "trashing" the victim can be fair game. We asked my old friend and investigator Billy Ware, who lived on a farm not too far from the Hagerstown penitentiary, to take on the case and dig into Pete Bunning's background by getting his institutional files and interviewing witnesses in the prison. It was probably a long shot, but we had nothing to lose.

Born in Jackson, Mississippi, Billy loved playing the "good ole boy" while playing guitar and singing Merle Haggard tunes in a deep baritone. He had been court-martialed out of the Army in Vietnam for striking an officer. As Billy told the story, "I really meant to kill the motherfucker before he got us all killed."

After the Army Billy drifted to Florida and Georgia where he got caught up in couple of armed robberies and ended up doing some serious time in Georgia and Florida state prisons. Although it took him awhile after his release, he got himself together, took on regular jobs, and eventually ended up going to and thriving in law school where I met him. With his felony background Billy had to fight hard after graduating to prove to the Maryland Bar authorities that he had been rehabilitated enough to be qualified to take the Bar Exam. The Bar authorities resisted him all the way, but after a long drawn-out battle, Billy won his case in court. During that time Billy and his wife Julie moved out to the country, raising two kids while he worked as a criminal investigator.

A couple of weeks later Billy called.

"Partner, you ain't going to believe this. Looks like our Pete Bunning was one human gay rape machine. His base file is all over gay sex shit. Wrote up many times for forcing himself on guys, with many fights.

"You gotta take a look at the file yourself. I'll drive down tomorrow; there's definitely some dudes I think we should try and talk to. Whether they'd be willing to talk about this shit with all the macho shit in the joint I don't know, but it's worth a shot."

The next day Billy stopped by and delivered Pete Bunning's base file. We gave each other a big hug as it had been far too long.

"Partner, it's some sad shit in there. Pete had it tough, just like Richard, maybe even worse. It shouldn't have been a surprise that one of them left that fucking cell in a box."

Billy had tagged the highlights with yellow post-its, but we had to read it all.

I went through each of the 108 pages of Pete Bunning's institutional life through reports and judgments from juvenile social workers, adult probation officers, psychologists, psychiatrists, prison guards, wardens, police officers, prosecutors, defense lawyers, judges, and the one forensic pathologist who examined the body that "left the cell in a box." My emotions ranged from horror at Pete's abused, neglected, and loveless life, to excitement for our defense as I checked off in red the pages of Pete's violent crimes and sexual assaults that painted the picture of a remorseless predator. In the end, though, I took in a deep and weary sigh for the lost souls like Richard and Pete, who never really had a chance in life.

We recognized that putting Pete's horrific past before the jury at trial would clearly suggest the possibility that Richard's and Pete's history of violence and aggression would inevitably end in catastrophe. Placing Richard at risk for sexual violence by Pete would not excuse the brutal murder, but it might make his actions more understandable, more human. It could possibly save Richard's life. And that was justification enough for my enthusiastic red lines through the words about the ravages of Pete Bunning's life that ended up with him face down in a pool of blood with forty-five stab wounds deep into his lifeless body.

When Pete was two years old his mother tried to kill him by hitting his head with a golf club. Years later an aunt was asked to try and account for his violent behavior. Referring to the assault with a golf club, she stated, "I think it was just that whack. He don't really know he's doing it."

His mother was a go-go dancer on Baltimore's Block, a strip of sleaze joints, and left him when he was five; his father, mostly unemployed and a drinker, couldn't take care of Pete and his four siblings. They were referred to the Department of Public Welfare when a social worker found that two of the Bunning children had been brought to Johns Hopkins Hospital in a state of anemia and malnourishment. All the children were placed into separate foster care homes.

One sister ran away from her foster home seventeen times and ended up in the juvenile court. Her whereabouts were unknown.

Pete spent a few years with an aunt, but his violence and lying made her return him to foster care where he was deemed "ungovernable." As a child, he spent three years in a mental hospital. He was called insecure and the victim of a starved childhood where there was never any permanence in his world—physical or emotional. He was considered "hostile toward the world" and "quite emotionally disturbed."

His education ended in the fifth grade, when he was suspended for fighting fellow students and "attempting to start a fire."

Pete was first incarcerated at eleven years old for stealing and setting fires. A string of other crimes quickly followed—breaking and entering, malicious destruction, arson, assault and robbery, armed assault with a knife—while he was in foster care, brief visits to a relative, various mental hospitals, and juvenile prisons.

His father resurfaced after remarrying and took Pete in. The new arrangement lasted but a few weeks when Pete sexually assaulted a younger stepbrother and a four-year-old girl in the neighborhood. It was noted that while home Pete had "cut the tail off a neighbor's cat."

Rather than return to foster care he was adjudged mentally handicapped and sent to the Spring Grove State Hospital for psychiatric treatment. His diagnosis was "unsocialized aggressive reaction of adolescence." At Spring Grove he was accused of sexually molesting younger and weaker patients. The mental hospital released him and at sixteen years old he was sent to the Maryland Training School for Boys in 1975, the same juvenile prison his killer would enter five years later, also when he was sixteen years old.

Reports stated that Pete "was evaluated by psychiatrists and psychologists many times during the past ten years and has been diagnosed as having severe emotional disturbance... sociopathic... seriously dangerous youth" and was considered a "potential threat... to the safety of others in the community."

Pete's out of control and violent behavior did not end while his was in juvie prison, but he was coming up on his eighteenth birthday and a report stated that "Pete had accomplished as much as he presently can in our program," and he was released to a psychiatric halfway house.

What bullshit. He had accomplished nothing except graduating to more serious and sexually abusive crimes. Like Richard, the system threw its collective hands up in the air with a seemingly incorrigible youth and gave up on him.

Pete never showed up at the halfway house and disappeared into the streets. His life of adult crime quickly followed. In the space of two months he was charged with malicious destruction, breaking and entering, assault and robbery. At eighteen years old he was sentenced to three years in an adult prison and released after serving his full term.

Two weeks after his release, Pete and another individual broke into a home and stole $7,000 worth of silver and other items. Trying to cover up their crimes, they set several fires in the home to eliminate their fingerprints. The fire threatened the lives of the four people who were asleep in their beds. Apparently the alarms of smoke detectors saved the sleeping residents as they were able to make good their escape from the burning house. Pete plea bargained his case; four counts of assault with intent to murder were dropped and he pleaded guilty to burglary and arson. Pete was only twenty-one years old and had spent almost all of his life past the age of four in various institutions. He was sentenced to fifteen years of hard adult time in prison by the Baltimore City Circuit Court.

Pete's violent assaults and aggressive sexual conduct continued while he was serving his sentence at a mental hospital and then the Maryland Correctional Institution at Hagerstown. His institutional file—the base file—contained over twenty-five serious disciplinary infractions: weapons possession, threats to officers and inmates, assaults on officers and inmates, and sexual assaults. As a result of his long history of infractions, he spent almost all of his locked-up life in solitary confinement.

Twice, he had smashed light bulbs and eaten the glass and was taken to the clinic, treated, and sent back to his cell.

One report summed up the sad human being that Pete Bunning had become, noting that from age six to the present: "He is polymorphous perverse, failing to differentiate between sexes and between children and adults. His sexual confusion has led to further ostracism and has reinforced his self-perception of inadequacy. The many months of seclusion, both at MCI and Patuxent, are symptomatic of this pathology. His antisocial behavior is seen as a means of retaliation against the environment to which he has become so alienated."

One report concluded: "This is an extremely dangerous, unsocialized man, whose stays at nine Maryland institutions over a period of sixteen years, have not demonstrated any substantial improvement in his behavior. He sets fires to homes at age twenty, just as eagerly as at age three."

In January of 1984, cries of "shank" filled the tier as Pete stabbed inmate Danny G fourteen times in the chest and left side of the body. He was never charged with a crime in court but was sent into disciplinary segregation. On June 28, 1984, a Classification Assignment Sheet reported that Pete was serving 1,161 days of disciplinary segregation and was scheduled to be released from solitary on February 17, 1987.

For reasons that were not explained in the records, less than a month later, on July 25, 1984, Pete was released from segregation and assigned to bunk with Richard Mason.

He was dead twelve days later.

## Trashing the Prison

There was no question the prison acted in gross neglect of its duties to provide a safe environment for its inmates. A psychologist said Richard would kill again. His mother said he would kill again. Richard said he would kill again. He even sent the Warden a letter specifically saying he would kill his cell buddy. And the prison did nothing but allow Richard to share a 6 x 9 foot cell with Pete Bunning, a man whose cruel upbringing, acts of violence and sexual assaults created a ticking time-bomb. As Billy said, it was no surprise that "one of them would leave that fucking cell in a box."

There was no doubt the prison system was partially responsible for the death of Pete Bunning. But could we use that to our advantage? Anything that took the focus away from Richard's conduct could possibly sway the jury that the prison also had to be held accountable for the murder of Pete Bunning.

## The State's Attorney

Other than introducing ourselves to the State's Attorney in a letter and short phone call, it was time for us to truly size up the competition. The murder took place at the Maryland Correction Institution in Hagerstown, Washington County. The trial would be prosecuted by the elected State's Attorney, Ken Long. In Maryland, the law allows the defense to automatically transfer a death penalty case from the county where the crime took place to another county to be selected by the Chief Judge of the State. This process helps eliminate potential bias of jurors in the county who may have strong feelings about a sensational murder, and who also may know the participants in the trial—defendant, witnesses, or lawyers. Richard's case had been transferred to Cumberland in Allegany County before the first trial. Notwithstanding the transfer of the case, the State's Attorney for Washington County would still prosecute.

There are cases where prosecutors are determined to seek a death sentence. Sometimes this passion to send someone to the gas chamber is a genuine and righteous belief that a defendant's crimes are so heinous that only an execution will protect society and give solace and a sense of retribution to the victim's family.

I disagree with those sentiments because I believe the death penalty doesn't deter murder, is arbitrarily imposed on the poor and people of color, and that innocent men and women have been sent to death row. I also think from a moral viewpoint that we have grown as a society and can do better and should join the vast majority of other countries that have outlawed capital punishment. But I understand the other view.

I don't respect, however, those prosecutors, and sadly, judges, who are hell-bent on seeking the death penalty for craven, political reasons. Reliable academic studies have shown what those in the trenches have always known: State Attorneys and judges in most states such as Maryland are elected and the pressure to be tough on crime while courting votes is a sure political winner. The studies have shown that the closer in time to an election, the more likely it is that prosecutors will seek the death penalty and judges will impose it.

In contrast, there are also State Attorneys who may believe in the death penalty, and will honor the fact that their constituents sent them to office in part to seek the ultimate punishment in a truly cruel and atrocious crime, but use their power reluctantly, judiciously, and cautiously.

Ken Long, the State's Attorney for Washington County, was such a prosecutor.

As Jerry and I had never practiced in Washington and Allegany counties, one of our first jobs was to do due diligence and scope out the reputations of the prosecutor and trial judge. Our conversations with fellow defense lawyers in Washington County all said the same thing. Ken Long was a totally decent, fair-minded man who was well respected by the entire legal community, including the defense bar. "A straight-shooter with no BS," was a common response to our inquiries.

This was high praise indeed from defense lawyers who by law have an adversarial relationship with prosecutors, and by nature are a skeptical and cynical lot.

Jerry and I decided to drive to Washington County and meet Mr. Long in person and make sure we had all available documents and evidence. Our main purpose, however, was to feel him out as to whether he would be willing to forgo seeking a second death sentence and have Richard sentenced to the alternative—Life Imprisonment.

As Richard would still be serving a thirty-year sentence for the Joe Wilson murder, an additional sentence of Life Imprisonment would effectively mean that he would never see the light of day and would die in prison.

But we had two problems. First, we had nothing to negotiate; we had absolutely no leverage and there was nothing we could give him. In 1990, when the trial was scheduled, a jury only had two options at sentencing—Life Imprisonment or Death. Unlike some other states, at that time a Maryland jury did not have a third option—Life Without Parole. This lack of a third option played into our second obstacle. A Life Imprisonment sentence meant that Richard could theoretically be released from prison on parole someday with the approval of the Governor. Richard's two murder sentences would make this legal theoretical possibility a fantasy in the real world, but the public perception that a killer who had killed twice in such a vicious manner could ever be released would definitely tie any prosecutor's hands.

We had nothing to lose. Ken was as decent as advertised; straightforward and friendly. He almost gave the impression that he'd rather be doing almost anything else but having to conduct a second death penalty trial for Richard Mason. He didn't reject out of hand our request that the State simply accede to a Life Imprisonment sentence.

"You have to give me a darn good reason to simply withdraw the State's position on the death penalty," he said. "You got to admit Richard could be a poster boy for capital punishment."

Ken Long's position was certainly fair enough.

Our team of psychiatrist Dr. Neil Blumberg, social worker Jerry Miller, and neurologist Dr. Jonathan Pincus had all completed their interviews and investigations and had prepared formal reports and we gave them to Mr. Long. We were hopeful that the horror that was Richard's brain-damaged life would help persuade Ken Long to forgo a second death penalty trial. It was a long shot as we had nothing to trade, but Ken Long was certainly a thoughtful guy and would give the request the serious consideration it deserved.

Several weeks later he wrote back.

"Try as I might, I cannot resolve in my mind that this matter is not worthy of meeting the State's request for the death penalty. I have reviewed Dr. Pincus's report several times; however, I continue to believe that if the State does not seek the death penalty in this case, it is highly unlikely there would ever be another case where the death penalty could be sought."

It was time to get ready for trial.

## Danny G and John Hansen

From Pete Bunning's file we were able to identify some of his victims in prison. Billy had also interviewed a number of inmates in the Hagerstown penitentiary who knew Richard and Pete. He called one afternoon while Jerry and I were going over the case.

"Partner," he said, "you have to talk to Danny G. He said Pete tried to rape him in the shower and when he fought back, Bunning stabbed him fourteen times with a shank. He's got photos of his wounds, in color and all. They're ugly and he's pissed.

"But getting him to testify, brother, is another thing. He doesn't want to be a punk, even if in his mind, Pete Bunning got what was coming to him.

"John Hansen was also hit on and assaulted by Pete. John says Pete started humping him when they were left alone in the rec room. When he told him to 'fuck off,' Pete grabbed a razor blade and sliced at his elbow.

"Guards walked in and stopped it before it really got real bloody. John didn't even want to have it written up. So he's gonna to be tough to come around."

Jerry, who's always quick with a quip, said, "Billy, that's why we're paying you the big bucks!"

"Thanks, Partner," Billy replied. "I'm on the case."

## Getting Ready

The last few weeks before trial we had lengthy trial preparation meetings with our "A" team of experts, Jerry Miller, Dr. Jonathan Pincus, and Dr. Neil Blumberg. Everything was set. They were all professionals and had extensive experience in court. Their individual reports and planned testimony were strong, and the State was not planning on calling its own experts to contradict them. We were good to go with them. Well aware that for political and economic reasons many states could not care less about defending death penalty defendants, we were incredibly grateful that the Maryland Public Defender was willing to support and pay for such distinguished professionals.

Billy and I drove to the Maryland Correctional Institution in Hagerstown, an old, dirty prison that looked to be right out of a B-grade movie version of prison hell.

We met with Danny G and John Hansen separately. Danny was not at all happy about getting involved in the case, but he didn't fight us and grudgingly agreed to come to court.

John Hansen was another story. John was a tall, lanky man with long, dirty blonde hair in a ponytail. He had tattoos up and down his arms.

As soon as we sat down with him he came right at us. There was no small talk.

"I know what you guys want and I ain't having it.

"If you haul my ass to court, I'll tell that motherfucking judge and jury that your boy was the bigger faggot, tried to fuck me and many others and always carried a blade. Pete Bunning was the same. Fuck 'em both and I hope they both rot in hell. When they carry your boy to the gas chamber, I'll say good riddance you faggot."

We tried to calm him down before talking about Richard and Pete, but as he said, he wasn't having it.

We could have dropped a subpoena on him and forced him to come to court and hope that he would come around. After all, we had documented proof that Pete Bunning had stabbed him. The last thing we needed, however, was an out of control witness saying Richard was a violent predator. Perhaps we could simply put into evidence at trial the detailed written reports of Pete's assaults. Live testimony would be much more dynamic and compelling, but the risk would be too great. We had to pass on John Hansen.

We turned our attention to Richard.

A defendant in a death penalty sentencing trial has the right to speak directly to the jury at the very end of trial. The great advantage is that Richard would not have to take the witness stand and be subject to cross-examination; just like a lawyer in closing arguments, he can stand before the jury and say his piece, whether an explanation of the crime or a plea for mercy, or both.

The decision to address the jury is the defendant's alone and not the lawyers' call. Richard had not talked to the jury at his first trial.

Driving up to Baltimore, Jerry and I discussed whether it would be advisable for Richard to exercise his right to speak to the jury and what advice we would give him. Richard was very articulate, and had a certain charisma about him. But it was a tricky issue. If the jury is turned off by the defendant, it could literally be curtains. On the other hand, by actually hearing his voice, jurors might make a human connection with him.

We spent many hours with Richard explaining our theory of the case and his right to talk to the jury. He didn't have to make a decision until the last minute, so we didn't press him, but suggested that he prepare a written statement so he would be ready, just in case.

## With Favor Wilt Thou Compass Us as with a Shield

Cumberland is a small city of about 20,000 people on the Potomac River in western Maryland, nestled in a valley of the Appalachian Mountains. The historic red-brick courthouse, built in 1894, sits in the center of the city and dominates the skyline with a spire and green turrets. Oil portraits of Chief Judges dating back to the nineteenth century line the staircase leading to the courtroom.

The courtroom is an old-fashioned classic; high ceilings with a chandelier, and dark mahogany wood for the walls and a lighter shade for the judge's bench, witness stand, clerk's desk, and jury box. There are dark brown leather chairs for counsel and the jury. The American flag and the State of Maryland flag stand at opposite ends of the bench where the judge's high-back chair sits in the center. On the wall above the chair is a huge twenty-foot circular Great Seal of the State of Maryland. The year 1632 is at the bottom of the Seal with the Maryland flag in the center with a crown on top draped by regal purple overhead cover. On either side of the crown stand two men—a farmer holding a spade and a fisherman holding a long fish.

There is Latin text encircling the Seal, *"Scuto bonæ voluntatis tuæ coronasti nos."* I learned later the words are from a verse in Psalm 5 and translate, "With Favor Wilt Thou Compass Us as with a Shield." The Lord will protect the righteous.

We're in the courtroom early waiting for Judge Frederick Sharer to take the bench and start the process of *Voir Dire*, the selection of the jury. Judge Sharer has a great reputation for fairness, patience, and courtesy. We have not had the occasion to have much contact with him leading up to the trial, but we've been very impressed so far as he has agreed to have a very robust jury selection that may take three to four days.

This is perhaps the most important decision the judge can make for us because in our experience in-depth questioning of prospective jurors may make or break a case.

*Voir Dire*, French for "to speak the truth," is not really jury selection, but in reality jury exclusion, as both the prosecution and defense try to eliminate potential jurors whose backgrounds and beliefs may incline them to vote against their side. The judge will excuse a potential juror for "cause" if the individual indicates that he or she can't be fair to either party. Even though the potential jurors are placed under an oath to tell the truth, most people want to present themselves to the judge as fair-minded, and very few will own up to their prejudices.

After the judge excuses potential jurors for "cause," each side has a number of "peremptory challenges," and may excuse or "strike" a potential juror without giving a reason. As long as a pattern doesn't develop showing that race, gender, or religion was the real reason for a lawyer's "strike," the decision to excuse a potential juror is unassailable.

The actual exercise of the strike in the courtroom in Allegany County can be awkward. During the first round, both sides interview the juror on the witness stand in a closed courtroom with no one present but the lawyers, judge, security officers, and defendant. After the juror leaves the courtroom, either party can move to strike the juror for cause. If the judge agrees, the juror is "struck" and is later advised outside the courtroom that he or she is excused and can go home. The juror will have no idea who moved to exclude him or her from the trial.

The second round is different. All jurors remaining are qualified to sit on the trial and are brought into the courtroom. The lawyers then exercise their strikes in open court in front of everyone. One by one a juror approaches the bench and the State or defense says to that juror that he or she is either "accepted" or "excused." Once twelve jurors, plus two alternate jurors are accepted, the jury is seated.

It takes time to select a jury to discover an individual's true beliefs, and many judges are time obsessed and in a hurry to complete the trial. In order to truly get to know a potential juror requires lengthy questioning about his or her family, work, positive or negative contact with the criminal justice system, feelings about the death penalty, and even religious beliefs. Even then, *Voir Dire* is more an art form than a science, and sometimes gut feelings will come into play.

Judge Sharer makes it clear that we will take the time necessary to select a fair and impartial jury in this most important of cases where a man's life is at stake.

*Voir Dire* takes five days. We make some tough judgment calls as to which jurors to strike, but we're reasonably confident the most hardcore believers in the death penalty have been struck, either for cause by the judge or on a peremptory challenge by us. You never know though. We go back and forth on one juror, a middle-aged woman, Mrs. Williams, who is very lively and opinionated, and professes to be very fair. She is a manager of a store, a boss, and we're cautious about having leaders on the jury because a strong leader can dominate group dynamics. Yet we like her and feel we can trust her. In the end, though, we play it safe and strike Mrs. Williams.

Ten women and two men make up the final jury. For better or worse, we're ready to start the testimony tomorrow.

The next morning Jerry and I are having breakfast in the downtown hotel we're staying in. Mrs. Williams, the prospective juror we had struck the day before, happens to walk in, sees us eating at our table and strolls right over with confidence, clearly intent on talking to us.

I brace myself for an ugly confrontation. We had just rejected her in the courtroom in a very public way. No one likes that.

She smiles at us as we clumsily stand up.

"You boys made a big mistake yesterday. No way was I sending your man to the gas chamber."

She's not mad, just surprised we couldn't figure that out about her.

We make some small talk with her. She wishes us well.

Jerry and I look at each other thinking the same thing. "We blew that one."

In the courtroom, Judge Sharer asks the bailiff to bring in the jury.

We all stand at attention as the jury files into the courtroom. Richard is wearing regular black slacks, a blue shirt, and black shoes.

Not one juror looks at him.

The judge instructs the jury that Richard had previously been convicted of First Degree Murder and that the jury had to accept that verdict. The jury's sole job is to determine Richard's sentence—Life Imprisonment or Death. All twelve jurors would have to agree before they sentenced him to death. One lone holdout would result in a life sentence.

This a great advantage for us. All we have to do is convince one person to stick to his or her principles and we can defeat the death penalty.

It is now time for the opening statements before the jury.

The judge turns to the State's Attorney.

"Mr. Long, you may proceed," he says.

Ken Long stands before the jury and methodically outlines the State's case—the facts of the crime, the impact of the crime on Pete Bunning's family, Richard's previous conviction for Second Degree Murder, and the State's responsibility of proving the aggravating factor that the murder of Pete Bunning took place in a prison. He says that the only just verdict is a sentence of death. Long is such a nice and honest guy that he naturally inspires confidence in people. It's a very effective opening statement.

It's now our turn.

Jerry paints a compelling story of a brain-damaged boy who had to endure a horrific upbringing and was left to the neglect of the juvenile social services and prison system.

Jerry does a great job explaining that there are two types of mitigating circumstances; some that are outlined in the official verdict form, but also some that the defense can suggest to the jury to write in. He also explains that both types of mitigating circumstances have equal value.

As for the crime, Jerry patiently explains that we accept, as we must, that Richard was convicted of murder, but there was much more to the story than the State's simplified version of events. Sadly, Pete Bunning also had a rough upbringing and, as tragic as that was, the plain fact of the matter was that Pete was a known violent sexual predator, and there was a great likelihood that Richard's conduct was in response to an aggressive sexual assault. He dramatically tells the jury that a razor blade was found under Pete Bunning's body. Finally, Jerry continues, the prison officials were out of their minds to assign Richard and Pete as cell buddies.

Even though the jury by law has to accept that Richard was guilty of First Degree Murder, the State is allowed to place the basic facts in front of the jury so that their sentencing decision could be placed in context of the seriousness of the crime committed.

The judge turns to Ken Long.

"State, call your first witness."

The State's case is short and to the point. Various correctional officers introduce photographs of the crime scene, including Pete Bunning's back and chest full of gruesome stab wounds. There is a photograph of Richard in handcuffs, looking straight at the camera, in shorts and no shirt. Blood is smeared all over his chest. He looks defiantly into the camera. HELTER SKELTER'S SON written by Richard in Pete's blood is photographed over the dead body in large block letters covering an area of the wall almost 4 x 5 feet. A bloody shank, the murder weapon, is photographed on the floor.

A forensic pathologist testifies as to the six stab wounds to the chest and the thirty-nine stab wounds in the back.

Cause of death: multiple stab wounds to numerous vital organs. Manner of death: homicide. He couldn't tell which stab wounds came first; the ones to the chest or to the back.

"So was it possible," I ask on cross-examination, "that the decedent could have been the aggressor and the defendant stabbed the decedent in the chest to defend himself?"

The pathologist refuses to play TV Medical Examiner and speculate as to who struck the first blow.

The State then points out on redirect examination that the crime scene showed that almost all the blood was on Pete's bed, in the words HELTER SKELTER'S SON above the dead body, smeared on Richard's chest, and a smattering on the floor.

The implication is clear. Pete was attacked while he was on the top bunk.

The letter from Richard to the Warden complaining about his visiting privileges and threatening to kill his cell buddy like he did to the "faggot" when he cut his eyeball out is read to the jury.

The social worker's and psychologist's reports calling Richard a hopeless sociopath with no redeeming qualities are admitted without the witnesses testifying. Although we could have objected and required the State to bring their experts into court, we're fine just having their reports entered into evidence without testimony. Paper reports, without explanation, can come off as flat. We will have our own experts in the courtroom, and think real live people before the jury will have a greater impact.

The State's case just takes a couple of hours and we're fine with that as well. As gruesome as the murder of Pete Bunning had been, such a short trial deprives the jury of the chance to truly invest their time, energy, and, most of all, passion to the case despite the magnitude of their decision. The first jury heard days of very detailed testimony and had to wrestle with finding Richard guilty before even considering a death sentence.

We're hoping this trial feels artificial to the jury, that they are just not feeling the righteous need for retribution or vengeance to send someone to his death. No matter how many times a judge instructs the jury to leave their passions behind, much of the appeal a lawyer makes to the jury in a death penalty trial is based on emotion. I think it demands too much of human nature to ask a person to dispassionately send someone to the gas chamber. I think there has to be a virtuous need for retribution, closure for the murder victim's family, or public safety, to convince someone to sign a verdict form with their name on it sending someone to die.

## "I'll Catch You Lunching"

Our experts, Miller, Blumberg, and Pincus, all testify to Richard's chaotic, ferocious, and neglected upbringing, including his being sexually assaulted by an uncle, and numerous fights in a home fueled by alcohol, anger, mental illness, and complete dysfunction. Dr. Blumberg also highlights Richard's paranoia as well as his long-standing attention deficit hyperactivity disorder.

Jerry asks Blumberg if he had read Pete Bunning's institutional file. Blumberg says he has.

Jerry asks how Richard would be affected if placed in a 6-x-9-foot cell for twenty-three and a half to twenty-four hours a day with a man who had a long history of violent homosexual assaults with shanks and razors.

In an understated, but forceful way, Blumberg states, "It would create about as explosive a situation as you can imagine. It would be like setting off an acetylene torch in a roomful of gasoline."

We've set up Danny G's testimony.

Dr. Pincus takes the witness stand. He is in his sixties, tall and thin, and has a pleasant, professorial manner as he tells the jury of his impressive education and position as Chairman of the Department of Neurology at Georgetown University.

He describes his interest in behavioral neurology, which involves the intersection of neurology and psychiatry. Breaking down medical jargon for his lay audience without dumbing it down, he testifies that lesions or growths in parts of the brain can cause remarkably violent and aggressive behavior.

Dr. Pincus testifies that after examining Richard, he concluded that Richard suffers from brain damage caused by multiple sources. He has a history of factors known to be associated with brain damage, including premature birth, low birth weight, a mother who abused alcohol, alternating strabismus, attention deficit hyperactivity disorder, and paranoia. Further, Richard also suffered multiple head wounds causing lack of consciousness from fights with this father, stepfather, brother, and boys he lived with in various orphanages and juvenile prisons.

Dr. Pincus goes through the injuries one at a time, a courtly professor teaching his class. The jury follows him in rapt attention.

Richard has a dent in his forehead after being slammed into furniture at the age of nine that can still be felt on examination; a V-shaped scar on his forehead after being kicked into a fan; a horizontal scar on his forehead after being hit by a baseball bat; a dent in the back of his head after being thrown into a wall, or when he was struck by a 2 x 4. There were numerous other blows to the head that didn't result in loss of consciousness.

The jury listens closely, some members bowing their heads when the more brutal assaults are being described in almost numbing detail.

Dr. Pincus tells the jury that Richard is very impulsive, liked to drive cars fast the short time he was a free man in society, and when he starts fighting, he loses control of himself and cannot stop. Richard admitted to him that he had been involved in acts of violence in which he feels that he overreacted.

And then Dr. Pincus testifies that he asked Richard to describe the events that led up to the murder. The jurors with their heads bowed now look up. All the jurors are intently focused on Pincus as he relates Richard's side of the story.

After smoking marijuana, Pete and Richard were gambling over a chess game with $20 at stake. Pete lost the game, refused to pay up, and angrily threw the chess pieces down. The two men started fighting with their fists until prison guards broke it up. They stopped the fighting, but continued cursing each other out. Richard said that he had been crushing Pete before the guards came over.

Pete told Richard, "I'll catch you lunching." Richard explained that in prison lingo this meant Pete would catch him off guard when he wasn't looking. Richard told a prison guard to get him out of the cell because his cell buddy had threatened him. The guard smirked and said he would move Richard away "after he sees blood."

Taking this threat seriously, Richard obtained a crude shank from another prisoner.

After seeing Pete take a razor and melt it to the end of a toothbrush, Richard and Pete started cursing and taunting each other, which ultimately led to the knifing.

We worry that allowing Pincus give Richard's side of the story might backfire. Pete was found face down on the top bunk. How could he be an immediate threat to Richard, even if he did have a razor blade?

In the brutal and harsh prison world, however, where the two shattered men barely existed, to say "I'll catch you lunching" means kill or be killed. We will soon call Danny G to the witness stand to breathe some life into that world.

Dr. Pincus testifies that if Richard's account of the events prior to the murder is accurate, then Richard, a paranoid, impulsive, brain-damaged individual under the influence of marijuana, believed his life was endangered by his cellmate. As such, Richard's actions could be seen as self-defense, albeit extreme and excessive. The multiple stabbings are evidence that he was out of control at the time of the murder.

Dr. Pincus concludes by stating that he believes Richard acted under considerable duress and provocation by his cellmate and that the murder was committed while his ability to act within the law was substantially impaired as the result of his mental incapacity

It is now time to call Danny G to the stand. Danny G is 6'1" and 230 pounds of hard muscle dressed in a short-sleeve white prison jumpsuit. He has long, black, oily hair parted down the middle and tattoos up and down both arms. He speaks in a guttural tone that reminds us of Marlon Brando in *The Godfather*. He's been waiting in a cell block down the hall from the courtroom. I inform the judge that Danny G is our next witness. Judge Sharer calls us to the bench, out of the hearing of the jury.

The judge offers to recess the trial for a few minutes and excuse the jury to their jury room. During the recess Danny G would enter an empty courtroom and have a seat in the witness chair and would be there when the jury returned. This courtesy extended by the judge would prevent the prejudice to our case of having Danny G menacingly parade right in front of the jury in leg irons and handcuffs.

It is a very thoughtful gesture by the judge.

We turn it down.

We want Danny G to look fearsome and threatening to the jury. We want them to be afraid of this tough and angry man.

I announce in open court, "The defense calls Danny G to the stand."

Each member of the jury turns their head as the door to the courtroom opens. Two beefy prison guards flank Danny G wearing a white prison jumpsuit as he lumbers into the courtroom right in front of the jury, his leg irons clanging and handcuffs binding him tight like Public Enemy Number 1.

The real life of prison enters the courtroom. There is utter silence. I look at the faces of the jury and see most of them are visibly uncomfortable, some with their heads partially down while stealing a glance at perhaps the most dangerous looking man they have ever seen in person.

Danny G wasn't in the movies or on TV.

Danny G was in Richard's world, a world of violence and fierce danger.

The clerk asks the witness to remain standing and administers the oath.

"Do you solemnly swear to testify to the truth, the whole truth, and nothing but the truth, so help you God?" says the clerk.

"Yeah," says Danny G.

"You may be seated."

Danny G sits down, his handcuffs clashing loudly on the small table on the witness stand. The sound startles everyone. A juror winces.

"Mr. G," I say, "please tell the jury your name."

"Danny G," he says.

"I see you are wearing a prison jumpsuit. Where are you in prison?"

"Hagerstown."

"What are you doing time for?"

"Armed Robbery and Kidnapping."

"How much time are you doing?"

"Twenty years."

"Do you know Richard Mason?"

"I know who he is. But I don't hang with him."

"Are you friends with him?"

"I told you, I don't hang with him."

"Did you know Pete Bunning?"

"Yeah, I knew him."

"How did you know him?"

"He tried to fuck me up the ass in the shower."

"Did you have any other dealings with him?"

"Yeah."

"What was that?"

"A few days after trying to fuck me, he stabbed me fourteen times in the chest."

"No further questions, Your Honor."

"No questions," says the State's Attorney.

"Mr. G, you may stand down."

Danny G stands up. With one leg iron crashing against another, and jangling handcuffs to boot, he shuffles right by the shocked jury and out of the courtroom.

I let the moment linger, wanting the jury to soak it all in. Everybody must be thinking that if Pete Bunning can assault such a large, well-muscled, tough man such as Danny G, imagine what he could do to the thin and small Richard Mason sitting right before them.

We enter into evidence Pete's prison institutional file, his base file, and read aloud selected portions to the jury highlighting his repeated history of violent sexual assaults.

We have one last witness, Richard's sister, Susan. She was coming from Baltimore that morning and we haven't seen her yet. We ask for a lunch recess and the judge grants it.

Outside in the hallway we see Susan and a scruffy looking man looking to be in his mid-fifties, thinning hair, and a beaten down craggy face. Susan introduces him as Jimmy Mason, Richard's father.

Susan says if we want him to, Jimmy is willing to testify at trial. Jimmy nods his head in agreement. We've never met him and don't know what he can add to our case, and whether any testimony from him might backfire and do more harm than good. Passing on lunch, we spend the time listening to Jimmy's story. We decide to go for it.

After lunch, Jimmy takes the witness stand. He looks much older than his stated mid-forties. He's spent most of his life in prison for armed robbery and other offenses. After marrying Richard's mother and fathering Susan and Richard, he abandoned them and quickly found himself in prison. He never played a role in Richard's life. He says he regrets his life's choices, but has connected with Richard now and wants to be his father, wants to make up to the son that he left behind. He says he can't do much, but he will do all he can to make it right with Richard. Jimmy says he hopes Richard will forgive him. It's never too late. He says Richard never had a fair chance in life.

It is poignant testimony that comes from the heart. It takes courage to walk into a public courtroom and say you failed in the most important thing a man can do—be a father to your children.

Susan is our last witness. She has long, sandy brown hair, works as a nurse's aide and looks straight at the jury. She tears up but remains strong as she describes in detail the beatings, sexual abuse, and horror that had been Richard's youth in East Baltimore, a cold and dark life. Her mother did her best, but could not cope with Richard's acting out and rebellion. Social services were a waste of time. She chokes up again as she tells the jury that she escaped to go to school while Richard was in a juvie prison.

Susan describes Richard as having a good heart but never had the love or guidance to make it in life. She says Richard means the world to her and she would be devastated if he were executed. With dignity, she takes a deep breath, and quietly pleads with the jury to save his life.

Susan steps down from the witness stand.

"Your Honor," I say, "the defense rests."

It is late in the afternoon, and the judge recesses court for the evening to resume tomorrow with his final legal instructions to the jury and closing arguments.

The jury silently files out of the courtroom.

Richard has been quiet and withdrawn throughout the trial, barely speaking to us. We've left him alone, not really imagining what he is going through.

We now spend extra time with Richard reviewing his planned speech to the jury that he wrote entirely by himself. It looks good. We don't change a word. He doesn't have to talk to the jury if he doesn't want to; it's totally his decision. We just don't want him to freelance and wing it.

That night Jerry, Billy, and I watch the Orioles on TV while we eat pizza in a local bar. Later in my hotel room, I go over my notes for the closing argument. I'm well prepared but worry that I will leave something out; that I will miss the critical argument that might reach the redemptive power of forgiveness in the jury.

## "A Beast Who Has Been Awoken"

The next morning Judge Sharer instructs the jury as to their role in making a decision and the law that applies. He takes his time and carefully defines aggravating and mitigating circumstances. All that is left are the closing arguments and Richard's speech.

State's Attorney Ken Long stands up and addresses the jury, and in a calm and earnest voice describes the brutality of the crime and the simple fact that this is the second time in Richard's young life that he had viciously killed someone. His closing argument borrows heavily from the first trial five years ago when he says it takes a special kind of person to kill the way Richard does. He reads the sad victim impact statement from Pete Bunning's family. Long does not contest that

Richard had a very hard upbringing, but he stays true to his argument that if this case does not warrant the ultimate punishment, virtually no case would. Ken Long sits down.

It's my turn. I highlight to the jury all of the strong points from our experts, Jerry Miller, Dr. Blumberg, and Dr. Pincus, the savage world of Danny G, the remorse of Richard's father Jimmy, and finally, the mercy sought by Susan. For after all, it is mercy and forgiveness, a recognition that no man is beyond redemption and grace that we are seeking to reach.

I close with John Donne's poem.

*Therefore, Never Send to Know,*
*For Whom the Bell Tolls,*
*It Tolls for Thee.*

I ask the jury to spare Richard's life and sit down.

I look at Richard as he gathers his papers. I realize that while I have spent countless hours talking with him about strategy for this trial, interviewed many key people in his tormented life, and studied hundreds of pages that document his road to standing before a jury and asking that they spare him from the gas chamber, I don't really know him. I don't think anyone does.

While I don't think he much likes or trusts lawyers, social workers, and shrinks, he has always been respectful and appreciative to every member of the team. I think all the positive energy and work by everyone on his team shows that people care about him, and believe he can be redeemed. He knows we all very much want him to live, while the forces in the only worlds that he knows—harsh prison life and a sometimes equally harsh criminal justice system—want him to die.

He stands up and faces the jury, papers in hand. His hands are trembling slightly as he takes a deep breath and begins in a sure and steady voice.

*Ladies and Gentlemen of the jury. I first like to extend my apologies for having you people to take time out from your personal lives and families and jobs and having to sit here patiently through this long process and having the burden upon your shoulders to play the role of God in deciding who shall live or die. But the fact remains that someone has to do it.*

*I've sat and pondered just how I can describe to you in mere words the brutal and violent effects prison has on a man, because in order to comprehend what I say one must physically and mentally experience it.*

*Over the years prison has changed its codes, values, and morals. At one time years ago, if you had a beef with a prisoner you'd tie your boots uptight, and go off in a corner for a few rounds of fist-fighting and may the best man win.*

*That has changed ladies and gentlemen; now-a-days they play for keeps by using weapons fashioned in many ways as primitive man made theirs. I've seen many a-man die a bloody death.*

*I witnessed a brutal, bloody attack on a prisoner that to this day has affected me psychologically. Some men sat around playing cards; one inmate had a habit of slamming down his cards each play. The inmate whom the cards belonged to asked him one time not to tear his cards up. A few hands later the same guy slammed down a card; the guy the cards belonged to stood up and asked if anyone wanted coffee. He then walked into the kitchen, and got a long steel soup paddle similar to an oar, and without a word struck the guy above the forehead knocking away hair, meat, and bones, which stuck to the wall behind the guy.*

*This incident impregnated in me a fear; a fear of being killed in a bloody fashion. This fear has mastered the art of instincts, when confronted with violence it immediately springs into action without thought, without feeling, and acts out as a beast who has been awoken.*

*This, ladies and gentlemen, is the beast Mr. Bunning had awoken on the night of his death.*

*I am in no way a coldblooded psychopathic maniac. I too feel and cry and hurt just as the next human being. I feel for the oppressed in third world countries and kids dying of hunger in Ethiopia. Women, kids, and old people being molested, and raped, and senselessly murdered.*

*I am not the same Richard Mason that I was six years ago. Since Mr. Bunning's death the prison has held me captive in solitary confinement and locked up in a cell the size of some of your bathrooms.*

*In that six years of solitude, I embarked on a journey of soul searching in search of the real Richard Mason, where I discovered a talented, compassionate, gentle, kind-hearted, caring, and loveable human being, who was capable of showing sensitivity towards mankind. I discovered an intellectual Richard Mason with a great sense of humor, but the sad part to all of this is that I can only open these doors to a very, very, select few. Because in prison, these types of traits must be introverted due to the fact that they are preyed upon as weaknesses.*

*A lot of attorneys will advise their clients to stand before a jury and Boo-Hoo crocodile tears with fake remorse. I cannot do that. For many years I was filled with bitterness and hatred towards Pete Bunning, but through the grace of God and maturity and wisdom and understanding, I am now at peace with him. My remorse goes out mainly to Pete's mother and then his loved ones and I can only say to them that*

*God knows if I could have done things any differently, I would have.*

*Let's talk about the options concerning life or death. If you give me death, I say give the prosecutor a can of turtle wax and a rag so he can polish up the chair and let's bring in a cleaning lady with a bottle of Windex so she can make sure the gas chamber windows are clear so the spectators will have a good view of me choking on cyanide gas. Then we can send the guard to the store and get me a box of Ritz Crackers, a jar of pig's feet, and an ice-cold diet coke, and of course dress me in my best Easter outfit and causally walk me to the gas chamber like Adolf Hitler did to the Jews.*

*Let's look at the option of life imprisonment. . . . I have a lot of goals and dreams and tasks that I will pursue. I'm planning on starting college this semester to get my B.A. I've been accepted in a school by the N.W.I.—National Writer's Institute because I want to be a successful writer someday. I will continue to participate in a prison program called "Project Turn Around" where our troubled youth come into the prison for a tour and one-on-one rap sessions.*

*I'm also in the process of starting a nationwide pen-pal group for our elders who are lonely and have been discarded in state-run old age homes to have people write letters and send cards. I just want to find things to do and give over the years back to society which will make a difference. And, lastly, I plan on marrying my beautiful fiancée who I love dearly, and who has showed me the true meaning of love.*

*Before I close, I'd like to share something with you that a seventy-eight-year-old nun gave to me a month before she passed away that changed my life completely and to this day hangs on my cell wall. It is called Desiderata.*

He reads Max Ehrmann's poem:

*Go placidly amid the noise and the haste, and remember what peace there may be in silence. As far as possible, without surrender, be on good terms with all persons.*

*Speak your truth quietly and clearly; and listen to others, even to the dull and the ignorant; they too have their story.*

*Avoid loud and aggressive persons; they are vexatious to the spirit. If you compare yourself with others, you may become vain or bitter, for always there will be greater and lesser persons than yourself.*

*Enjoy your achievements as well as your plans. Keep interested in your own career, however humble; it is a real possession in the changing fortunes of time.*

*Exercise caution in your business affairs, for the world is full of trickery. But let this not blind you to what virtue there is; many persons strive for high ideals, and everywhere life is full of heroism.*

*Be yourself. Especially do not feign affection. Neither be cynical about love; for in the face of all aridity and disenchantment, it is as perennial as the grass.*

*Take kindly the counsel of the years, gracefully surrendering the things of youth.*

*Nurture strength of spirit to shield you in sudden misfortune. But do not distress yourself with dark imaginings. Many fears are born of fatigue and loneliness.*

> *Beyond a wholesome discipline, be gentle with yourself. You are a child of the universe no less than the trees and the stars; you have a right to be here.*
>
> *And whether or not it is clear to you, no doubt the universe is unfolding as it should. Therefore be at peace with God, whatever you conceive Him to be. And whatever your labors and aspirations, in the noisy confusion of life, keep peace in your soul. With all its sham, drudgery and broken dreams, it is still a beautiful world. Be cheerful. Strive to be happy.*

Richard looks up from his papers and faces the jury one more time.

"Thank you, ladies and gentlemen. I wish you well in life."

Richard returns to his seat, exhausted, and near tears. I know some criminal defense lawyers like to show some physical contact with their clients—put an arm around a defendant's shoulder, even hug them in the courtroom in front of the jury, to show the accused is worth touching, worth affection. But I think it can look phony and I don't do that. But yet still, I put my hand on Richard's back and lean over to whisper to him.

"You did good, man. I'm proud of you."

He nods back to me.

It's done. Over. We gave it our best shot, and it is now out of our hands.

I can't read the jury at all as they file out of the courtroom to the jury room, except to say they all seem withdrawn, as the true weight of their responsibility is about to become a reality.

It is now time to wait. Richard shakes our hands and says, "Thanks guys. I know you fought hard for me."

He doesn't ask our opinion as to the verdict. I don't know what I could say. We feel like our case went as well as it could, but we couldn't predict the verdict. The Deputy Sheriffs take Richard back to the cell block in the back of the courtroom.

Jerry, Billy, and I go back to the pizza joint for lunch and talk sports and music, anything but the case. An hour later we're walking the hallways of the courtroom, killing time with small talk. Richard's sister and father do not wait for the verdict. They go back to Baltimore.

Three hours after the jury began deliberations, the judge's clerk enters the hallway and asks us to come into the courtroom.

Richard is already in his seat, rocking back and forth in his chair. We sit beside him silently. There is nothing to say.

State's Attorney Ken Long walks in and sits down.

"All rise," says the Clerk as we stand up. Judge Sharer takes the bench.

The Judge says the jury has sent a note indicating that they have reached a verdict

"Are we ready to take the verdict?" Judge Sharer.

"Yes, Your Honor," says Ken Long.

"Yes, Your Honor," I say.

There is a long and quiet silence as the bailiff goes to escort the jury into the courtroom. I try and control my breathing as I stare at the Great Seal of Maryland. "With Favor Wilt thou Compass Us As with A Shield." The Lord protects the righteous.

Richard's head is bent down between his legs as he stares at the floor.

The door leading to the jury room swings open as the jury slowly walks into the courtroom to their seats in the jury box. I can't read them at all. I never can. No one is smiling or looking relieved.

We stand out of respect for the jury and then sit down.

Judge Sharer asks the foreperson to please rise.

A middle-age woman stands up holding the verdict form nervously in her hands. She's looking straight at the judge.

Judge Sharer looks straight at the Foreperson.

"Madam Foreperson, as to the aggravating circumstance number 1—the defendant was a principal in the first degree to the murder—does the jury find beyond a reasonable doubt that aggravating circumstance to be proven or not proven?"

"Proven," says the Foreperson in a loud clear voice.

"Madam Foreperson, as to aggravating circumstance number 2—the defendant committed the murder at a time when confined in a correctional institution—does the jury find beyond a reasonable doubt that the aggravating circumstance to be proven or not proven?"

"Proven," she says.

Here we go. We couldn't do anything about the aggravating circumstances. The jury's findings on mitigating circumstances will determine Richard's fate.

The judge turns again to Madam Foreperson.

"Madam Foreperson, as to mitigating circumstance number 1—the defendant has not previously been found guilty of a crime of violence—how does the jury find?"

The Foreperson reads from the verdict form and says, "We unanimously find by a preponderance of the evidence that the above circumstance does not exist."

"Madam Foreperson, as to mitigating circumstance number 2—the victim was a participant in the defendant's conduct or consented to the act which caused the victim's death—how does the jury find?"

The Foreperson says, "We unanimously find by a preponderance of the evidence that the above circumstance does not exist."

*Damn*, I think, Danny G's testimony and Pete Bunning's base file suggested that Pete may have been a participant in the events leading up to the murder.

The judge goes on.

"Madam Foreperson, as to mitigating circumstance number 3—the defendant acted under substantial duress, domination, or provocation of another person, though not so substantial as to constitute a complete defense to the prosecution—how does the jury find?"

The Foreperson reads from the verdict form and says, "After a reasonable period of deliberation, one or more of us, but fewer than all twelve, find by a preponderance of the evidence that the above circumstance exists."

She doesn't raise her head but looks down at the verdict form.

*Damn. We wanted all twelve jurors to find this mitigating circumstance. A least we got one or more jurors, but is that enough? We just need one juror to hold out against death. Do we have that person?*

The judge goes on.

"Madam Foreperson, as to mitigating circumstance number 4—the murder was committed while the capacity of the defendant to appreciate the criminality of his conduct or to conform to the requirements of the law was substantially impaired as a result of mental incapacity, mental disorder, or emotional disturbance—how does the jury find?"

The Foreperson reads from the verdict form and says, "After a reasonable period of deliberation, one or more of us, but fewer than all twelve, find by a preponderance of the evidence that the above circumstance exists."

*How many jurors do we have?* I wonder. *It's key.*

"Madam Foreperson, as to mitigating circumstance number 5—the defendant was of a youthful age at the time of the crime—how does the jury find?"

The foreperson reads from the verdict form and says, "We unanimously find by a preponderance of the evidence that the above circumstance does not exist."

*Oh shit*, I think. *He was only nineteen years old at the time of the murder. What the hell do they want?*

The judge continues.

"Madam Foreperson, as to mitigating circumstance number 6—the act of the defendant was not the sole proximate cause of the victim's death—how does the jury find?"

The foreperson reads from the verdict form and says,

"We unanimously find by a preponderance of the evidence that the above circumstance does not exist."

We were hoping to get at least one juror to agree that Pete Bunning helped cause his own death. We're getting creamed.

One more statutory mitigating circumstance to go. But it's the most important.

"Madam Foreperson, as to mitigating circumstance number 7—it is unlikely that the defendant will engage in further criminal activity that would constitute a continuing threat to society—how does the fury find?"

The foreperson reads from the verdict form and says, "We unanimously find by a preponderance of the evidence that the above circumstance does not exist."

I try and sit straight up in my chair, but I feel like collapsing. The jury just rejected Richard's claim that he has changed his life over the last six years of solitary and found the compassionate and peaceful soul that could never show itself. The jury believes that Richard will commit further serious crimes, that he is a continuing threat to society.

The judge now goes to the write-in part of the verdict form.

"Madam Foreperson, does the jury find by a preponderance of the evidence any additional mitigating circumstances exist?"

The Foreperson looks at her verdict form.

It's not a simple "no." She wouldn't have to be looking at the verdict form if the answer is "no."

She reads from the verdict and says,

"We find,

"1) Parental abuse and neglect, as well as inadequate parental care, and

"2) Inadequate treatment in the Maryland Juvenile System."

*Maybe we have a chance*, I think. It's not all Richard's fault. All twelve believe that Richard was a broken youth who was not well served by his family or those officials in charge with his care.

The judge goes on to the last section of mitigating circumstances.

"Madam Foreperson, does any one or more of the jurors, but fewer than all twelve, find by a preponderance of the evidence any additional mitigating circumstances exist?"

The Foreperson again looks at her verdict form and reads:

"One or more of us, but fewer than all twelve find,

"1) Neurological brain dysfunction and paranoia, and

"2) Conditions at MCIH, and the decision to place Pete Bunning and Richard Mason in the same cell."

*We have a chance*, I think again. *At least one juror, maybe more, believes Richard was brain damaged, and that the prison was partly at fault. But I don't know what the verdict will be. They found he would be violent again! But they also found mitigating circumstances. It could go either way.*

The Foreperson rolls up the verdict form in her hand. She won't have to read from it again. The next question only requires a word, "yes" or "no"; the question after that, a word, or hopefully, two, "Life Imprisonment" or "Death."

The judge looks nervous now. Calm and collected the whole trial, he is now taking his time and getting himself together as he prepares to ask the next question.

Richard raises his head and looks defiantly at Madam Foreperson, like if you're going to send me to the gas chamber, do it to my face. The Foreperson only looks at the judge.

The judge clears his throat.

Everyone in the courtroom is silent and still.

"Does the jury unanimously find that the State has proven by a preponderance of the evidence that the Aggravating

Circumstances marked proven outweigh the Mitigating Circumstances?"

The Foreperson does not look at Richard but keeps looking straight at the judge.

"No," she says in a clear voice.

"What is the jury's sentence?" asks the judge.

"Life Imprisonment," says the Foreperson. She sits down.

Richard bows his head.

I stare straight ahead.

The judge thanks the jury for their service and talks about the value of the jury system to the community, but I'm not really listening. My mind is pretty much blank. I don't feel joy, only relief.

The judge finishes his remarks to the jury and excuses them. They stand. We all stand out of respect, but Richard remains sitting in his seat, his head bowed.

The jury walks out of the courtroom. The judge thanks all counsel for their professionalism and says that court is in recess. He steps down from the bench and out the door behind the courtroom.

Ken Long walks over to us and shakes Jerry's, Billy's, and then my hand, and says "well done." We thank him for his professionalism. He leaves the courtroom.

Richard stands up, looks us in the eye and says, "Thanks guys." We all shake hands.

Two Deputy Sheriffs walk over and put handcuffs and leg irons on Richard. They escort him out of the courtroom.

Four years later, on May 17, 1994, John F. Thanos was the first man executed in the State of Maryland in the modern era.

### Fade to Black

Richard and I had corresponded a little after the trial, mainly about his request for access to various court records, but eventually lost touch. Our professional relationship had ended. Although I maintain some correspondence with some former clients, Richard had no desire to do so.

Richard did keep up for a time with a pen pal, Michael Webb. In a letter written on January 22, 1999, nine years after his second trial, Richard complained that he was not receiving adequate care for his HIV and "my eye balls have sunk back in the sockets and I'm down to 135 lbs."

Richard wrote and dedicated a poem to Michael.

*Fade to Black*

*Life, it seems, will fade away*
*Drifting further everyday*
*Getting lost within myself*
*Nothing matters no one else*
*I have lost the will to live*
*Simply nothing more to give*
*There is nothing more for me*
*Need the end to set me free*

*Things not what they used to be*
*Missing on the inside of me*
*Deathly lost this can't be real*
*Cannot stand this hell I feel*
*Emptiness is filling me*
*To the point of agony*
*Growing darkness taking dawn*
*I was me, but now he's gone*
*No one but me can save myself, but it's too late*
*Now I can't think, why should I even try*
*Yesterday seems though it never existed*
*Death greets me warm, now I will just say goodbye*

*One love forever, your friend, Richard Mason*

◊ ◊ ◊ ◊ ◊

Several months later, the *Baltimore Sun* reported that in August of 1999, Richard Mason was severely beaten into a coma by four members of a gang over a drug debt at the Maryland House of Corrections in Jessup, Maryland. The article reported a drug gang in the prison dealt to inmates nearly two ounces of marijuana, a half-ounce of heroin, and a third of an ounce of crack cocaine. Richard had not paid what he owed and was pounded nearly to death. As of November of 1999, four months later, Richard was still hospitalized.

Michael Webb and Richard's stepfather later told me that as a result of the beating Richard was rendered a quadriplegic and lost the use of his legs, arms, and hands. Richard could still talk, but no longer write. He had assigned prisoners who washed, fed, cleaned his bodily parts, and wrote letters at his dictation.

Records of Richard's life thereafter are scarce. On September 9, 2004, he received a Certificate of Achievement in Psychology from the Maryland State Department of Education.

Richard's letter to Michael in 2004 thanked him for sending money to his account. He ended by saying, "Please keep faith in me, like I will keep in you. Love, Richard for life."

On, December 12, 2004, Richard completed a Living Will. The signature line read: "X—Mr. Mason unable to sign."

After a while, Richard stopped corresponding with Michael.

The Maryland Death Index shows that Richard died on July 4, 2010, in the Western Correctional Institute in Allegany County. The cause of death is unknown.

I would like to think that in his twenty years of life after his trial, despite his serious illness and catastrophic injury, Richard kept his promise to the jury and went to college and became a writer, and a pen pal to lonely senior citizens, and helped troubled youth learn from his mistakes. I would like to think that Richard found some inner peace and lived his life to the fullest.

This chapter is dedicated to Billy Ware who passed away in 2006. Thanks, Partner.

# Death on the Ho Chi Minh Trail

◊ ◊ ◊ ◊ ◊

## A Green Baseball Field

We played baseball in black and white in the late fifties and early sixties in New York City and the suburbs. Stickball games were played against a white handball wall with a field of black-tarred pavement. We played pickup games in sandlots of half-built homes and used T-shirts as bases.

My older brother Jeff and I hunched over the small TV in the den whenever we could and watched the Yankees in grainy black and white on WPIX Channel 11.

One Sunday afternoon we walked up a ramp in Yankee Stadium in the Bronx, my father holding my hand on one side and Jeff's on the other. Slowly reaching the mezzanine section, we left the ramp and suddenly there was this blaze of green grass that seemed to last forever. My ten-year-old eyes had never seen a more beautiful sight. Hector Lopez and Mickey Mantle were casually shagging fly balls in practice, gliding over the perfectly manicured grass. This was how baseball should be played, and I dreamed that someday I would play on this field.

But for now, I was content with being the star catcher in Little League.

Most Little League games were played on dirt infields and outfields at local elementary and junior high schools. Little League was organized like Major League Baseball. There were the minor leagues—Single-A, Double-AA, and Triple-AAA—roughly based on a kid's age and ability. It was expected that by the time a boy reached the maximum age of twelve he would be in the Majors, but there was no guarantee.

"Making the Majors" was a very big deal. Some kids never made it. If you finally made it to the Major League, you played at Wrights Field on Mott Street with a grass infield and outfield. Wrights Field even had dugouts, just like Yankee Stadium.

One late afternoon Jeff and I rode our bikes over to Wrights Field to watch the Major Leaguers, hoping to play there someday.

I was an above-average player and one of the better players on any team that I played on. I could play any position but preferred to be the catcher, the toughest position on the field.

The catcher was the captain on the diamond as he called the pitches to be thrown, and directed the players on the field. No one wanted to play the position that compelled using "the tools of ignorance," a term allegedly coined by the legendary Muddy Ruel. It highlights the irony of a position requiring the player with the most intelligence to play, but still be stupid enough to squat down in an uncomfortable position the whole game. Not only that, but despite shin guards, chest protector, and a mask, you still got hit with foul balls all over your body. It was the only position on the field where you had to wear an athletic cup.

I loved playing catcher since I was in all the action, but also knew that nobody else wanted to play the hardest position. It was also well known that the fastest route to the Little League Major Leagues, not to mention Yankee Stadium, was being an excellent catcher.

I was playing above my age group on the Triple-AAA team called Henri's Deli. My older brother Jeff wasn't a very good baseball player and was playing down, below his age, on the same Triple-AAA team. He should have been in the Majors. One day before practice Coach Marino told me that Ed Murphy, the Major League coach, was coming to watch me play and planning on bringing me up to the Majors. Coach Marino said I was a special player, much better than my age, and would make it all the way.

Before practice started, I told Jeff that Coach Murphy was there to watch me and that I was going to make it to the Majors before he did.

He just looked at me and ran onto the field to play catch with anyone he could.

## Left Back

We were only eighteen months apart but different in many ways. Today Jeff would have undoubtedly been diagnosed with a learning disability, probably dyslexia and ADHD. Back then he was labeled stupid and got left back in school. I was the smart one.

Although strong and powerful, he wasn't a very good athlete. I was the athlete. As he entered his teenage years he began hanging around the "hoods," and joined the Paragons, a rough bunch of guys who mainly hung out, wore leather jackets, smoked cigarettes, drank beer, and sometimes stole cars for joy rides.

I was embarrassed by him.

We didn't talk much, but if we ever got into an argument, as brothers inevitably do, I wouldn't be shy about rubbing in my baseball heroics and good grades. I'm sure he felt like slugging his stuck-up little brother, but Jeff never laid a hand on me and would just walk away.

Because Jeff had been "left back," we were in the same sophomore homeroom class in high school. Sitting alphabetically side-by-side, we sat in small wooden desks, both stewing in different ways. When the bell rang I ran from the class and left him behind. I hated every morning homeroom class and used any excuse I could to skip it. Although we never talked about it, I'm sure he felt the same.

As that school year was ending in the spring, I went to my adviser and pleaded with her to separate us for the fall semester. She complied.

My junior year was a lot easier for me. Jeff and I were not in any classes together and I barely saw him at our large high school with about 900 in our class alone. The separation lessened the stress for both of us.

At home we each had our own third-floor bedroom. We would walk separately to school. Because of after-school sports, I missed many dinners at home and often ate by myself. We didn't argue much; just stayed out of each other's way. That was okay by me.

I didn't know what he was going through and, wrapped up in my own world, I didn't care. But while I was easing into school life, his year was falling apart.

He came home one night and knocked on my bedroom door. I was sitting at my desk scribbling algebraic formulas.

"Yeah, what's going on?" I said.

He came in and sat down on my bed. This didn't happen very often. He wore what we called back then a white sleeveless "wife beater" T-shirt. He turned his body to show off a tattoo on his right shoulder with a red devil and pitchfork circled in black with the word, "Paragons."

"They flipped out," he said. "Told me they'd pull me out of school and sign me up in the Army if I didn't get my shit together."

He paused.

"I don't give a fuck. Fuck 'em," he said.

"What the fuck are you doing anyway?" I asked.

"I'm hanging with the Paragons. Just because they're not Joe college don't mean shit," he said while looking me straight in the eye.

"But do you want to go into the Army?"

"I don't know what the fuck I want to do. Dad said he could put me to work at his station. I don't want to work at his fucking gas station."

"But what do you want to do?"

"I don't know, man." He stood up, looked me in the eye again, and left.

Two weeks later I was in my bedroom and heard Dad shouting at Jeff downstairs in the den. Dad rarely lost his temper so something big was going on.

I opened the door and heard them screaming back and forth at each other, but couldn't make out what they were saying. Suddenly the shouting stopped and I could hear Jeff climbing the steps to our upstairs bedrooms.

I stood outside my room as he walked onto the landing. He was again wearing his white wife beater T-shirt. He turned and sneered at me, showing off a new tattoo on his left shoulder; another red devil circled with the Paragons. Without a word, he walked into his room and slammed the door shut.

Two weeks later he was arrested for malicious mischief. The charges were later dropped, but the die was cast.

Two weeks after that, in the company of my parents, he enlisted in the Army on December 5, 1965.

The body count in Vietnam in 1965 was approximately 2,000 Americans, 11,000 South Vietnamese, and at least that number, if not more, for the North Vietnamese and the Viet Cong.

On December 14, 1965, Jeff reported to Ft. Hamilton in Brooklyn for induction. He was seventeen years old. He had never been away from home.

My parents later told me the Army had a special program for volunteers and would honor Jeff's request to serve in Europe. He would not be sent to Vietnam unless there was a national emergency.

Six months later we visited him in Nuremberg, Germany for four days. Jeff and I shared a hotel room together and talked through the night about life in the Army. Smoking a cigarette on his bed, he told me about the rigors of basic training while getting into shape to run two miles with a full pack and rifle slung across his back.

"It was rough. I'd never been able to run much, but I got through it. Can probably even beat your ass in a race right now," he said with a smile.

He told me about his mechanized unit of the infantry where they trained on armored personnel carriers and infantry fighting vehicles for maximum flexibility and protection in combat. He casually called them APCs and IFVs. I had never even heard of APCs and IFVs.

Without saying so, we both realized that he was now the older brother teaching me about a man's life in the tough world of the military while I was still trying to get a date as a junior in high school.

We had never had that kind of relationship, and I knew he was proud. And I was proud of him.

Jeff told me about his buddies from Oklahoma and Chicago, but he still seemed homesick and lonely. Some of his buddies were gung ho to volunteer for Vietnam. The Army would kick in combat pay and you got thirty days of leave before they shipped you out.

I pleaded with him to stay in Germany. There was always time to sign up for the war later if he wanted. He had only been away from home a short time.

Several months later he and his buddies volunteered to serve in Vietnam. I'm sure he had no idea where the hell Vietnam was. He was home for a month's leave, but I rarely saw him. He hung with the Paragons at night and slept through the day while I was in school. We had some family dinners, but no one talked about Vietnam. It was like he was just returning to Germany. Everything would be fine.

I don't remember the last time I saw him. We had no special good-bye. We acted like everything was okay, no reason to make a big deal about it.

He wrote us a postcard from Hawaii in January of 1967 saying they had a two-day stopover before they arrived at their unit. He landed in Vietnam on January 14, 1967.

We wrote to each other every month or so and talked about pooling our money and buying a car together when he returned home.

On September 16, 1967 around eight-thirty in the morning, my sister Stacy burst into my bedroom hysterically crying.

"Stacy, what's. . . ."

She interrupted me.

"Two soldiers are downstairs," she screamed through her tears, "Jeff's been killed. Mom is with them now."

She turned away and ran downstairs.

"Oh God, no!" I shouted.

*Where's Dad?* I wondered, hoping somehow that he could make things right.

I slipped on some blue jeans and a T-shirt and went downstairs.

Sitting stone-faced at the dining room table, wearing only a bathrobe, Mom sat across from the two soldiers in full-dress uniforms. She smoked her Pall Mall without saying a word.

Stacy sobbed next to her while holding her hand.

The two soldiers stood up and extended their hands .

I shook each one.

"I'm Major Forbes," he said. "This is Major Crenshaw. "We're very sorry for your loss."

"Thank you," I said.

We all sat down at the table.

Without saying a word, Mom passed me a folded piece of paper in front of her, a Western Union telegram.

I opened it. It said that Jeff "died in Vietnam on 14 September 1967 as the result of a gunshot wound received while on combat operation when hit by hostile small arms fire."

I took in a deep breath and looked at Mom.

"Can I make you some coffee?" Mom asked the officers.

"Ma'am," Major Forbes replied, "let us take care of that. We'd like to help."

"Thank you, but no," Mom said.

Major Forbes nodded his head. "Yes Ma'am."

Mom looked at me with small tears starting to run down her face.

"Russ," she said, "call your father. He should be at the station by now."

She stood up and went into the kitchen. Stacy followed her.

Scared and in shock, I couldn't move from the table.

Major Forbes looked at me and gently asked, "If you want me to, I'll make the call."

I wanted him to make the call. I could not imagine Dad's voice on the line. He would know immediately. Why would I be calling at this time? I should be in school.

I slowly stood up.

"Thanks, Major, but I should call my Dad," I said softly. Both officers looked at me with concern.

I walked downstairs to the den and sat on the couch next to the phone.

I had not cried and I wondered why.

*How can I possibly call him at his gas station and tell him?*

My heart was racing. I took some deep breaths to try and calm down. It wasn't getting much better but I felt I just had to pick up the phone.

I slowly dialed his number.

He picked up immediately.

"Hello, American Oil.

"Dad."

"What's wrong?" he demanded in a curt voice.

"Dad. Two soldiers are here. Jeff was killed in combat. He's gone."

Total silence.

My father was a tough man who had endured much in his life.

I couldn't think of anything else to say. I couldn't comfort him.

More silence.

I heard him crying for the first time in my life.

"We lost him. We lost him. We lost him," I heard him say through his tears.

"Please come home, Dad. Please come home."

"I'll be there soon," he said and we hung up.

I climbed the stairs to the kitchen but only Stacy sat with the officers.

"She went to her room," Stacy said and nodded to Mom's bedroom.

Mom did not leave her bedroom for three days and only then to go to the funeral. After the funeral, she returned to her bedroom and didn't leave for days.

Stacy and I sat at the table in silence with the officers and waited for Dad to come home.

A letter from President Lyndon Baines Johnson arrived a few days later. Letters from Senator Robert F. Kennedy and Senator Jacob Javitts followed.

Letters and records from the Army came as well.

They weren't much.

A form condolence letter from the Battalion Chaplain Thomas J. Downes.

I doubted that the Chaplain even knew Jeff.

A certificate dated September 18, 1979: The AWARD OF THE BRONZE STAR—Theater: Republic of Vietnam; Reason: "For meritorious service in connection with military operations against a hostile force."

A September 30, 1967, letter from a General Wickham, unsigned with his name stamped in, indicating that he had "the honor to inform you that the Government of the Republic of Vietnam has awarded posthumously to your son the Military Merit Medal of the Gallantry Cross with Palm."

On October 3, 1967, we received another letter from General Wickham, again unsigned with his name stamped in, advising that the Secretary of the Army "exercised his authority to promote your son posthumously ... to the grade of Sergeant..." The General also advised the family that "I have the honor to inform you that the Purple Heart has been awarded posthumously to your son."

He concluded by saying that "It is my earnest hope that your son's fine record of service will be a source of comfort to you in the days to come."

That the form letters from General Wickham were unsigned pissed the hell out of me. He didn't have the decency to put his damn signature on the letters.

There were a number of miscellaneous documents regarding funeral arrangements and the payment of modest death benefits. That was it. The documents told us next to nothing. We had no details as to where he died and who was with him. No commander or unit member ever contacted us. The Bronze Star Medal indicated that he was with "Co A, 1st Bn (Mech), 5th Inf, 25th Inf Division." That was military mumbo jumbo to me.

What I didn't know haunted me. I couldn't shake the aching feeling that he died alone with no one to comfort and care for him in his last minutes.

Years later, in 2001, I sent away to the military archives in St. Louis for his complete military records. Twenty-seven bureaucratic pages eventually arrived in chronological order. Many of the documents were repeats from our file.

The first new document, however, was the most devastating. In all capital letters:

DECEMBER 5, 1965, "A CONSENT, DECLARATION OF PARENT OR LEGAL GUARDIAN.

"THE ABOVE APPLICANT HAS NO OTHER LEGAL GUARDIAN THAN US, AND WE HEREBY CONSENT TO HIS ENLISTMENT IN THE SERVICE COMPONENT OF THE ARMED FORCES... WE CERTIFY THAT NO PROMISE OF ANY KIND HAS BEEN MADE TO US CONCERNING ASSIGNMENT TO DUTY OR PROMOTION DURING HIS ENLISTMENT AS AN INDUCEMENT TO US TO SIGN THIS CONSENT."

It was signed by my parents on the date of Jeff's enlistment.

I was grateful this CONSENT form had not been in the meager file I took over from my parents. They would have had to review the file those first few months after his death for documents relating to the funeral and death benefits. Their grief for his loss and their guilt for agreeing to his enlistment were already so overwhelming that they didn't need to see their signatures on a military consent form.

They never consented to his death.

I closely read the other documents:

December 14, 1965: Oath of Enlistment, with fingerprints attached, to Elections of Amount, Beneficiary Designation and Settlement Options for Servicemen's Group Life Insurance.

"EXTRACT" documents designating various units, transfers, and ranks in military bureaucratic jargon.

November 8, 1966: EXTRACT from Headquarters, 3rd Support Brigade, noting "Oversea Voluntary Asg" with order "to report to USARS Oakland, California by 12 Dec 66."

It hurt to see "Oversea Voluntary Asg." In a hotel room in Nuremberg he had talked about volunteering for Vietnam with his buddies. I couldn't talk him out of it.

June 15, 1967: Enlisted Qualification Record, a four-page document that recorded aptitude tests, military education, specialized training, qualification in arms, physical status, foreign service, "appointments and reductions and from PVT E-1 to E-2, E-3 and finally to SP4 on 15 Jun 67." The Record of Assignments noted that he worked as a cook in January of 67 when he arrived in Vietnam, and then was transferred to "Lt Wpns Inf on 9 May 67."

Why he transferred to "Lt Wpns Inf" was not explained. Did he volunteer?

September 16, 1967: Report of Casualty; "Indiv. died as result of gunshot wound received while on combat operation when hit by hostile small arms fire." Date of death—14 Sept. 67; time 2115 hrs."

The Report of Casualty simply repeated the Western Union telegram and I wondered how was it possible that there was no further information or details.

September 19, 1967: Casualty Report Work Sheet had basic biographical information and noted in bold under Selective Service Number: **N/A Underage**.

I couldn't stand the sterile bureaucratic language.

October 23, 1967: Survivor Assistance Report documented various funeral arrangements on September 21, 1967, and noted that Gold Star Lapel Buttons were to be given to my parents, grandparents, my sister Stacy, and me.

That was the last document.

A life and death in the military in twenty-seven pages. The complete record.

His death still remained a mystery.

My parents and sister never talked about him. Neither did I.

## The Virtual Wall

One late afternoon in June of 2001, Stacy emailed me at my chambers at the courthouse to say that she had been doing some internet research with her teenage son Gabe for a school paper on the Vietnam War. She said they had come across a website called the Virtual Wall, which had an individual page for each soldier who had been killed in action. She asked me to call her.

I picked up the phone.

"What's up?" I asked.

"I looked up Jeff's page on the Virtual Wall. A photograph was posted just last week. It's of Jeff in the field posted by someone named Allen Chaney. It's a photo I've never seen before. It's incredible. You have to see it. You probably don't use the net, do you?"

She didn't wait for a response. She knew me well.

"I'll walk you through it."

I followed her lead and clicked away.

A slightly blurry black-and-white photograph filled the screen. A soldier in the center with short, curly, dirty-blond hair was half-sitting and half-standing astride sand bags three to four feet tall that appeared to form a bunker. One leg was straight to the ground, while his other leg was bent at the knee. He was in profile with his left hand outstretched to another soldier who was sitting off camera, except for his boots and hands. It was Jeff. He looked older than the teenager he was.

Two other soldiers were inside the bunker with him. One soldier wore sunglasses and stared straight into the camera. The other was shirtless, back turned, and appeared to be using his hands to pack something up.

"I can't believe it," I said. "I thought I had all of the photos of him in Vietnam, but I've never seen this one."

I kept staring at the computer screen, waiting for the photo to come to life. It was frozen in a lost time, some thirty-four years ago.

"Who's Allen Chaney?" I asked.

"I don't know, but I have to believe he was in Jeff's unit. Maybe he's one of guys in the bunker with him. I've got to go. Play around on the net to see if you find something. Keep me posted."

"Okay. I'll do my best. This is wild. I'm kind of nervous about what we may find out after all these years."

I clicked away again, feeling the hidden universe of the internet come to life at my fingertips for the first time. Just when I thought I was out of my depth, I came across an Allen Chaney website. There was a formal headshot photograph of him in his early twenties, dressed in his Army uniform, looking serious and maybe a little scared.

*Getting closer*, I thought.

I scrolled down. The Allen Chaney website said that he was from Texas, and served in the 25th Infantry, Tropic Lightning's, 1st Battalion, 5th Infantry Bobcats. The Bobcats were stationed near Cu Chi. Same as Jeff. This had to be the Allen Chaney who posted the photograph. The website said he had been wounded three times, January 8, 1967, April 4, 1967, and September 14, 1967.

September 14, 1967. I looked again. "Jesus Christ," I said out loud to myself. September 14, 1967 was the date that gripped my gut. The date Jeff was killed in action.

Was Allen Chaney with Jeff when he was killed?

The website said Chaney was now a master mechanic working for the government. It listed an email address.

I took a deep breath. I tried to slow down and take in the moment. My long and frustrating quest to learn more about Jeff's death was possibly within my grasp. I typed a message for Allen Chaney.

*Dear Mr. Chaney,*

*My name is Russ Canan and I am the brother of Jeff Canan who was killed in action on September 14, 1967. For the past few years I have been trying to find out information concerning my brother and the circumstances of his tour of duty and death in Vietnam. I used the services of Delta Force Associates to retrieve his military records, but the records were not very helpful.*

*By coincidence, my sister Stacy was assisting her 15-year-old son on a research project on Vietnam and came across Jeff's picture on the Virtual Wall. I have now read your site and greatly appreciate your posting that picture. Needless to say, it was very moving for us and we would like to learn more about your relationship with Jeff and any other information you or others may have about him. I noted specifically that you were wounded the same day Jeff was killed—September 14, 1967. Is it possible that you were with him on that day?*

*Again, our deepest thanks for your consideration in posting the picture. We look forward to hearing from you. Russ*

Several days later, Allen Chaney's name popped up on my email screen.

*Dear Russell,*

*My name as you know is Allen Chaney and I live in TX. I am now retired after serving 31 years in the US Army and the Army National Guard.*

*I was a member of the same night ambush patrol on which Jeff was killed. I was in a different position than Jeff and I was hit by Viet Cong automatic rifle fire. Our patrol was counter ambushed and Jeff was hit by, I was told, one of our claymore mines that the Viet Cong had turned around and then detonated toward his position. We were then fired at by a number of VC until a relief force from our unit arrived. The VC then continued to harass us with sniper fire.*

*I learned that Jeff had died prior to the arrival of the medivac helicopter. Jeff and I were loaded on the helicopter and flown to the 25th Infantry Division's base camp at Cu Chi. After arriving, Jeff was taken away and that was the last time I saw him.*

*Jeff and I were friends during our tour, as were the others. Jeff has been in my memories since that fateful night. I love him as a brother.*

*God bless you and Stacy and all of Jeff's family.*

*I hope these few words will be of comfort. Please let me hear from you again.*

*Allen*

I teared up. I wanted to grab hold of him. Reach right through the computer to keep this feeling going, but afraid it's way too much, way too soon, even after all these years.

"Thank you, Allen," I wrote back. "Would you mind if I call you some time? Just to talk. I totally understand if you'd rather not.

"Best, Russ."

My eyes remained glued to the screen.

A swift response.

"Sure, call anytime." Allen.

I replied right away.

"Thank you again, Allen; seeing the photograph and meeting you is overwhelming. I wish you the best. Talk soon. Russ."

It was only around 5:00, but I headed out of my office stopping to tell my judicial assistant, Mary Davey, "I'm going for a walk. See you tomorrow."

I almost never left that early.

Mary looked at me closely; she has great insight into people and knows me well.

"You okay?" she asked.

"I'm okay, just need to take a walk and stretch my legs."

She nodded and stared down. She didn't want me to know that she saw me crying.

"Okay, see you tomorrow."

I nodded and walk out.

Leaving the courthouse, I crossed Pennsylvania Avenue. I walked on the National Mall heading for the Wall.

It felt good to walk. It felt good to know that Allen Chaney loved Jeff like a brother, that he did not die alone.

He loved him like a brother. Jeff had a brother there. That's good. I can see them laughing in the mess. On patrol together, scared shitless, having each other's back, sharing a helicopter ride in the dark night back to Cu Chi base.

I should have loved him more like a brother.

I walked to the V-shaped black granite wall nestled into the lush green park with the Lincoln Memorial in the background. The late afternoon light glowed on the 58,000 names of the American men and women who died in the war.

I went to panel 26e, line 70. I placed my hand on his name, Harold J. Canan, and gently rubbed each letter of his name. He was named after my Uncle Harold, who we never knew; killed in action in the Philippines during World War II, just three years before Jeff was born. My mother said he was always called Heschi.

"Rest in peace, brother," I whispered. "Allen Chaney brought you alive today. Thank you, Allen. I'm sorry I don't think of you every day; I get caught up in the day-to-day. I remember Mom saying that she sometimes went whole days not thinking of Heschi. I'm doing the same, I guess. Moving on with life, I guess. You have four nephews, my sons Lukas Jeffrey, named after you, and Ethan Ware, named after Dad, and Stacy's sons, Gabriel and Nathan. You also have a niece, Stacy's daughter Marisa. They're all still very young, but we've told them about you and they've put their hands here with you. They will remember, I promise. We will try and do our best."

## Plugging a Hole in the Ho Chi Minh Trail

A few years later I was invited by Vietnam's judiciary, in conjunction with the United Nations, to work with Vietnamese judges on a rule of law program to compare and contrast our very different legal systems.

The training would be held for judges in Hanoi and then repeated for judges in Ho Chi Minh City, which I still think of as Saigon. I'm going on my own to Hanoi, but my wife Lee and the boys will meet me in Ho Chi Minh City, where we will travel after my work responsibilities are completed.

I was drawn to find out where Jeff was killed in action, to pay homage to him and the others who served and sacrificed. Quick research showed that the 25th Infantry Division base in Cu Chi was only an hour or so northwest of Saigon. I had assumed Jeff was killed near the base but really had no idea. I wanted to go there and lay some flowers, breathe the air, feel him again, kneel down in respect.

I called Allen Chaney. We had talked a few times since Stacy discovered his posting of Jeff's photograph on the Virtual Wall. He's a quiet man, seemingly willing to talk, but at the same time reticent.

"Allen, I'm going to Vietnam to work with their judges and will be in Hanoi and Saigon. I know that Cu Chi is only about thirty kilometers from Saigon. Was he killed close to base or in another part of the country?"

"Russ, we were pretty close to base," he said.

"Is it possible you can help me find the exact area where Jeff was killed? I know it may be a long shot, but I'd like to go there and pay my respects. I'd like to kneel down on the spot."

"I can't remember exactly where, but if you go to the Bobcats archives, I believe it will tell you where he was killed. There's also a description of the type of search and destroy operations that we were patrolling back then.

"God Bless you. Kneel down for me too."

"Thank you Allen, I will."

"Godspeed, Russ."

I clicked away on the Bobcats website again. I found the overall battle plan for 1967.

*In January, 1967, the battalion shifted operations from Cu Chi to Tay Ninh Province, some 48 kilometers to the northwest. Tay Ninh was an exit point for the Ho Chi Minh Trail which was used by the enemy to transport troops, weapons, and military equipment from North Vietnam through Laos and Cambodia and from there to points further south. The 25th Division was placed there to plug the hole. The 5th Infantry participated in daily search and destroy operations in an effort to interdict the movement of supplies to the Saigon area. When the Viet Cong celebrated Tet 1968 by increasing offensive operations around Saigon, the battalion was shifted south to deal with troubles in the Boi Loi, Ho Bo Woods and Filhol Plantation area.*

I learned for the first time that Jeff's job with the 5th Infantry was to help try and "plug" the damn hole in the Ho Chi Minh Trail, a hole that could never be plugged. A verse from the John Prine song, *Hello in There*, came to mind and hit me hard:

*We lost Davey in the Korean War.*
*I still don't know what for.*
*It don't matter anymore.*

I kept digging deeper into the archives and found the daily log.

It was all there.

*On September 14, 1967, the battalion continued security operations and also conducted saturation ambush patrolling in the area of Loc Giang. At 0515 hours, an ambush patrol from Company A engaged 2 VC with negative results. At 2220 hours, an ambush patrol from Company A, located 500 meters south of the junction of Highways 10 and 6A, received small arms and automatic weapons fire at XT 435157. One Bobcat was killed and two were wounded.*

## French Colonial Architecture

Several weeks later I landed late at night in Hanoi. The air was thick and moist and I was sweating even before I could hail a cab to head downtown to my hotel. The taxi drove through crowded streets, teeming with motor scooters with riders constantly beeping their horns while wearing colored bandannas to cover their noses and mouths. As we weaved through tree-lined boulevards, lights illuminated French colonial buildings of light ocher and mustard yellow, over-hanging rust clay tiled roofs, and wrought iron balconies. Classical columns were flanked on either side with dark green shutters.

Arriving at an upscale hotel, I was back in the west again with businessmen and tourists crowding around the art deco bar. Hanoi was thriving and commerce was hot; there were corporate deals to be made and tourists wanting to explore the city that was once called the Paris of Asia.

It's 2:00 a.m. in Hanoi but I was in a far distant time zone, so I sat on my veranda with a whiskey in hand looking down the street at another pristine example of French colonial architecture. The building had been restructured and modernized, but the original colonial walls were still there. I stared at the remnants of Hoa Lo Prison, which is Vietnamese slang for "Hell's Hole." The American prisoners of war called it the "Hanoi Hilton."

After catching a few hours' sleep, I walked over to the building, now a small museum, with a slate gray outside sign, *Maison Centrale*, formed in an archway against a light yellow background. The French built the "Central House," in the nineteenth century to terrorize Vietnamese prisoners, particularly political activists. A prison built for 500 once housed 2,000 men and women in squalid and deplorable conditions.

Inside, next to a diorama of the entire complex, a massive steel gate door known as the "mouth of the monster," dominated the room as the original entrance to hell. The harsh exploitation of the Vietnamese by the French until their expulsion in 1954 was carefully documented with a guillotine and crude instruments of confinement and torture on display.

One exhibit demonstrated twenty life-like human models in light green pants and no shirts shackled together by a continuous piece of metal steel with slots to clamp their ankles in as they spent their days and nights bound side-by-side. The metal bar that connected them was called the *barre de justice*.

A narrow and dark dungeon, or *cachot*, with the look of a medieval torture chamber, housed an emaciated dangerous prisoner/model chained to a concrete floor.

In another room a guillotine stood alone, the head block where the accused breathed his last breath was low to the ground. An old black-and-white photograph depicted three severed heads.

The exhibit led to an outside corridor that displayed a huge sewer tunnel where five prisoners condemned to death crawled through while escaping on Christmas Eve in 1951.

A solemn memorial garden with large drawings of Vietnamese prisoners etched into gray stone honored the martyrs and victims of French repression. Vietnam's history dates back thousands of years but is only widely known in the West through the two wars the Vietnamese call the French War and the American War. The Ho Loa Museum was primarily a tribute to the fallen of both wars.

One gallery graphically showed America's devastating bombing campaign which dropped over seven million tons of bombs over Vietnam, Laos, and Cambodia. The museum made it clear that this carnage doubled the bombing tonnage inflicted on Asia and Europe during World War II. Black-and-white photographs documented the random killing of women and children amid the wreckage in the countryside, villages, and the cities.

The Hanoi Hilton view of history had a gallery devoted to the humane care given to the American POWs. Senator John McCain's flight suit and parachute were carefully placed in a separate display, hung from head to foot, and one can almost see a young pilot standing proudly in uniform.

I walked around the rest of the gallery viewing photographs of POWs playing chess and volleyball. One print states, without any irony, that the Americans called the prison the "Hanoi Hilton," because they were so well treated.

The American POWs had another story to tell. As noted in Stanley Karnow's classic, *Vietnam: A History.*

> *Though the North Vietnamese had acceded to the Geneva Convention of 1949, which holds that prisoners of war are "victims of events" who merit "decent and humane treatment," they followed the Soviet lead in making an exception for "crimes against humanity"—their portrayal of the U.S. bombing of their country. They confined many of the Americans to solitary cells for long periods, submitting them to such brutalities as a rope torture that yanked their limbs out of joint. They abused the captives for declining to broadcast prepared antiwar statements—often excerpted from the American press—or for rejecting other requests for "cooperation."*

Karnow goes on to note the South Vietnamese savage treatment of captured North Vietnamese and Viet Cong, as well as critics of their own government. There was no honor on either side of this war.

I thought back to my Senate confirmation hearing during which Senator John McCain tried to derail my judicial career because I had represented death row prisoners. In the course of the proceedings, however, Senator McCain changed his view of me and wished me good luck. He was the first person to ever call me "Judge."

I sat down in the hallway of the exhibit and thought of Senator McCain's relationship with student radical and anti-war protester David Ifshin.

I had met David Ifshin a few times while attending Syracuse University. He was the president of the school's student government in 1970 and heard that my brother had served in the Army and been killed in Vietnam. He sought me out because he was about to lead a student strike in protest against the war and ROTC on campus. Ifshin wanted me to be one of the speakers at a rally he was organizing and thought my talking about Jeff's death would speak to the crowd in a forceful way.

I told him no. Although I was against the war and supported the strike, I simply could not talk about Jeff in public. It was hard enough to share his story privately; there was no way I could do so in front of a crowd.

He said he understood, and if I changed my mind, I should contact him. The door was open.

Later, in the spring of 1970, four students were killed by the National Guard at an anti-war protest at Kent State University in Ohio. Many college campuses went into revolt. Ifshin started organizing a shut-down strike on campus. He again sought me out to speak at a rally.

"You have a powerful story to tell that would inspire others. We're hoping to do more than just shut down the school. We want to shut down the war so no more sons and brothers are killed. You can add a strong voice to our movement," he said.

"David, I'm sorry, man, but it's just too raw for me right now. I just can't do it in front of so many people. I can barely talk about him to close friends. I couldn't make it through a speech. Sorry. I'll be out there, though, supporting the strike."

He looked at me thoughtfully. I was expecting a lecture.

"I understand," he said. "We appreciate whatever support you give us to shut it down."

We shook hands. It was the last time we ever talked.

I attended the rally on campus and watched him address the crowd with passion, intelligence, and leadership. I admired him. I regretted I didn't have the courage to step forward.

The next I heard about David Ifshin, he was on the cover of *Life Magazine* in 1971 with Jane Fonda, her fist in a power salute. Ifshin was part of a student delegation that traveled to Hanoi to protest America's involvement in the war. While in Hanoi he gave a speech railing against America and its fighting soldiers.

I thought Fonda and Ifshin had gone way too far. It was one thing to criticize America's policy in going to war. It was another thing to go to Hanoi and dishonor the incredibly brave men and women who felt it was their duty to serve.

One of those men was John McCain. Ifshin's speech was played relentlessly in the Hanoi Hilton where McCain lay in his cell. In 1967, he was shot down in a Navy jet flying over North Vietnam. He had serious injuries to his knee, both arms, stabbed by a bayonet, and was a wreck of a man. He had been tortured in that cell—hung by broken arms for many hours and subjected to other despicable acts. Down to 100 pounds, his cellmate compared him to a Nazi concentration camp survivor.

As the son of an Admiral, the North Vietnamese offered him an early release for propaganda purposes. Military code dictated that the first to be captured was the first to be released. It was not John McCain's turn and he refused a return home before his time. As one writer of the time put it, he could not be tortured into going home early.

This part of the narrative of John McCain's life was well known. Three years after my confirmation hearing with Senator McCain, I was now a sitting judge and read an article by Michael Lewis in the *New Republic*. It is a story of grace and forgiveness.

The story told how David Ifshin had gone establishment. He became a lawyer and worked for AIPAC, the American Israel Public Affairs Committee. He got into mainstream American politics and at times worked on the Mondale and Clinton campaigns. At one point during the Mondale campaign, McCain denounced Ifshin and his conduct in Hanoi.

Years later Ifshin felt repentant and saw McCain at a social event and went over to apologize to him. McCain started first, however, and said he was sorry for his attack on Ifshin during the Mondale campaign. Ifshin, though still steadfast against the war, sincerely apologized for his speech and conduct in Hanoi. They forgave each other, became friends, and helped establish the Institute for Democracy in Vietnam.

Several years later they went together to a ceremony at a Memorial Day event at the Vietnam Wall. Several protesters denounced Ifshin. McCain later went on the Senate floor to defend him.

Tragically, several years later, David Ifshin, only in his mid-forties and a husband and father to three young children, was diagnosed with a fatal cancer. John McCain stood by his friend and comforted his family. He was quoted as saying, "I thought, thank goodness we didn't waste any more time in anger. You can't put off setting your life right."

At David Ifshin's funeral, John McCain gave a eulogy explaining why he defended David against the protesters who had condemned his radical actions.

"I wanted the protesters to know that they were bearing false witness against a good man. That this small gesture meant so much to David, meant even more to me. David

Ifshin was my friend. His friendship honored me and honors me still."

As I left Hoa Lo Prison, I thought that America's war with Vietnam was so complex and the suffering by so many on both sides so devastating, that my private journey to connect with Jeff almost seemed trivial. And yet, as I slowly walked down Hai Ba Trung Boulevard, I somehow felt that reconciliation with Jeff, and the Vietnamese, was in keeping with John McCain's sentiments of redemption.

That night I sat at the Le Club Bar at the Hotel Metropole. Built in 1901 in the French colonial style with a white façade and green wooden shutters, the five-star Metropole had a sedate lobby and bar with a brown motif of deep leather chairs, dark chocolate furniture and bar top, cross-beamed ceilings, and marble and wooden floors contrasted with soft cream pastel walls.

A number of dignitaries and celebrities stayed at the hotel during French colonial rule. Somerset Maugham was a frequent guest and Charlie Chaplin and Paulette Goddard honeymooned in one of the luxurious suites. Jane Fonda stayed at the hotel during her anti-war speeches and reportedly had to use an air raid shelter when sirens were sounded.

I felt the spirit, however, of Graham Greene in the building. Greene covered the Indochina war while staying at Metropole, and wrote his masterpiece, *The Quiet American*, in 1955 sitting at the bar and lobby in the Hotel Metropole.

A political and romantic triangle taking place in Saigon during a Communist uprising against the French in the early 1950s, *The Quiet American* is a parable of American innocence, arrogance, and complicity while clashing with a cynical and fading European empire, both seeking the riches and beauty of a woman and country that were never theirs to possess in the first place.

Graham Greene was remarkably prescient in seeing that the folly of America's early days in the conflict would lead to tragedy and despair. As his world-weary British journalist said of the enigmatic and idealistic young American at the core of the story, "I never knew a man who had better motives for all the trouble he caused."

The next morning I walked over to meet the Vietnamese judges and my Thai counterpart at the Ministry of Justice to prepare for our program. Through an interpreter, we outlined a series of lectures and discussion groups to highlight the differences and similarities in our legal systems. We also discussed the potential for reforms for the arrest, trial, and punishment of accused criminals.

The Vietnamese judges were friendly and appeared to be serious about making their legal system more transparent and equitable. They welcomed the opportunity to work with foreign judges and planned to have approximately twenty judges from Hanoi and the rural countryside participate in the workshop.

The program went as planned and appeared to be well received by the judges. On our last night in Hanoi, the five host judges, led by Judge Tran, took us out to dinner, and though talking through an interpreter can be stilted, the evening was sociable and warm. Toasts with rice wine and vodka were liberally made to our newfound friendship and partnership.

Conversation was light and mainly law related until Judge Tran asked about my children and their names. Judge Tran, a gray-haired man with thick black glasses and a soft voice, was a senior judge and afforded much respect and deference by his fellow judges. He was very interested in how parents named their children in the United States since the practice was a treasured and honored tradition of family life in Vietnam.

Judge Tran explained that first names in Vietnamese are often literal and symbolize an attribute such as peace, modesty, or beauty that parents aspire for their newborns.

I had to hesitate. I didn't want to be rude and skirt the question, and on the other hand I didn't want to open raw wounds. My gut told me Judge Tran and the others would be open to a frank discussion, even if it brought up painful memories.

I explained that in the Jewish tradition parents named their children after deceased loved ones, with either the name itself, or a common initial.

"My younger son, Ethan Ware, was named after my father Eli.

"My oldest son, Lukas Jeffrey, was named after my brother Jeffrey."

They nodded thoughtfully.

"If you don't mind, we would like to know about your father," Judge Tran said.

"My father was a working man, dropped out of school at fourteen to work during the U.S. depression in the 1920s to help support his family and mainly worked in gas stations, finally owning a gas station in New York City. He was very proud that I became a judge."

"And your brother, you are young to have lost a brother."

"My brother Jeff was in the Army and was killed near Cu Chi in 1967. He was eighteen when he died. After our program is completed in Ho Chi Minh City, I hope to be able to visit where he died."

They all shook their heads sympathetically. Judge Tran stood and walked over to me and shook my hand warmly.

"We are so sorry for your loss. It is a terrible thing to lose a brother so young. If you need help in Ho Chi Minh City finding a guide and driver, we will assist you."

"Thank you, my friend. I would appreciate your help," I said.

"Consider it done, my friend," he replied.

## Search and Destroy Operations: 500 Meters South of the Junction of Highways 10 and 6A

The next day our group of judges flew to Ho Chi Minh City to get ready to repeat our program for the twenty local judges in the area. Since Lee and the boys were arriving in a few days, I found a hotel with an awesome crystalline blue swimming pool on the roof. The weather was extremely hot and humid and I knew the pool would be a cool sanctuary for young children.

Having finished my own swim around sunset the day of my arrival, I walked around the rooftop and could see the new U.S. embassy. The old embassy during the war, on the same grounds, had been demolished. I could only see, however, the searing vision of helicopters on the roof with desperate South Vietnamese struggling to get on board during the fall of Saigon. That photograph of desolation rivaled the graphic images of an execution in the streets of Saigon, and the sight of the girl in the picture running down a hill in napalm flames as the iconic symbols of a futile cause.

I was delighted several days later to return to the airport and meet my family. We were cramped on two beds at the Sofitel, but the boys loved the swimming pool and seemed ready for adventures. We planned a canoe trip down the Mekong Delta and a trip to the beaches of the South China Sea. Meanwhile, I had a few more days of our program to finish while Lee and the boys explored the city.

Judge Tran took a special interest in me and though he was not fluent in English, we were able to communicate easily through our interpreter. He was pleased that our program was going well and hoped other such events could be held in the future. On our last night after we finished our work, the judges again took us out to dinner with Lee and the boys in attendance. Again rice wine and vodka were flowing and good-hearted toasts of friendship were made by all.

Judge Tran had made arrangements with a guide and driver to take us on our journey to the junction of Highways 10 and 6A the next day. He suggested we stop by and see the tunnels of Cu Chi, which were along the way. I thanked him for his graciousness and courtesy and we awkwardly hugged good-bye the next morning as we met our guide and driver.

We drove over paved roads through the city streets and suburbs of Saigon. After about an hour we traveled through small towns, rubber tree farms, and rice fields until we arrived at a sign in Vietnamese and English that said "Welcome to the Cu Chi Tunnels." The tunnels were part of an extensive maze of underground passageways, some dated to the Viet Minh nationalists' war against the colonial French. A generation later, the Viet Cong, the communist guerrilla fighters in South Vietnam, extended the tunnels over 150 miles almost to the Cambodian border in order to live, hide, and fight in the rice paddies, just miles away from Jeff's 25th Infantry base.

Strategically located near Saigon in an area where heavy vehicles could operate in the summer monsoon rains, the Cu Chi District was also a link to the Ho Chi Minh Trail where supplies came down from North Vietnam. The Cu Chi District had been a stronghold for the Communists in their resistance to the U.S. military.

British journalists Tom Mangold and John Penycate's book, *The Tunnels of Cu Chi*, highlight the importance of the tunnels to both the Viet Cong and the American forces. The book quoted Mai Chi Tho, a leader of the Viet Cong in the tunnels:

> *Cu Chi was a springboard for attacking Saigon, the enemy's brain center. It was like a thorn stabbing*

*in the eye. The enemy had to find some way of sweeping Cu Chi... clean; the fight was a fierce one. We used the area for infiltrating Saigon—intelligence agents, party cadres, sabotage teams. The Tet offensive of 1968 [on Saigon and other towns] was prepared—the necessary troops and supplies assembled—in the Cu Chi tunnels. The Americans appreciated the area's importance because it constantly threatened the security of Saigon, of their own headquarters. If they could not solve the problem of the tunnels of Cu Chi, how could they deal with the problem of Vietnam?*

The book quoted an anonymous American general stating that the tunnels of Cu Chi were "a dagger pointing at Saigon."

The American response to the "problem of the tunnels" was predictably ferocious. In Mangold and Penycate's words:

> *The District of Cu Chi... became the most bombed, shelled, gassed, defoliated, and generally devastated area in the history of warfare. For years, most of Cu Chi suffered the fate of being a "free strike zone." That meant that random artillery fire, known as "harassment and interdiction" rained upon it by night; bomber pilots were encouraged to offload unused explosive and napalm over Cu Chi before returning to base.*

Jeff's night patrol on September 14, 1967, set out to search and destroy the tunnels of Cu Chi.

The tunnels were now a tourist destination.

A local guide escorted us into a room and showed us a large diorama model, some four feet by four feet, of the complex and multi-level web of bare bedrooms, kitchens, weapon caches, conference rooms, communications centers, and medical quarters for the Viet Cong to get respite and sustenance before they struck again.

The sheer scale and scope of the tunnels of Cu Chi showed the Viet Cong's determination and resolve like nothing else. Outside, the boys, ages nine and seven, were allowed to enter the tunnels and explore for a few minutes. At 6'2" and 200 pounds, I was way too big to even think about entering the three feet high and two feet wide tunnels. Next to the tunnels there was a destroyed U.S. tank, preserved to symbolize the defeat of the Americans.

There was also a shooting range with stationary AK-47 and M-16 rifles for hire. I had never fired a weapon before but saw that the boys were fascinated. Paying a couple of dollars to fire ten rounds, I squatted down and let each boy separately wrap his arms around me and put his finger on the trigger. Five rounds a piece. Taking turns, each boy got to play pretend soldier as he fired off the AK-47. The boys were jazzed, but I was quiet and reserved, thinking about the times Jeff and I played soldier at home wearing helmets and carrying realistic looking toy rifles.

Our guide said we were only fifteen to twenty minutes away from the junction of Highways 10 and 6A. He asked if we wanted to take a very short detour to Trang Bang to see the "Napalm girl." I thought I knew what he meant but wanted to be sure.

"Who is the Napalm girl?" I asked.

"The Napalm girl, the Napalm girl," he said. "The girl who caught on fire running down the hill by the temple."

"Does she live there?" I asked.

"No, but her brother has a café, and you can see the temple that got bombed, and follow her as she ran away." The guide's English is good, but I wasn't quite sure I understood what he was trying to tell me.

"If she's not there, what is there?" I asked.

He looked at me quizzically and turned his head. "She was there," he said.

I got it then.

"Yes, of course, let's go."

This will be hard to explain to the boys, but I hope they will understand.

The guide called her the "Napalm girl" but to me she was always "The Girl in the Picture," the most unforgettable photograph of the Vietnam War, or maybe any war. A screaming nine-year-old girl running naked down a dirt road with her arms outstretched. A napalm bomb had just exploded and her back had been savaged by the burns.

Fifteen minutes later we drove along dirt roads and entered the small hill town of Trang Bang. The driver stopped at a small café at the bottom of a hill. We were told the café was run by the girl's brother and he was often there. We went inside and saw an elderly Vietnamese couple sitting in chairs by one of the five or six tables. They looked at us with interest, nodded their heads, and then politely turned away. Sitting down at a table, we ordered some soft drinks from the middle-aged waiter. I also purchased a biography, *The Girl in the Picture: The Story of Kim Phuc, the Photograph, and the Vietnam War*, by Denise Chong.

Our guide talked to the waiter and advised us that he was not Kim's brother. As we sipped our drinks, I saw a television mounted on a wall running a loop of a British documentary of the bombing on June 8, 1972, with a video of its aftermath with Kim and other villagers fleeing the bombing of Trang Bang. I had only seen the still photograph of her running naked while burning in the back from napalm. The video was shocking in its own way as Kim and other screaming children ran down the hill looking for safety. I closely watched my sons as they saw the horror on the screen and quickly turned away and asked to go outside and play.

Kim Phuc was nine years old when South Vietnamese pilots, thinking they were bombing the Viet Cong, mistakenly bombed a group of children and villagers fleeing a Cadoi temple. Four villagers, including Kim's three-year-old cousin, were killed in the bombing. AP photographer Nick Ut clicked off the Pulitzer Prize–winning photograph of Kim, but also saved her life and another child's by taking them to a hospital in Saigon. Kim was in the hospital for over a year and had to endure skin transplantations and over fifteen surgeries. We watched the documentary as it looped around.

After we finished our drinks our guide took us outside the café to the approximate spot where photographer Nick Ut snapped his photograph. I took out my camera. Dominating the center a dirt road gradually slanted downhill with bumps and a water puddle.

Slightly to the left of center, approximately where Kim Phuc fled fiery napalm thirty-three years ago, a girl about nine or ten on a bicycle, headed down the hill dressed in white. She had short dark hair above her shoulders. A younger girl, maybe five or six, sat in the rear holding on to the bike, her long hair flowing in the breeze. The girl driving the bike was intent and serious as she headed down the hill. I snapped off a photograph.

Chong's book details Kim's remarkable life after the photograph that shocked the world; first as a propaganda tool for the Communists, and later studying medicine in Cuba where she met her future husband. She converted to Christianity, and the couple ultimately defected to Canada, where they lived a quiet life until her presence was discovered by the press.

Kim dedicated herself to the plight of children at war and was named an UNESCO Goodwill Ambassador in 1994. Two years later, Kim spoke movingly at the Vietnam Wall on

Veterans' Day and shared her message of hope and forgiveness moving forward.

In 2006, in an NPR piece called "The Long Road to Forgiveness," Kim gave her hopeful vision of the future.

> *Forgiveness made me free from hatred. I still have many scars on my body and severe pain most days but my heart is cleansed. Napalm is very powerful, but faith, forgiveness, and love are much more powerful. We would not have war at all if everyone could learn how to live with true love, hope, and forgiveness. If that little girl in the picture can do it, ask yourself: Can you?*

It had already been an emotional day and I had some reservations about our going onward. What was I hoping to accomplish? Was I seeking some sort of catharsis to cleanse my soul for my own shortcomings and role in driving a seventeen-year-old boy into the Army to die by a claymore mine on the Ho Chi Minh Trail? I don't really believe much in "bringing closure" to sad and tragic events. Jeff's death shook our family to its core, and that was never going to change. And yet I felt that going to the place of his death would help honor and respect his memory. I felt that my sons, as young as they were, would understand the beauty of paying homage to a loved one.

We were all worn out as I gazed over the horizon at the lush green rice paddies. I thought, however, it was time to go forward and complete our journey. Slowly driving along the dirt roads for about ten minutes, we came to the junction of red clay Highways 10 and 6A, surrounded by more rice paddies. Due south, I could see a small hamlet with about ten wooden homes and thatched huts gathered together. We got out of the car and walked toward the hamlet, counting the meters as we went. I didn't see anyone in the fields or by the houses. As we walked, I tried to see the open and lonely road

and fields at night as terrified young men gripped their rifles while trying to hide their fears, praying for the mission to be over so they could return to base. Step-by-step we slowly and quietly approached the huts. Even the boys, usually rambunctious and noisy, walked in silence. I counted 500 meters and stopped just outside the small huts clustered together. I looked around for a suitable place and walked over to the edge of a rice paddy. In the distance I could see men in the fields with a water buffalo hauling a plow.

It was a peaceful place, with a deep verdant green field. Lee and the boys placed on the ground some flowers, a photograph of Jeff in his dress uniform, a photograph of Jeff, Stacy, and me as small children, and his Purple Heart medal. We gathered around in a circle and knelt. I slowly read in English the words of the mourner's Kaddish:

*May the Universe of Creation be recognized in your lifetime*
*And throughout your days, and during the lifetime*

*of the entire House of Israel, soon.*
*So let us acknowledge, honor, celebrate and sing to the*
*Sacred Source, though transcendent and truly beyond*
*songs*
*and blessing.*
*May the source of peace grant us peace, and let us say:*
*Amen*

As I finished the Kaddish, I looked around and could see a number of villagers talking with our guide, no more than twenty yards away.

I looked to Lee and the boys and said, "I think we're ready to go home." They all nodded. I fought back tears and we started to leave.

As we walked back to the car, our guide approached. He pointed to the group of villagers. "Do you see the old grandmother over there?" he asked.

"Yes, I see her." She looked to be in her eighties with gray hair and a simple brown dress.

"She says 'the American was killed over there.'" He pointed to a place in a woodpile, across the dirt road about fifteen yards away.

I looked at the elderly woman and nodded and mouthed the words "Thank You."

Was this the place where Jeff was actually killed? When she said, "The American," how did I know it was Jeff? It didn't matter.

"Let's walk over there," I said to the boys.

We slowly walked across the dirt road and gathered in the woodpile, logs, and wood chips scattered over the grass.

The boys again placed the flowers, photographs, and medals on the ground. Once again we knelt as I read the mourner's Kaddish.

We left the flowers on the ground and picked up the photographs and medals and headed back to the car.

The elderly woman and the other villagers closely looked at us. I placed my hands together in the Buddhist way and leaned over and bowed to them.

They placed their hands together and bowed back in return.

## The Gift of a Photograph

The days go by upon our return to the U.S. I email Allen Chaney and send him some photographs from our journey, and thank him for all his guidance and support, but he does not respond. The email does not bounce back. Several months later I call his number, but he does not pick up. I leave a message on his voice mail.

"No need to call back," I say. "Just checking in; hope all is well."

No response. I hope that he's all right.

September 14 approaches. I do not want to intrude in Allen's life, but also want to connect again to thank him. Share

Jeff some more. Once more I email. Another phone call. But no response. I search the Bobcats' website and the internet universe. Nothing comes up. Allen's website is still there but nothing has been added since we left for Vietnam. It is time to respect his privacy. Sadly, I leave it alone.

The years pass by as the boys play soccer and basketball and go through the ups and downs of middle school, high school, and then off to college.

Lukas, with his love of music, wants to go to Austin, Texas, to check out its vibrant country, blues, and rockabilly scene. We carve out a few days and make our plans. With thoughts of Texas, I think of Allen and once again send off another email.

The email bounces back. His phone number has been disconnected. I send an old fashioned letter to the only home address I have. It is returned to sender. I scour the internet for information; Allen's website is there but nothing new had been posted in years. I fear the worst, but see no obituary online.

I email the Bobcats webmaster for information and he sends back a different home address in the general Waco area. Two weeks before we are scheduled to leave, I send another letter to the new home address. No reply.

Three days before we fly out, my cell phone rings.

"This is Allen Chaney. Sorry I have not been in touch. Your letter to my last home was forwarded to my new address. I'm living with my wife on her family's old farm.

"Thanks, Allen. So good to hear from you. I certainly don't want to intrude, but if you have time my son and I are coming to Texas and we would like to come out and pay a visit, it that's okay with you."

Allen does not hesitate.

"Russ, I'd be honored to meet you and your son. Come anytime. Other than some early chores in the morning, I'm retired from the government now so come when you can. We're happy to see you anytime."

Several days later Lukas and I are listening to rockabilly as I drive our rental Ford down Highway 35 to Waco. Usually we talk almost non-stop in the car, but we're both quiet, lost in our thoughts. At the small town of Valley Mills we realize we are lost and I call Allen as his farm appears to be off the GPS grid. Shows what a city boy I am as I didn't even know it was possible to be off the grid. He instructs us to go up a hill several miles away and he would meet us in his truck.

Winding our way over dusty and hilly country roads, Allen meets us at a junction in the road. He gets out of his pickup truck and shakes my hand, averting his eyes. Lukas shakes his hand. Allen is about five-eight or so and stocky. His face looks nothing like that of the young man in his early twenties in his dress uniform on his website, ready to go to war. Even though I had stared at his photo many times, I never would have recognized him.

We follow him the few miles down the road to his farm. It is a hard scrabble property that seems too dirt-packed for the grazing of cattle, but what do I know?

A heavy tractor sits in a wooden shed. The gray shuttered farmhouse is worn, but also comfortable and inviting. Allen introduces us to his wife and we sit down on a couch. Allen sits right across us in a stiff steel chair. His wife offers us coffee, soft drinks, and some biscuits. There's a quiet silence in the room.

I glance at some faded photographs and needlepoint on the walls. I start talking about the drive down from Austin. It's small talk, I know, but I don't know how to begin.

Remembering that we brought gifts, we give them wrapped presents from the White House gift shop, a photo book on the history of the White House and the year's Christmas ornaments. His wife thanks us. Allen has not said a word.

We make some more small talk about our bouncing around Austin—watching the million bats at sunset fly away from the Congress Avenue Bridge overlooking the Lady Bird Lake, listening to country and rockabilly in the Little Long Horn Saloon, exploring the LBJ library. I start to talk about visiting the watchtower on the University of Texas where ex-Marine Charles Wittman took an M1 carbine and other weapons, climbed to the observation deck, and opened fire, killing sixteen persons and wounding many others in one of the first mass shootings in the United States.

*What am I doing?* I think. In August of 1966 when Wittman climbed the tower, a very disturbed soldier, Allen had been in Vietnam then. He already had been wounded by rifle fire. My gut told me Allen was keeping a mystery inside, maybe best left unsaid. We were about to go into another dark time. I take a deep breath.

"Allen, thanks again for helping us, starting with the photo on the Virtual Wall and guiding me to the Bobcats archives to find the exact location where Jeff was killed. Would you like hear about our trip there?"

"Yes, I would like that," he says.

I tell him about my work with the Vietnamese judges in Hanoi and Saigon. We talk about our trip to the beaches off the South China Sea. I describe our journey to the tunnels of Cu Chi, Trang Bang, and finally to the quiet spot 500 meters south of the junction of Highways 10 and 6A.

Allen listens quietly and doesn't ask any questions. I have photos on my phone of the rice paddies where Jeff was killed and Allen was wounded. I keep the phone in my pocket. Does he want to see these pictures? He seems very fragile. I don't know what to do and decide to wait and see.

We sit in awkward silence.

"Have you enjoyed your retirement?"

"Yes, I worked many years for the government and finally got a disability retirement. Came to realize way too late that I had PTSD. It's better now, but I still struggle.

"It's been hard on me coming home and I needed some help. Always kept a job and in the reserves, but I was hurting inside."

His wife sits down and nods silently.

This is much harder than I thought it would be. I get the feeling that we may be straying into painful memories that are better kept within.

I will take my cue from Allen.

"Do you mind talking about Jeff?"

"No. It's good for me."

"Were you close with him?"

"We were all close. What I remember most about him was that he was always in a good mood. Many of the guys were so down all the time or ripped, but not Jeff."

"Were any of the other guys close to him? Guys I maybe can call on?"

"We were all close. I don't remember anyone in particular."

"I see the Bobcats have reunions sometime. Do you think I could attend?"

"Sure. We'd love to have you and Lukas. I'll give you the information. We always have a memorial service."

"Thanks, we'd like that.

"Allen, do you mind talking about the night Jeff was killed? I certainly understand if you don't want to, so no problem either way."

Allen's wife is looking on sympathetically. I get the feeling she would just as soon he not talk about September 14, but she says nothing.

"I don't mind, Russ. Not much to say really that you don't know. We often went on night patrols and we were kids scared silly. We knew the VC might be out there."

His voice is very low and trails off as Lukas and I lean in to hear.

"Jeff was up front when I heard the explosion. 'Mine! Mine!' I heard someone screaming. I was heading for a ditch when I got shot in the leg. I fell in the ditch and a medic came quickly and patched me up. He shot me up with morphine. I could hear the radio calling for the chopper. They put me on a stretcher and we waited. Two other guys came over with Jeff on a stretcher. We laid there side by side waiting. Jeff was all covered up. He was dead. I heard one of the guys say 'Claymore.' The chopper landed and I could see the blades twirling above me. They lifted us both into the chopper and we lay side by side. I never saw his face. That's about it. After we landed, they took Jeff away. I never saw him again."

He pauses and looks down. We all wait for a few seconds in silence.

"Thanks, Allen."

"You bet, Russ."

"Can I ask you one more question? September 14th was the third time you were wounded and yet you signed up for another tour. You could've gone home, but you volunteered to stay. That took a lot of courage."

"Russ, I always felt the Lord was looking out for me. I wish things could have been a little easier coming home, but I only regret losing my brothers like Jeff over there. I think I did the right thing for my country."

"Thank you, Allen, for being such a friend and brother to Jeff and now to my family. I can't tell you how deep I will hold this day."

"You're welcome, Russ. Please stop by any time for a visit. I hope you can come to a reunion."

I look at Allen's wife and she returns my smile. They are friendly, lovely folks, but it's time to leave.

I stand up and Lukas and Allen follow my lead.

"Would you mind taking a photo?"

Allen nods his head

I give Allen's wife my phone.

Allen stands in the middle of Lukas and me. We don't throw our arms around each other, but stand stiffly as she snaps off a couple of photos.

"Before you leave, I have something I want to give to you," Allen says.

He goes to his den and returns and hands me the blurry black-and-white photograph of Jeff in the field with his fellow Bobcats in the sand bunker in Cu Chi, the photograph he had posted so many years ago on the Virtual Wall.

"Please take this photo. This is for you and Lukas."

"Oh no, Allen, this belongs to you."

"It's for you and your family, Russ."

"Thank you, Allen."

I take the black-and-white photograph and place it in my shirt pocket and carry a bit of Jeff home with me.

# Rough Justice

◈ ◈ ◈ ◈ ◈

*What the hell,* I thought. I reread the note from the jury in chambers. "If we find the defendant not guilty of Assault with Intent to Kill While Armed, can we still find him guilty of Assault with a Dangerous Weapon?" The note was signed by the Foreperson, Juror #10.

How could they be asking this question? I had already told them twice they could do just that in my final legal instructions, right before they began their deliberations. I had also given them this instruction in writing to take back to the jury room. It was also crystal clear on the verdict form.

The jury apparently needed to hear again that Assault with a Dangerous Weapon, or "ADW" in courthouse slang, is what's called a lesser-included offense of Assault with Intent to Kill While Armed (AWIK w/a). The jury could indeed find that although the defendant had not intended to kill the victim, as required for AWIK w/a, he assaulted the victim with a dangerous weapon without intending to kill. There could be no mistaking. The answer to the jury's question was clearly yes.

The jury's confusion about a very straightforward matter provided a rare glimpse into their decision-making process. Once this point was settled, their inevitable decision would just be a matter of time. And I was in shock. How could the jury possibly convict the defendant of ADW? Had the case been tried before me without a jury, I would have found him not guilty of both charges. It looked like I was going to have to accept a verdict that I personally disagreed with. This happens occasionally, though most of the time I agree with the jury's verdict, or, if not, I understand how they came to their conclusion in a rational way.

I could not understand this one, though. It didn't make sense to me at all. To make matters worse, there was no principled way for me to prevent the jury from reaching what I considered to be the wrong verdict. But it wasn't the possibility of an ADW conviction I was really worried about. It was the other charge in the case.

The defendant was also charged with Possession of a Firearm during a Crime of Violence (PFCV). Both AWIK w/a and ADW are categorized as crimes of violence in the District of Columbia, and a conviction for either one of them meant a sure conviction for PFCV. That was the real problem because PFCV, unlike ADW, carries a mandatory five years in prison, and there was nothing I could do about that either.

At least for the ADW charge I could place the defendant on probation, and he wouldn't have to go to jail. He was in his forties with no criminal record. He was a single parent to two teenage girls and held a steady job. Sending him to prison would be devastating to the girls. But even more than that, I believed he was innocent. I could see a miscarriage of justice coming down soon.

During judicial trainings judges work through all sorts of hypothetical sentencings. A classic scenario is a brutal rape and torture, where the accused sets the victim on fire and leaves her in a deserted field to die. A conviction for such a depraved crime would call for a very harsh punishment, probably a life sentence. Hardly anyone would disagree. But what if you thought the jury got it wrong, and you believed the defendant was actually innocent? Not that the government's case was weak or that there was a reasonable doubt as to the accused's guilt, but that you firmly believed he did not commit this vicious crime. As the sentencing judge you have wide discretion and could lock him up for life. There is, however, no mandatory sentence for this crime, and you could also place him on probation with no jail time at all. Do you respect the jury's judgment and impose the harsh sentence? Or do you use your own judgment and effectively go around the verdict by not locking up the defendant at all?

I think most judges defer to the jury's verdict and impose the harsh sentence, no matter how much it offends them. To do otherwise would turn our jury system upside down. But I wasn't faced with this difficult philosophical question. I was in real time with no discretion and no legal authority to reject the jury's verdict. Because the crime of PFCV carries a mandatory sentence, I would have to impose a five-year prison term.

The problem is that under the law, the standard for a judge taking a case from a jury and issuing a not guilty verdict is very high. After the prosecution puts on all of its evidence and completes its case, defense counsel routinely moves the court to acquit the defendant and throw out the charges. The law requires the judge to review the evidence in the light most favorable to the prosecution and allow the jury to make all credibility decisions. Simply put, the jury is the judge of the facts. The trial judge determines the law; the jury finds the facts, and the court must defer to the jury's judgment on them.

There is a very narrow exception that allows the judge to throw out a case if the government's case is so incredible that no reasonable person could find the defendant guilty. This is an exceedingly rare occurrence and was not the case before me.

I thought back to a case when I was defense counsel and a judge took a case away from a jury in a child rape trial because he just didn't believe the young girl's version of events. I, of course, was delighted for my client, as I believed he was innocent, but was still shocked the judge had freed him. The prosecutor was beyond ticked off, and when the judge left the bench he told me, and anyone around who would listen, that the judge was lawless and violated his oath of office.

Should I do the same in this case? Should I take the case away from the jury? I had the power to do so, and the government did not even have the legal right to appeal my decision to our court of appeals. The case would be over. Defendant forever cleared of the charges.

The facts were pretty straightforward. A community party was being held in the local neighborhood hall in a middle-income neighborhood of D.C., and many neighbors were in attendance. The defendant, who I will call Sam Johnson, was usually the DJ at parties and provided the music with sophisticated amplifiers. His teenage daughters were there, as were a number of young men in their early twenties, including best friends Joe and William. As the party went on, Joe insisted on taking over from Sam the role as DJ. Sam refused as he was worried Joe would blow out the speakers. Joe persisted because he didn't like the music Sam was playing. Sam relented but warned Joe not to play the music too loud to save the speakers.

The party went on, but at some point Sam saw Joe flirting with his fifteen-year-old daughter. Sam and Joe had words, but nothing came of it. Later on, Joe cranked up the music and blew out the speakers, just as Sam had feared. A loud argument followed but no violence. Sam had had enough. He decided to leave the party and pick up his gear later.

Outside the hall, in the fresh air, Sam encountered William, Joe's friend, and they immediately had words. William later claimed at trial that Sam pulled a gun and threatened him. William said he turned to run when Sam fired and hit him in the front of his thigh. He couldn't really explain how he was shot in the front when he had turned his back to flee. Maybe he got shot first and then turned to run. Everything happened so fast it was hard to remember exactly. William testified that Sam got in his car with the gun, sped away, and did not return. In my view, William was not very believable and came off as both arrogant and aggressive.

The law allows the opposing party the right to impeach or discredit a witness by confronting him in front of the jury with prior convictions of certain crimes. William was impeached with several serious crimes.

No other eyewitnesses to the shooting testified for the prosecution. There was no scientific, physical, or electronic evidence presented to corroborate William's story. The gun was never recovered, and no evidence was presented that Sam had ever owned or had access to a gun. Sam made no incriminating statements to the police or anyone else.

At the close of the government's case, all the jury had was William's very shaky version of events, bad blood between Sam, William, and Joe, and Sam's flight from the scene with the gun. Had the case ended right there, with no defense evidence, I would have easily found reasonable doubt and declared Sam not guilty. But this was a trial by jury and the jury would have the last word.

As expected, the defense made a motion for judgment of acquittal claiming the government had not proved its case. I had to deny the motion; it was the jury's responsibility to believe or not believe William. They could also find as a motive that Sam was angry because of Joe's flirtation with his daughter and the destruction of his speakers. Finally, the jury could conclude Sam acted like a guilty man because he fled the scene with the gun rather than call an ambulance and the police.

It was now the defendant's turn to put on evidence. I'm sure the jury wanted to hear Sam's version of these events. That seemed, however, unlikely. The conventional wisdom from the defense viewpoint is the accused should not testify at trial. While there are, of course, exceptions, the theory is the defense is generally better served attacking the prosecution and poking holes in the government's case. Once the defendant takes the stand and is cross-examined, the jury's focus and decision-making shifts to analyzing whether or not he should be believed. Many an accused has stolen defeat from the jaws of victory by putting on evidence after the prosecution rested its case.

The decision to testify is the defendant's alone. Counsel is there to advise, but the accused can testify even if his lawyer recommends otherwise. Sam's lawyer was very experienced and savvy, and I'm sure she read the case the way I did and saw the dangers of Sam's testimony. Plus, she had an ace in the hole.

Her first witness was a working man in his thirties who parked right across the street from the hall waiting for his date to come out of her home. He had a clear view of the scene under well-lit conditions. He didn't know Sam or William and didn't even live in the neighborhood. He had a regular job and no criminal record. There was no evidence that he was using drugs or alcohol. The perfect witness.

He saw William and Sam arguing face to face. He couldn't quite hear what they were saying, but he clearly saw William bring out a gun from his jacket and point it at Sam. Sam grabbed the gun, and they tussled. A shot rang out, and William went down. No turning of the back and running. The witness saw Sam run away. He saw many people run out of the hall to aid William. He knew enough to know that he didn't want to be a witness in a shooting and get caught up in a police investigation, so he left with his date. Sometime later, Sam's investigator knocked on his door. Apparently, his date had mentioned to others in the neighborhood that he had seen the shooting. Although he really didn't want to be involved, he understood the importance of testifying.

I could see the prosecutor was surprised. Unfortunately, too much of a criminal case is trial by ambush. The government is required by law to turn over to the defense physical evidence, such as photographs and expert reports, but generally is not mandated to turn over the names of witnesses or their prior statements to the police or the grand jury until trial begins. The law does require evidence that is favorable to the defense be turned over by the prosecutor before trial in time for the defendant to adequately prepare his case. But, in general, the defense basically has to do its own investigation.

The defense obligation to disclose information to the prosecution is even less. While a defendant also has to turn over to the prosecution physical evidence and expert reports, he is under no obligation to identify any witness to the crime before the day of trial and may even keep under wraps altogether any witness who may hurt rather than help his case. I'm sure Sam's lawyer thought long and hard as to whether she would make this witness available to the prosecution before the trial in an effort to have the government dismiss the case well before trial. The prosecutor was well respected and very fair minded. Faced with such a good defense witness and no strong corroboration of William's side of the story, it's possible the prosecutor could have been convinced to dismiss the case.

In any event, it seemed to me a weak government case had now gotten worse. Surely all the testimony was over. It would have been entirely prudent for the defense to rest its case at this point. But Sam wanted to testify. His lawyer kept a poker face, but my guess was Sam's testimony was against her advice. Sam did well, though. He was originally from rural North Carolina and had a country way of talking. He came off as a hard-working man who was raising his two daughters alone. His testimony pretty much tracked the eyewitness. He admitted he ran because he was scared William's friend Joe would be after him, and he also didn't want to face the police. He hoped William would not press charges or give up his name and it would all go away. He tossed the gun in a sewer.

With all the evidence in, it was now up to counsel to give their closing arguments to the jury, followed by my instructions of law. This was a slam-dunk case for the defense. I expected a quick "not guilty" verdict, probably within an hour. It was, however, almost 5 p.m., and I had to recess the trial before the jury could begin its deliberations. I could sense the jurors were disappointed and wanted to get right at it, but I sent them home for the evening and asked them to come back at 9:30 the next morning.

Shortly after 10:30 the next day, Mr. Van Hook, the deputy courtroom clerk, came into chambers and said the jury had sent a note.

"If we find the defendant not guilty of assault with intent to kill while armed, can we still find him guilty of assault with a dangerous weapon?" It was signed by the Foreperson, Juror #10.

I had already instructed them in open court and in writing. The answer was clearly yes. That was the easy part. But I had a pit in my stomach and was deeply concerned.

Mr. Van Hook, a quiet and reserved man, rarely gave opinions on cases. He saw my response and said, "This one's a real surprise, isn't it?" We both shook our heads. "I'll call the lawyers to come to court," he said. Thirty minutes later he called and said all parties were in the courtroom and ready.

As I walked into the courtroom, Mr. Van Hook stood and announced, "All rise. This honorable court is now in session. The Honorable Judge Canan, presiding. Please be seated and come to order." As he is performing this ritual, I always take a deep breath, reminding myself of the important work ahead.

Mr. Van Hook called the case. Counsel and the defendant stepped forward and identified themselves for the record. I announced that the jury had resumed their deliberations at 9:30 that morning and at 10:38 sent a note. I read the note out loud: "If we find the defendant not guilty of assault with intent to kill while armed, can we still find him guilty of assault with a dangerous weapon?"

I could see the surprised look on the lawyers' faces. Sam dropped his head.

"Counsel, I think we all know the answer to the jury's note is a simple 'Yes.' It's in both the jury instructions and on the verdict form."

I looked to the lawyers. "Counsel, what's your position?"

"I agree," the prosecutor said.

"I agree, as well," said defense counsel.

I wrote the word "Yes," signed my name, date, and time on the jury note, and asked Mr. Van Hook to send it back to the jury.

The note had been addressed, and there was no more business before the court. I hesitated. Ordinarily, I would leave the bench and wait for the inevitable verdict. But the reality of what was about to happen caused us all to pause. It was very quiet in the courtroom. No one was moving, but there was nothing to be said or done. Or was there anything else I should be doing? Perhaps I should suggest to the prosecutor and defense counsel that they should consider reaching a plea bargain to avoid the mandatory sentence. Was it even appropriate for me to make such a suggestion, especially at this stage in the trial? I was not sure what to do, so I decided to do nothing and left the bench.

Back in chambers I contemplated a judge's role in plea bargaining. The Superior Court Rules of Criminal Procedure generally follow the federal rules. Specifically, Rule 11 says that the prosecutor and defense counsel "may discuss and reach a plea agreement." As for the role of the judge in plea bargaining, the rule is quite specific: "The Court must not participate in these discussions." This rule is based on the principle that a judge's power and prestige would have undue influence in the bargaining process and could easily intrude on the prosecutor's prerogative to charge defendants and, at the same time, subtly coerce defendants to waive important constitutional rights and plead guilty.

In many state courts the judge plays a critical role in the horse trading that plea bargaining has become. When I was a defense counsel, I occasionally took cases in other states. The custom in many counties was for the judge, prosecutor, and defense counsel to meet in the judge's chambers and "try and work it out." The defendant was not present, and the discussion was off the record. Usually there would be some small talk—courthouse gossip and telling of tales from past cases—and then we would get down to business. The prosecutor would generally open with the offer. I would make a counteroffer, and then the judge would start twisting arms.

Many times the judge leaned on the State to soften its offer by either allowing the defendant to plead to a lesser crime or agreeing to a lesser sentence. Many times this would work to the defendant's advantage. The prosecutor generally appears before the judge every day, and, in order to keep good relations, the State would usually go along with the judge's recommendation. The State also knew that even if it turned down the judge, should the defendant be forced to go to trial and lose, the ultimate sentence would often look like the rejected deal in chambers. If that were the case, what was the point of going to trial?

Sometimes, of course, the judge leaned on the defendant to be "reasonable." Usually left unsaid was the leverage the judge had to ultimately punish the defendant should he reject the offer, insist on going to trial, and then lose. Some judges were known for "hammering" a defendant at sentencing for exercising his constitutional right to go to trial. The consequences for going against the judge's recommendation could be harsh.

More often than not, a bargain would be reached with the main charge reduced and a specific sentence agreed upon. We would then go into court and finalize the deal, but that was a formality. Although the deal would be cut behind closed doors and out of sight from public view, for the accused it offered a sure thing rather than risking the wrath of an angry judge. For the State and the victims, it offered finality and a sense of closure when weighed against the uncertainty of trial, where anything can happen.

My own view is that transparency is almost always the right way to go. Judges should not be placed in a situation where it would be all too easy to abuse power against either side. The Superior Court proceedings are always on the record in criminal cases. They are both audiotaped and transcribed by a court reporter in open court. We never bring the parties in chambers and negotiate pleas in private.

Scholars and government researchers generally agree that roughly ninety to ninety-five percent of all criminal cases, both federal and state, end in guilty pleas. That being so, keeping the judge out of the process preserves judicial neutrality and prevents the court from exercising undue influence over the government and the defendant.

As I considered these basic principles I reassured myself that the safest and easiest thing to do in this case was to do nothing. The jury was obviously coming to the end of their deliberations, and the forthcoming verdict would be their considered judgment, a judgment I was legally bound to accept. However, I was faced with presiding over what I considered a grave injustice.

Before a trial begins, I always ask the prosecutor and defense counsel if there is any plea offer on the table that could resolve the case short of trial. More than a few times in the past, there was movement from one or both sides on the morning of trial. If I felt the parties were close to a deal I would remind them the court has no role in plea bargaining but could encourage them to reconsider their positions and make decisions that would be in their best interests.

I had never even gone that far while we were in the midst of a trial, much less while the jury was deliberating. By bringing up a plea now, would I be going outside my role and skirting, if not violating, the rule against judges participating in plea bargaining? Was I seeking to achieve some type of rough justice? Do the ends justify the means if the ends are just? After further consideration, I saw no harm in raising the possibility of a plea with the parties, and in my view I would not be violating Rule 11. I concluded that simply reminding the prosecutor and defendant that they could consider reaching a plea bargain was not participating in the discussions of the plea itself.

I asked Mr. Van Hook to call the parties back to the courtroom.

This would be new territory for all of us.

I believed I could bring up a plea without violating my oath of office. It probably wouldn't work anyway. The government was holding all the cards, and the defense had no leverage. The thought of sending Sam to prison for five years still bothered me deeply. I decided to go forward.

Mr. Van Hook came into chambers and said everyone was present.

I returned to the courtroom.

"Counsel," I said, "I'm well aware of the court's limited role under Rule 11 for plea bargaining, and I cannot participate in any discussions. I think, though, we all know the import of the jury's question and what the verdict will be in this case. The defendant has no record, is raising his children, and works. I just can't see where a five-year mandatory sentence would constitute justice. I strongly urge both sides to consider a plea, even at this late stage."

The lawyers looked at me and nodded their heads.

The prosecutor said, "I'll see what I can do."

Defense counsel said, "I'll try."

An hour later I was called into the courtroom. Remarkably, they had reached a deal. Sam could plead guilty to Assault with Intent to Kill, and the government would drop the AWIK while Armed, as well as the Possession of a Firearm During the Commission of a Crime of Violence. The key to the deal was that while AWIK was a major felony and carried a maximum sentence of up to fifteen years in prison, there was no mandatory jail time. I could, theoretically, and probably would, sentence him to probation. He would not have to go to prison.

But now came the hard part. Sam had to get through the plea in open court.

Sam had just testified under oath that the gun was not his and he acted in self-defense in the struggle for it. He was now going to have to state, again under oath, that it was in fact his gun and that he intended to kill William with it. The lawyers were in the courtroom, but Sam was just outside, in the adjoining witness room. I could hear him crying and hear his daughters crying with him.

I looked at counsel. Defense counsel shrugged her shoulders and opened her hands as if to say, "What can I do?"

We all just sat there, waiting for Sam to pull himself together.

I wished the prosecutor would simply dismiss the case, though I knew that was unlikely.

Then I heard two loud knocks on the door leading to the jury room. We all froze. Mr. Van Hook got up, opened the door, and was handed a piece of paper by the jury foreperson.

He closed the door and walked back to his desk next to the bench. He wrote down the date and time on the note and handed it to me. The jury would remain in the jury room until we had all the parties in the courtroom. I read the note and then announced it to counsel. "Counsel, the note reads: 'The jury has reached a verdict.'" It was signed by the Foreperson, Juror #10.

I looked to defense counsel. "Counsel, I'm willing to wait a reasonable amount of time, but if it's not going to happen, we will have to take the verdict. Please consult with your client."

She walked back to the witness room. Several minutes later Sam walked in, followed by his daughters. They were all sobbing. Sam walked into the well of the court and stood next to his lawyer while the daughters sat in the first row of the audience.

The taking of a guilty plea is very routine and almost automatic.

Mr. Van Hook placed Sam under oath.

Next, defense counsel announced the terms of the plea bargain. In exchange for Sam's plea to AWIK, the government would dismiss the AWIK w/a, ADW, and the PFCV. The prosecutor agreed the terms were accurate.

It is then the judge's role to go over the terms of the plea agreement personally with the defendant and make sure his pleading guilty was done knowingly, intelligently, and voluntarily.

Routinely, I asked him his age, level of education, and whether he was born in the United States. He said he went as far as the ninth grade and was born in North Carolina. I asked a few more preliminary questions:

"Are you taking any medication or used any drugs or alcohol in the last forty-eight hours that would make it difficult for you to understand or follow these court proceedings?"

"No, Your Honor."

"Have you had enough time to discuss this case with your lawyer and think about your decision to plead guilty here today?"

"Yes, Your Honor."

"Mr. Johnson, I'm taking this plea under oath and what that means is if you lie under oath you could be charged with the crime of perjury or making a false statement. Do you understand?"

"Yes, Your Honor."

"You do not have to plead guilty and if you do plead guilty you will be waiving or giving up certain constitutional rights. Do you understand?"

"Yes, Your Honor."

We went through each of his rights mechanically.

"You would be presumed innocent and would remain innocent unless and until the government proved the case against you beyond a reasonable doubt. If the government could not prove the case against you, you would be found not guilty and free to go. "Do you understand?"

"Yes, Your Honor," he said.

"Next, you have the right to be tried by a judge or jury. A jury is twelve members of the community who would hear the case and decide if you are guilty or not guilty. If a jury didn't hear the case, a judge would. If you plead guilty you would be waiving or giving up the right to a jury or judge trial. Do you understand?" I asked.

"Yes, Your Honor," he said.

We went through all of his rights individually: right to defend himself through counsel, right to testify, right not to testify, right to cross-examine the government's witnesses, right to present witnesses of his own, and right to appeal. He understood all his rights. He was willing to give them all up.

He was advised that the maximum sentence for AWIK was fifteen years and a fine or assessment of not less than $100 and not more than $5,000 that went to a fund for the victims of violent crime. He said he understood.

"Are you satisfied with the services of your counsel?" I asked.

"Yes," he said.

"Has anyone forced, threatened, or coerced you to plead guilty?" I asked.

He looked straight at me, or perhaps through me.

"No," he said.

"Other than the plea agreement that was announced by your lawyer, has anyone promised you anything else?

"No," he said.

"Has anyone promised you what sentence you are going to receive?"

"No," he said.

I paused. While I hadn't promised him a light sentence, I certainly communicated to both his lawyer and the prosecutor that I thought five years in prison was not fair. Of course his counsel would have told him that the judge thought a sentence of five years was too long. So, in reality, he thought I had promised him, through the back door, a sentence of less than five years. And he was right. I had not made an explicit promise, but everyone in the courtroom, including me, knew that the promise was implied. If for some reason I changed my mind at sentencing and imposed a prison term of five years, or more, he could rightly think I misled him. In the pressure of the moment, I did not realize I had made a side deal with the defendant.

I thought about scuttling the plea. I had gone over the line. But we had come so far, and I thought the plea was the right thing to do.

We pushed on.

"Are you pleading guilty to the charge of Assault with Intent to Kill because you committed this crime?

He looked straight at me again.

"Yes." He then looked down.

"Mr. Johnson," I said, "I'm now going to ask the prosecutor to state in open court what evidence the government would have presented if this case came to trial and then ask you if that's what happened."

This is always the hardest question when I take a plea. Because we had already had a trial, the absurdity of this situation was not lost on anyone.

The prosecutor summarized the facts of the trial we just had: that Mr. Johnson had been in a verbal argument in the parking lot and then pulled and shot a gun at William with the intent to kill him.

Sam looked down the whole time.

"Mr. Johnson, is what the prosecutor said accurate?"

He hesitated and mumbled, obviously reluctant. He muttered something, barely audible.

Normally, in a routine plea if it appears the defendant is reluctant, or unwilling, to admit he committed the crime, I say to him something like "It appears to me that you are reluctant to take this plea. Please understand that no one is forcing you to do this. If you want a jury trial, you have that right. Because if I take this voluntary plea, it is final, and you can't come back tomorrow, next week, or next year and try and take the plea back because you don't like my sentence or for any other reason."

Everyone, however, wanted the plea to go down—the defendant, his lawyer, myself, and even the prosecutor.

I didn't say anything.

I looked at his defense counsel as if to say you know I can't accept this plea unless he says yes. She completely understood.

She whispered to him for a few minutes. He wiped away some more tears.

He looked at me and said softly, very softly, "Yes."

Almost by rote I launched into what I say at the conclusion of every plea that I have ever taken.

"The court finds that the defendant was advised of all his rights and with competent counsel has knowingly, voluntarily, and intelligently waived and given them up and that there is a factual basis for the plea so, therefore, I accept it."

I think everyone in the courtroom breathed a sigh of relief. It had been difficult, but we all got the right result. Sam would be guilty but would not be going to prison. The end justified the means. But was this really justice? Maybe rough justice.

I asked Mr. Van Hook to bring in the jury. They looked very solemn as they took their seats.

I said, "Ladies and gentlemen of the jury, I want to bring to your attention a development that just took place in the courtroom. Mr. Johnson and the government have entered into a plea agreement where Mr. Johnson pled guilty to a charge, and the government dismissed other charges. Usually this kind of thing happens before trial, but, in this case, it happened while you were deliberating, and I just accepted the plea a few minutes ago. As such, we will not be taking your verdict."

I continued, "I very much appreciate your service to the court and community, and please be assured that even though we took the time to go through this trial your time was not wasted, and we now have a final resolution of this case. On behalf of the court and the community, you have my deepest thanks and you are now excused."

The jury looked at me quizzically. They got out of their seats slowly, surely confused as to what had just happened. Perhaps I should explain to them in detail all the circumstances, but I rejected that idea since it would be hard to communicate all the dynamics without communicating to them that I thought they were about to make a tragic mistake.

I didn't do anything, and they left.

I turned to the parties and routinely, almost again by rote, set a date for sentencing two months in the future, before which I would receive a presentence report from the probation office. Not that I really needed any additional information to render a decision on Sam's sentence, but we were now playing it by the book.

I returned to chambers. I needed to take a break from this drama, and, besides, I had to prepare for my next trial, a burglary where the defendant was accused of breaking into a home at 1:00 a.m., tying up a seventy-year-old man, former director of a local choir, and pushing him into a closet while the burglar cleaned out the house of all valuables.

I thought about what one of my colleagues said when I was about to go on the bench and start presiding over criminal cases: "We get to see a human parade of misery and try and make some sense of it all. Try to do justice as best we can."

I looked up and saw Mr. Van Hook standing quietly at my door. I had been lost in my thoughts. He asked to come in, and I said, "Of course."

He said, "I found this in the jury room. Thought you should see it."

It was the jury verdict form. It read:

*We, the jury, find Samuel Johnson:*
*Assault with Intent to Kill while Armed: Not Guilty*
*Assault with a Dangerous Weapon: Not Guilty*
*Possession of a Firearm During a Crime of Violence: Not Guilty*

It was signed by the Foreperson, Juror #10.

We looked at each other, and I slowly shook my head. Although, technically, the lawyers didn't need to know about the verdict form because it was now an unofficial document, I asked Mr. Van Hook to call the lawyers and let them know.

He said, "I think they already do since I saw them talking to some jurors in the hallway."

"Please call anyway and send them copies of the verdict form."

I sat back in my chair and gazed out the window. I looked at a lush, green park across the street and saw people coming and going into the courthouse, all, no doubt, consumed by their important cases.

I guess this goes down in the "no good deed goes unpunished category," I thought to myself. I didn't have time, however, to think this through. I had to prepare for the burglary trial. Mr. Van Hook went out to make his calls.

Two days later I received a motion from Sam's lawyer seeking to withdraw his guilty plea. As grounds for the motion, she said I had put in motion, out of a sense of justice, of course, a process that was, in the end, coercive and threatening and that her client's plea was involuntary as a matter of law and should be vacated. She said that, as a result of the intense pressure brought to bear on Sam, he deserved a new trial.

The government filed an opposition and rightly pointed out that if the verdict had been what we all thought it was going to be, the last thing Mr. Johnson would be doing was seeking to withdraw his plea. The government also noted Mr. Johnson took his plea under oath, that this fact alone should be given great consideration, and that maybe, at the end of the day, his acceptance of the facts during the plea was the truth after all, notwithstanding the jury verdict that was never formally accepted.

A few days later they all came back to court to hear my ruling. This was an easy decision. Sam's lawyer was right of course. I had orchestrated a turn of events that scared Sam—at the threat of five years of hard time, and with the unsaid promise from me that he would not go to prison—into pleading guilty to something I felt he did not do. I had crossed a line to do the right thing under severe pressure in exceptional circumstances.

I granted the motion to withdraw the guilty plea. We were back to the beginning of the case. I looked to the prosecutor.

He said: "Your Honor, the government moves to dismiss this case."

"Motion granted," I said.

I looked at both counsel. "Counsel, I appreciate your high level of competence and professionalism in this difficult case."

I turned to Mr. Johnson. "Good luck, Mr. Johnson. Your case has been dismissed, and you are free to leave."

Faced with the same case today, would I do the same thing? Sitting back in the comfort of my home it is easy to philosophize and say of course not. But would I be writing a different story if the jury had found him guilty, as we all thought they were about to do? I would be thinking of him doing five years in prison for something I thought was unjust. I would be thinking of his daughters.

A judge takes an oath to follow the law, an oath I take very seriously and like to think I have always done to the best of my ability. I skirted the line in this case and rejected the jury's prerogative to determine guilt or innocence to avoid what I thought would be a miscarriage of justice. Was justice ultimately done? I think, in the end, it was, but at a cost to my fidelity to the law. I don't think I would do it again.

# The Right to Live; The Right to Die

Is a viable fetus a person under the law? Does it matter if the fetus is born alive or is stillborn? Can the estate of Baby Boy Smith sue the driver of the car that caused his death before he left the womb?

Should a trial judge order electroconvulsive therapy, formerly called electroshock therapy, and authorize a doctor to send electrical current through the brain to treat a profoundly depressed patient in a mental institution? The patient does not have the capacity to make such a decision for herself. Should I make it for her?

Does a patient in a nursing home have a right to refuse to have his leg amputated so that he may have a good chance to live? Without the amputation, gangrene will spread through his body and he will surely die in a matter of weeks, or even days. The law says he has the right to refuse treatment, even to save his life. But is he capable of making this decision? Should I go see him in the nursing home and convene court there to find out?

These are questions I had to answer in the last few months before *In the Matter of Y.P.* was filed in the Superior Court.

One decision allowed a mother to sue a negligent automobile driver for the death of her stillborn son.

One decision authorized a doctor to perform electroconvulsive therapy as a last resort measure to essentially bring to life a severely depressed woman when all other treatments had failed.

One decision concluded a patient was unable to make life or death choices for himself and authorized the amputation of his leg to try and save his life.

These were all deeply troubling decisions to make, each of which prompted a careful examination of the very meaning of life and death. The Court must always respect a person's right to make decisions for herself, even if it leads to her death. But what if that person is incapable of making such a choice? What happens if the person is incapacitated and had never expressed a view as to her end-of-life care?

It is one thing to authorize medical intervention, arguably against a patient's wishes, to allow hope that someone would live. If I make the wrong call, at least that person is alive. It is quite another thing, however, to authorize removal of life support to allow someone to die.

It was this decision I faced in the case of Y.P.

On June 4, 2014, fifty-one-year-old Y.P. suffered cardiac arrest following a drug overdose. She was transported to the emergency room at United Medical Center in the District of Columbia and was in cardiac arrest upon arrival. Despite heroic efforts to revive her, she remained unresponsive.

Y.P. sustained massive brain damage due to prolonged oxygen deprivation and was placed on a ventilator. Repeated efforts to wean her from the ventilator were unsuccessful. She would never be able to breathe again on her own.

While at the hospital, Y.P. developed bacterial pneumonia, which worsened her respiratory condition, and renal failure, which was successfully treated. When reasonably stable, Y.P. was transferred to a long-term care facility. She remained on the ventilator and received artificial nutrition and hydration through a feeding tube.

At the time of her hospitalization, Y.P. had not signed an advance directive expressing her wishes for end-of-life care, nor had she asked a trusted family member or friend to serve as a power of attorney to make decisions for her in case she ever became unable to do so for herself.

Y.P.'s three adult children, four siblings, and a niece were all very active in her life. Although married at the time of her hospitalization, she was estranged from her husband and they apparently had no ongoing relationship.

On March 27, 2015, nine months after her cardiac arrest, Y.P.'s long-term care facility filed a petition in court requesting appointment of a general guardian to make medical and other decisions for her. A report by her primary physician indicated Y.P. had chronic respiratory failure and profound encephalopathy secondary to anoxic brain injury. In more common terms, Y.P. was in a persistent vegetative state and completely lacked cognitive function.

Reading over the petition and the various medical reports in chambers, I thought about the fragility of life and the loss of loved ones during the natural course of time. Our era of medical magic, however, has extended the bounds of life beyond the course of nature. I didn't know where Y.P.'s case would go or how her family would feel about her future. I only hoped the family would be united in whatever course of action was chosen. A court hearing would have to be convened to find out what was known of Y.P.'s wishes, the family's view as to how to proceed, and the facility's position in terms of the futility of further treatment.

The guardianship process is designed by the law to balance protecting vulnerable adults who are cognitively impaired with the right of self-determination. Appointing a guardian over a person's objection is a profound interference with the basic rights of a citizen and is only done when the need to do so is clearly shown by the State, person, or hospital bringing the case to court. Counsel is appointed for the individual and she is afforded many due process protections, such as the right to call witnesses and challenge the case against her at a trial. If, and when, a guardian is appointed, he or she is authorized to make legal and medical decisions on behalf of the individual, who is now called a "ward."

In such cases, the Court is called upon to make a number of decisions. First, is the person incapacitated in the sense that she lacks the ability to make fundamental legal, medical, or financial decisions? If the Court indeed finds her incapacitated, who is the appropriate person to serve as the guardian? The law prefers that a family member assume the role of guardian. Sometimes dysfunctional family dynamics make the appointment of a particular family member unrealistic and a member of the bar or a social worker is called upon to assume the role of guardian.

I contemplated the court hearing that was scheduled in three weeks. The medical reports overwhelmingly demonstrated Y.P. was incapacitated. Unless there was some truly amazing reversal before the court date, my finding that she would need a guardian would be no more than a formality.

The papers also indicated that her older daughter, who I'll call Jane, had the support of her siblings to act as guardian. Jane was in her early thirties, had a job, and appeared to be well-grounded. One of Y.P.'s sisters lived in the D.C. area, while the rest lived in Panama. Since Y.P.'s husband was not in the picture, by law Jane would have priority to serve as the guardian over Y.P.'s sister. It appeared that as sad as the situation was, my decision would be easy. The appointment of Jane as guardian appeared to be a formality as well.

I appointed a lawyer, Ronald Dixon, to represent Jane as well as a lawyer to represent Y.P. Finally, because Y.P. was in a persistent vegetative state and unable to communicate, I appointed an attorney to serve as a guardian ad litem to articulate her best interests. A guardian ad litem, or GAL, is a short-term appointment that is usually held by an attorney or a social worker and designed to assist the Court in an objective and impartial manner make decisions regarding incapacity and appointment of a specific guardian.

Having taken care of the administrative tasks of appointing counsel and a guardian ad litem, I couldn't help but think that this might be the type of case where at some point I would be asked to authorize the termination of life support.

My thoughts turned to Judge George Greer and the famous Terri Schiavo case that was fiercely litigated in Florida from 1999 to 2005.

In that case Ms. Schiavo, a young woman of twenty-seven, had been in a persistent vegetative state for a number of years. After years of fighting to bring her back to life, her husband believed that she would not want to continue on life support any longer in such a condition. He was also ready to move on with his life. He sought permission from the court to remove the ventilator and hydration intubation that kept her alive.

Ms. Schiavo's parents objected on a number of grounds; they claimed against all medical evidence their daughter was conscious, and they asserted their religion taught them that life was sacred and only God would know when a person was ready to pass away.

Judge Greer convened a number of hearings and ultimately concluded that Ms. Schiavo's condition was irreversible and that she would not have wanted to continue living in her present condition. He approved removal of life support.

What followed next was a maelstrom of international news amid the collision of politics, the Right to Life movement, social media, and religion. Florida Governor Jeb Bush and the Florida legislature tried to intervene. President George W. Bush called Congress into a special Easter session to allow the federal government to interfere in what was quintessentially a state court decision. Pope John Paul II issued a proclamation on "Life Sustaining Treatments and Vegetative State: Scientific Advances and Ethical Dilemma," making it clear that Catholic doctrine forbids the removal of life support. The case was reviewed numerous times by state and federal courts. All courts agreed with Judge Greer. Life support was finally withdrawn and Terri Schiavo died.

Judge Greer, a humble man and by his own characterization, a religious, conservative Republican, received death threats and was placed in 24/7 security and had to leave his home. Most galling to him, however, was when he was told by the pastor of the church he had attended for years that it would be better if he not return. He became the unlikely symbol of judicial independence.

I had been chair of our judicial training committee at the Superior Court and invited Judge Greer to talk to our judges, not so much about the decision itself, but about staying resolute and principled in the face of such unrelenting opposition. I thought warmly of the dinner we shared the night before he spoke to the Superior Court judges.

The court hearing on the Petition for a Guardian on April 28, 2015, was quiet and sad. At this point Y.P. had been on life support for more than ten months. I expressed my regret to the family about Y.P.'s condition and they nodded in appreciation. Y.P.'s attorney acknowledged that she was incapacitated and supported the appointment of Jane as the permanent guardian. Jane accepted the responsibility as guardian but indicated she was considering removing her mother from life support.

Y.P.'s sister, who I will call Rosanna, had been sitting quietly in the courtroom, but then raised her hand. I invited her to come to counsel's table. Rosanna passed Jane at counsel's table to stand at the microphone. Aunt and niece pointedly did not look at each other. Rosanna said that she strongly opposed such a decision. This was the first indication that the family was divided on Y.P.'s future.

I needed to make sure everyone stayed calm and fully understood their rights and responsibilities. I informed the family that any guardian appointed would need to obtain court authority to terminate life support. Understanding this, Rosanna did not object to Jane's appointment as general guardian.

I was relieved the family treated each other with respect and appeared to understand the limits of the guardian's power. I wished them well under these trying circumstances and recessed court.

Walking back to chambers I thought it very likely Y.P.'s case would return to court and I would have to squarely face a decision I had hoped to avoid.

Eight months later, on December 4, 2015, Jane filed a Petition seeking Court permission to withdraw her mother's ventilator and feeding tube. Y.P. had been on life support for one year and six months.

Given the gravity of the situation, I reappointed counsel Dixon to represent Jane and appointed guardian ad litem Katherine Wiedmann, a very experienced lawyer, "to determine Y.P.'s best interests, insofar as they are relevant to the question of whether she would have consented to the withdrawal of life support." I also appointed Suzanne Wynne, a knowledgeable and experienced licensed social worker, to evaluate the case and provide the Court with up-to-date information on "Y.P.'s prognosis and, to the extent possible, to investigate her position vis-à-vis removing life support." I advised everyone that I also wanted to hear testimony from Y.P.'s primary care doctor.

My law clerk, Jessica Westerman, and I studied the law and procedures concerning termination of life support. Generally speaking, the law dictates the Courts apply the principle of "substituted judgment" in considering whether someone has the right to die. The term "substituted judgment" is misleading in that it implies that someone else, usually the guardian, should substitute her judgment for that of the incapacitated person. In reality, the term means the Court should honor, to the extent possible, the decision the patient would make had she the ability to articulate her wishes today.

The law covering removal of life support embraces the principle of substituted judgment, and decisions from our Court of Appeals have supported its use in other contexts as "the only way to pay full respect to the individuality and dignity of a person who has expressed clear, deeply felt, even sacred preferences while competent."

In researching the law, I was reminded of one of the most wrenching cases a trial judge on our court was asked to decide. A hospital petitioned the court for authority to allow doctors to perform a cesarean section on a woman pregnant with a viable fetus, but dying of terminal cancer.

Before falling unconscious, the woman had expressed contradictory wishes as to whether she wanted doctors to perform the cesarean section—which would hasten her death—in the event she could not deliver the baby naturally. At a hearing convened at the hospital, the judge weighed the State's interest in protecting the potentiality of human life against the woman's interest in prolonging her own life. The trial judge ultimately ordered the cesarean section be performed. The Court of Appeals denied an emergency motion to halt the order and the cesarean was performed. Sadly, both mother and child died shortly thereafter.

In light of the importance of the issues raised, and in order to give guidance to the legal and medical community in the future, the Court of Appeals took the unusual step of reconsidering the case despite the death of the mother and child. The Court concluded the trial judge insufficiently considered the mother's previously expressed wishes, past decisions concerning medical treatment, and value system. The Court then set aside the cesarean order.

From reviewing the law as it has developed, it was clear that my decision in Y.P.'s case would not be to side with either the daughter's or sister's respective wishes or perspectives. The ultimate decision would rest on a finding of what Y.P. would have wanted under the circumstances. Every person has the right under the law to accept or refuse medical treatment. The right of bodily integrity and self-determination belongs equally to persons who are competent and those who are not.

But what would happen if I could not determine one way or the other what Y.P would have wanted to do? I knew she hadn't signed an advance directive setting forth her views on end of life care. She also had not asked a family member or friend to serve as a power of attorney authorizing someone else to make the decision for her in case she was unable to do so for herself. It was also possible that after the court hearing I still would not know with any degree of reliability what Y.P. would have wanted. What then? We started looking at that possible scenario as well.

For the typical decisions a guardian has to make on behalf of a ward, the law in the District of Columbia is straightforward. If the ward's wishes are unknown and remain unknown after reasonable efforts to find them out, the guardian's decision is made on the basis of the ward's best interests.

As an example, a guardian may be faced with the dilemma as to whether an elderly ward should leave his home and go into some type of nursing facility. If the ward, now incapacitated and unable to communicate in a rational way, had never made his feelings about nursing homes known, the guardian would have to consider the ward's best interests as to where he would receive the safest and best quality of life.

But the law was not as clear as to the extraordinary decision regarding the removal of life support that a guardian is called upon to make. Specifically, the statute addressing termination of life support did not instruct trial courts to consider a ward's best interests, much less describe or define what that standard actually means in the case of a person in a persistent vegetative state. Ending a life is a very different thing from altering the quality of a life.

Our Court of Appeals had not specifically addressed the standards when the ward's wishes were unknown. In the cesarean section case, the Court stopped short of instructing the trial court how to proceed under these circumstances. The Court, however, suggested that a trial judge should consider objective criteria by "determining what most persons would likely do in a similar situation." In another case involving a mental hospital's request to administer psychotropic medication to a schizophrenic patient, the Court also suggested that a trial judge could "fill in the gaps" by taking into account "what most persons are likely to do in a similar situation."

I wasn't totally comfortable going forward on a case of this magnitude without doing further research as to how other states handled the issue. Research showed there were two approaches to what seems like an intractable problem, and I quickly realized the view I adopted could very well mean the difference between life and death. Guardians are entrusted with making many decisions on behalf of a ward that do not require court approval. For the termination of life support, however, a guardian must seek a court order before instructing a hospital to remove life support. As such, the ultimate decision is the judge's call.

A small minority of states apply what is called the "purely subjective standard," under which judges must decline to authorize withdrawal of life support absent clear and convincing evidence of an individual's pre-injury desire to withdraw it. These states deny requests to withdraw life support if the incapacitated patient's wishes were unknown or conflicting. This approach also refuses to approve termination of life support when the patient was born with a severe cognitive or intellectual disability, and thus was never able to articulate his wishes on end of life care. One case, for example, denied a mother's petition to discontinue life-sustaining blood transfusions because her son never was competent to express a desire to forgo them, despite his obvious dislike for and discomfort during the transfusions.

Other states apply a variation of the purely subjective standard by attempting to infer an individual's wishes from her philosophical, religious, and moral views; life goals; values about the purpose of life and the way it should be lived; and attitudes toward sickness, medical procedures, suffering, and death. The proponents of this approach argue that by limiting the inquiry to evidence of an individual's actual wishes and maintaining a high evidentiary threshold, this standard theoretically accords maximum respect to individual autonomy by honoring the patient's right to control her own life, and not what a reasonable or average person would have chosen to do under the circumstances.

Supporters of the purely subjective standard argue that introducing objective factors such as an individual's age, prognosis, or capacity for pleasure or pain lets a judge determine a patient's quality of life, which would, as one case stated, undercut a patient's "right of self-determination and inviolability of the person upon which the right to refuse medical treatment stands."

Perhaps the strongest of all these arguments to me was that allowing a judge make a quality of life determination, at all, strikes at society's core beliefs and should therefore be made by a legislature and not the courts.

For instance, concluding in one case that life support should be withheld from an individual in a persistent vegetative state whose wishes are unknown could result in a similar finding in all such cases. Are judges supposed to make this overall policy decision? Are judges capable of making such a judgment?

And what is "quality of life"? Left unsaid in this calculation is the role religion plays in forming public policy by electing like-minded representatives. I knew that some religions, or more precisely, sections of some religions, strongly believe that only God has the power and wisdom to let us know when it is time to die.

These were all weighty concerns as I turned to consider another approach.

In contrast with the minority of states that apply some variation of the purely subjective standard, the majority of states use objective factors to determine the course of action that is in the individual's "best interest"—that is, the one she mostly likely would have chosen for herself—when her wishes remain unclear.

When there is insufficient evidence of an individual's wishes, these states look to the hypothetical reasonable person and consider factors such as a person's natural instinct to live, pain and suffering with and without a proposed treatment; capacity for physical pleasure, emotional enjoyment, and intellectual satisfaction with and without treatment; life expectancy; prognosis; level of functioning; degree of humiliation and dependency; ability to interact with the environment; potential relief from suffering; function preservation or restoration; quality and extent of sustained life; age, as related to responsiveness to treatment; ability to cooperate with treatment; and the potential side effects of treatment, to determine whether a "reasonable person" would, under the circumstances of that case, want life support withdrawn.

Since our Court of Appeals had strongly suggested in the cesarean section and psychotropic medication cases that trial judges should follow the majority approach and utilize the objective/reasonable person test, it appeared that my path to making a decision was to follow the conventional line of cases. My reservation, however, was that ordering action to preserve human life is qualitatively different from making the irrevocable decision to end it.

I also reflected on the exercise of judicial power and its far-reaching consequences. I have permanently taken a child away from her abusive parents, and sentenced a rapist to life in prison who gratuitously killed his victim. I have also evicted a mother and her children from their home where the mother's only sin was that she was too poor to pay the rent. In protecting a child and giving her a chance to thrive in another loving family, or protecting the community from reprehensible violence, judicial power can be a righteous force for good; in evicting a poor family from their home, judicial power feels like a reluctant, validating force for legal and economic order. On either end of the scale, the scope of the consequences is profound, and I have a healthy respect for the magnitude of the decision I have to make.

The judges I most admire and aspire to emulate not only have the intellect to understand the complexity of the law, but, more importantly, have reached a balance in their lives to appreciate the limitations of a person's ability to make life-altering decisions while embracing the responsibility to do so. Call it the "getting of wisdom," if you will. To entrust a judge with the power of life or death, whether in sentencing a convicted murderer to the electric chair or lethal injection, or in authorizing the withdrawal of life support, is perhaps a power the law should not ever allow to one person. It was helpful to take these basic principles to heart. I had accepted the duty to take on the case of Y.P. and I resolved do my best.

On February 9, 2016, all the parties gathered for the court hearing. Y.P. had now been on life support for a year and eight months. As I entered the courtroom I could see Jane and what appeared to be her siblings on one side of the aisle. On the other side I saw Rosanna with four other women with headphones on. I also saw our Spanish-speaking interpreter next to the four women with a miniature microphone at the ready.

At the beginning of the hearing I asked if we could proceed informally and just let everyone say their piece, or if there was a need for a contested trial with witnesses placed under oath and subject to cross-examination. Everyone agreed that going forth informally was fine. I was relieved to hear that; a bruising trial with harsh cross-examination would undoubtedly only further tear apart an already fractured family.

I asked Jane to step up to the microphone at the lectern in the courtroom.

"Is there anything you want to say? You don't have to say anything if you don't want to. I don't want you to feel like you must, but if you want to say something now would be an opportunity."

Strong and self-assured, Jane took a deep breath.

"I'm Jane. I'm Y.P.'s daughter and her guardian. I think it's just really time to remove life support from her. I think she's been on it long enough. I've seen for myself. It's just becoming more disturbing that she sat this long and some people are okay with it. I'm not. And I'm speaking for myself. I just think it's time. It's a time to heal and this just needs to come to an end, just closure."

I understood her personal viewpoint but I wanted to address the legal question that would ultimately guide my decision.

I looked at Jane. I didn't want to put her on the spot or make her feel uncomfortable, but if anyone had insight into what her mother would have wanted, she would probably be the best person to know. I decided to simply ask her what she knew.

"Is there anything that your mother said or did that would give you some indication as to what she would have wanted?"

"No," she said. "She's young. I don't think she thought that far ahead."

Next, her brother, who I will call James and who was in his late teens or early twenties, stepped up to the lectern. Unlike his sister, James seemed fragile.

I gently asked if he wanted to say anything, once again making it clear he didn't have to if it was too much for him.

"I just feel like permission should be granted to my sister just so it's in our hands. That's all I have to say."

According to guardian ad litem Wiedmann, James previously had stated he "didn't think his mother would want to be kept alive on life support because she was a vibrant and caring, loving person; deprived of the ability to visit regularly with family and to engage is not how she would want to spend the rest of her life."

I invited Y.P.'s siblings to come forward. One sister stated "Yesterday when we arrived from Panama we went directly to the hospital. We spoke with her. She was moving her hands, she was moving her mouth. She was crying. You could feel that she has life. She is not dead. That's all."

I thanked her under these difficult circumstances.

Another sister quietly approached the lectern. "This is a very difficult and painful family situation. But my position is that we have to give her an opportunity at life. I visited her last night. She moves her hands. She opens her eyes. She was crying. She moves her feet. In other words, there is life there. She is not dead."

I thanked her as well.

A third sister came forward. She stated, "What I would like is for my sister to be given more time. We went to go see her last night. We went to see her today. We saw her cry. We saw her move her eyes. And I don't have anything else to say and I thank you very much."

"Thank you, ma'am. I know how difficult this is. Thank you."

Rosanna, the sister who resided locally, related a phone conversation with Y.P. two days before Y.P. was hospitalized during which they discussed plans to fly to Panama to renovate their mother's house. And then a few days later, she was in the hospital.

"When this happened," Y.P.'s sister explained, "I started praying and talking to the Lord."

Rosanna also described dreams that she, her brother, and her daughter had had in which Y.P. was "out of bed, walking and talking… That she's going to come back. That she's going to talk and walk and be a normal person. It's coming to me. And even today I feel very peaceful. Everything is going to come through. That's how I feel. Thank you."

I thanked her and saw guardian ad litem Wiedmann step forward. Referring to Rosanna, she said "this sibling feels extremely strongly that a miracle will happen and that Y.P will be walking, talking, and will resume her life as it was before."

Y.P.'s niece, who also traveled from Panama, came forward.

"I do believe that if my aunt were meant to die she would have died by now… and we are believers. I do believe that God is doing something in my aunt's life. And I do believe that she should be given another… opportunity, more time. I do wish and do believe that everybody should come together and her kids should come together. They don't see her, there is no love. I don't think that they should be asking that she be disconnected. She was somebody who loved life. She was Christian. She was a believer even though she stepped away for a while, but she believed in God. And that's my opinion, and thank you."

"Thank you, ma'am."

Although I wanted to hear directly from Y.P.'s primary care physician at a later proceeding, I asked guardian ad litem Wiedmann to sum up her review of the medical record, including her discussions with Y.P.'s doctor. I was not sure if the relatives from Panama were going to be able to attend a future hearing with the primary physician, so I wanted to make sure they fully understood Y.P.'s medical condition and prognosis from the view of her doctor.

She confirmed that Y.P. had given no written or oral indication of her wishes regarding end-of-life care.

Next, the GAL, quoting from the doctor, stated that Y.P.'s brain injury is "profound and severe, and she requires total assistance with all activities of daily life"; Y.P.'s prognosis is "dismal, with no chance of recovery"; and that "continuing medical treatment in this case is futile."

Based upon conversations with Y.P.'s family members, the guardian ad litem also stated that although Y.P. "was religious... did go to church... and did share with her sister some religious beliefs," Y.P. had at some point left her sister's church to join a different church. Her reason for doing so remained unclear. Y.P. was a member of the new church at the time she was hospitalized.

Y.P. had no condition requiring ongoing medication and had not previously been hospitalized. Based largely upon Y.P.'s primary care physician's finding that continued treatment would be futile and concluding that, under these circumstances, a reasonable person would not want to remain on life support, guardian ad litem Wiedmann concluded it would be in Y.P.'s best interest to grant the guardian's petition to remove the breathing, feeding, and hydration tubes.

I had appointed Suzanne Wynne, a very experienced licensed social worker, to review Y.P.'s case. I asked her to step forward and summarize her written report. I thought it very important that the whole family hear out loud the expert reports. I understood that if I ultimately chose to terminate life support, they would be devastated and hurt. Nothing would change that. But they would have all the information out there and at least, hopefully, understand any decision I would make.

Upon her review of Y.P.'s medical chart, social worker Wynne, reported, "it is evident that Y.P.'s care is palliative." Although various therapists would exercise and stimulate

Y.P.'s muscles, "these efforts were intended to retain some muscle tone and were in no sense oriented to restoring cognitive functions." Y.P. also experienced sporadic acute care issues, including a bacterial infection that caused "severe, persistent diarrhea," requiring hospitalization to restore her baseline health.

I had seen a photograph of Y.P. before her injury. She appeared in that snapshot of her life happy and with a broad smile. The fact that, in addition to everything else, she suffered such a degree of diarrhea struck at me hard. Many disabled adults, particularly the elderly, have to wear diapers. They adapt, they go forward, and embrace a value in the life that they have—family, friends, reading, music, TV, you name it. The richness of life can be wonderful, even under the most challenging of circumstances. But to suffer the indignity of severe, persistent, diarrhea while enjoying nothing that life has to offer seemed to me an existence with no meaning.

I knew immediately I had to be careful here. It was not my personal views or philosophy of life or death that mattered. I had to follow the law as best I could.

The social worker concluded that her review of the chart indicated "the massive damage that Y.P.'s brain sustained offers no hope that her brain can recover life-sustaining functions."

She also said that the primary care physician told her that Y.P. was beginning to experience organ failure. At some point the "kidneys begin to fail and that sets off a whole process of toxicity. And she's at the beginning of that process. And that is one of his reasons for believing that it would be kind to let her go."

There was no more testimony. I indicated to the parties that in light of the gravity of the situation, I wanted to have the primary care physician appear in court. I also wanted to review the state of the law again. I recessed court and set a further hearing in a few weeks.

In chambers, it appeared to me the two critical factual issues had largely been resolved. The medical records and reports from the guardian ad litem and social worker were very compelling. First, Y.P. was in a persistent vegetative state, did not respond to external stimuli, and had no cognitive functioning. Her very existence was totally dependent on a ventilator and hydration and nutrition through a feeding tube. Despite her siblings' and niece's testimony, I didn't believe she recognized her family or had any interaction with them. I didn't believe any reflexive movements were voluntary.

Nonetheless, I wanted as much information and certainty as possible. As such, we made arrangements to have the primary care physician appear in court and testify as to Y.P's condition, prognosis, and whether any future medical treatment was futile. Although it seemed highly unlikely that new medical evidence would be presented at a future hearing, I thought there was also value for the entire family in hearing the doctor testify in open court.

The resolution of the second issue was also clear to me. Y.P. had not made known in a formal legal document, or through family or friends, what she actually would have wanted to be done in her present situation. I realized that somewhere deep inside I had wanted clear evidence to emerge that would make the ultimate decision for me. But the evidence was not there and I realized, with dread, that ultimately I would have to make the decision without guidance as to what Y.P. would have wanted.

Having determined the facts of the case, I realized the decision as to whether Y.P.'s life support would be withdrawn depended on which philosophy of law I chose to adopt. The majority of states that have wrestled with this dilemma defer to objective factors that the hypothetical reasonable person would consider. It was also the approach our Court of Appeals had suggested that trial courts—like my court—should follow in making critical decisions about a patient's well-being. The path to making a judgment seemed strongly to weigh in following the majority view.

Although I had to remain intellectually honest by keeping my personal philosophy out of the decision-making process, it was also my personal view as well. No way would I want to exist in a persistent vegetative state, only surviving on medical technology, while my family grieved but could not heal. So, while I was getting more and more comfortable with the legal decision I had to make, I wanted to confront the minority view again.

The principle that troubled me the most was, strangely enough, one of faith. I don't consider myself a religious person. Raised in Reform Judaism, I belong to an eclectic and progressive Jewish community that attracts interfaith couples, such as my wife and me, and to the extent it has a philosophy, it sees Judaism as an evolving value-culture that honors humanism and spirituality. There is an emphasis on what is known as *tikkun olam*, or repairing the world in one's everyday life and the life of the community. Folks have very different concepts of God, if they have any concept at all, while most probably see the "divine" within each of us and all of life. Although I have a great interest in world religions, and tinker with Zen Buddhism as a meditative way to relax, I'm certainly no scholar in belief and grace.

I did know, however, that branches of Judaism, Christianity, and Islam have very strongly held views on life support that are predicated on the belief that all life is sacred and is to be protected at virtually any cost. For instance, on the holiest of Jewish holidays, Yom Kippur, the Day of Atonement, it is expected that a Jew fast from sundown to the next sundown in order to allow for reflection and repentance for one's sins. It's one of Judaism's strictest commandments; but if a person risks death from fasting on Yom Kippur, not only may she eat, she is required to do so.

Not only is all life revered, these religious beliefs embrace the concept that there is no measuring the "quality of life." Having been created by God, all human life is equally holy and sacred. There is no distinction between a child, a healthy adult, the disabled, or the terminally ill. All three religions have suffered pernicious persecution where an adherent's very humanity has been taken away, as if the believer's very existence had no meaning. Less than human, a follower could be tortured and murdered with impunity. Having suffered such virulent outside forces of destruction, these branches of faith refuse to denigrate anyone's life.

Respect for life has led these religious beliefs to condemn as a murderer anyone who assists in performing an act of euthanasia on a dying person, even one in great pain. Is there any difference between giving medication to a dying patient to hasten death, and withdrawing the breathing and eating support that allows one to keep living? Are both acts of murder?

Citing scripture in the Bible and the Koran, some rabbis, priests, and imams would say that it is not for the courts, or the legislatures for that matter, to determine if a person's "quality of life" has meaning or purpose. How do we draw the line between those we think may have a reason to live and those who don't? Although a life artificially existing in a persistent vegetative state may not have a purpose to the "reasonable person," it is a life that is precious to God. When faced with either injustice, or the cruelties of suffering upon the innocent, my friend Sister Joseph Beatrice used to say, with a rueful smile, that "God works in mysterious ways. It is not for us in our limited wisdom to understand. God understands and that is enough."

I wondered how a religiously observant judge, who passionately adhered to these beliefs, would feel in my situation. If the law required termination of life support, could that judge actually sign her name to the judicial order allowing Y.P.'s death? I was struggling enough as it was trying to resolve two very different legal approaches to what seemed to be an irreconcilable problem.

I thought of a scenario that would have affected me personally. Several years before I joined the bench, the citizens of the District of Columbia soundly rejected a referendum proposal for the death penalty. What if somehow the politics changed and the death penalty returned to the District? In light of my strongly held moral views against capital punishment, could I fairly and impartially sentence someone faced with the possibility of execution? The oath of office I took required me to do so. But could I carry it out? Could I really say out loud in an open courtroom, with the victim's and defendant's families in the front rows, along with the public and media, and my conscience to reckon with, "Mr. Jones, the Court hereby sentences you to death by lethal injection."

I respect those who believe their lives are blessed with the grace of God. In weighing which legal approach to follow in a termination of life support case, I suppose a religiously observant judge would have to recuse herself from this type of case if, as seemed clear, the law of the District of Columbia favored the objective, "reasonable person" standard. I had to admit to myself that I was relieved to not be burdened with such deep religious convictions.

I reviewed all the statutes and cases again. Particularly in light of the Court of Appeals' apparent openness to "filling the gaps" in a court's knowledge about an individual's wishes by "taking into account what most persons are likely to do in a similar situation," the logical and ineluctable conclusion was that the District of Columbia followed the majority of states to have addressed this issue, meaning that I would have to determine what a reasonable person in Y.P.'s circumstances would choose.

I also consulted with other judges whose views I deeply respected. Although this was to be my decision alone, having the support and backup of my colleagues' experience and wisdom was reassuring. In the end I believed following the objective, "reasonable person" standard was the correct interpretation of District of Columbia law. Absent a surprising turn of events from the primary care doctor or other evidence coming to light at the next court hearing, I concluded that all the key objective factors—diagnosis, prognosis, and quality of life—all weighed heavily in favor of allowing Y.P. a dignified death. I started drafting my opinion authorizing the withdrawal of her ventilator and hydration intubation.

Several weeks later I walked into the courtroom and took a deep breath as the clerk asked everyone to rise and called court into session. I could see at once that Rosanna and the niece from Panama were present. Everyone introduced themselves for the record.

It was very quiet and somber in the courtroom. It felt like everyone knew what was going to happen and were giving the moment the quiet and dignity it deserved.

Jane's lawyer asked to call Y.P.'s primary care doctor to the witness stand.

Y.P.'s doctor testified that she had been under his care for eighteen months. He further stated that, among those ventilator-dependent patients he had treated, Y.P. stood out for the profoundness of her anoxic injury, the result of lack of oxygen to the brain. She had "no brain function whatsoever" and "no response whatsoever to stimulation." Contrary to the assertions of Y.P.'s siblings, the doctor had not seen Y.P. cry nor move her hands or mouth in the eighteen months he had treated her. He further testified there was no doubt in his mind that Y.P. had lost the ability to recognize family members. He described Y.P.'s prognosis as irreversible and stated that she was not going to recover. He stated that, ultimately, her condition would be terminal.

Moreover, the doctor testified Y.P. had developed a sacral ulcer as a result of being on her back for so long and her extremities had contracted from lack of mobility. Her bones had become so brittle that her ribs would fracture during emergency chest compressions if her heart failed.

Were Y.P. to be removed from life support, doctors would enact a protocol designed to prevent distress. She would die peacefully in a matter of hours.

The doctor ultimately recommended that based upon the principle of medical futility—the bioethical concept that a physician has no duty to continue treatment proved to be ineffective—life support should be withdrawn.

I asked if anyone else wanted to address the court.

Jane and guardian ad litem Wiedmann had nothing further to say. Their position had not changed. Jane's lawyer said that if the Court granted the petition, Jane would give the family time to say their good-byes.

Y.P.'s sister raised her hand. She slowly approached the lectern.

After taking a deep breath, she said softly, "I just want to ask you to just let her wake. She will wake up."

Without looking at me, she turned her back and went back to her seat.

I recessed court and asked the parties to wait a few minutes while I reviewed my notes.

The doctor's unwavering testimony only reinforced my decision. I had already drafted an outline of an opinion and decided to announce the judgment in open court. As Jane had said, it was now a time to heal. There would be time later to publish a formal opinion in writing. I knew it was going to be impossibly hard for Y.P.'s sister to hear my decision, but I didn't want to shy away from it either. I took the time I needed to integrate the doctor's testimony into my draft opinion. I was ready to rule.

I went back into the courtroom and made no eye contact with any of the participants.

I slowly and methodically went through the facts that showed without question that Y.P. was in a persistent vegetative state with no cognitive or physical awareness of life around her.

Turning next to the philosophical debate in the law about which approach to follow when a patient had not previously expressed her views about end-of-life care, I concluded as a matter of law that the District of Columbia followed the majority view and would look to objective factors that a reasonable person would consider in this situation.

Given Y.P.'s diagnosis and prognosis, I stated that no reasonable, competent person, who did not have religious or other views to the contrary, would want to be maintained on artificial breathing and feeding machines while not enjoying any quality of life as we know it, and being subjected to the indignity of her body being totally dependent on medical science.

As I was finishing my opinion, Y.P.'s sister stood up and silently left the courtroom. She did not look at me as she left.

I granted Jane's petition to allow her the authority to withdraw life support.

I announced that Court would now stand in recess and left the bench.

Y.P.'s sisters and niece did not appeal my decision.

Jane had said earlier that before she would actually sign the document authorizing the hospital to withdraw life support, she would allow family members the time to say their goodbyes. Jane was an honorable person, and I assumed that she lived up to her word.

A little over a month after I ruled, I received a Notice of Death from Jane stating Y.P. died on April 11, 2016. May she rest in peace and her memory be a blessing to all who knew her.

This chapter is dedicated to my mentor and friend, Judge Leonard Braman, who counseled with wise advice during this case. Judge Braman passed away in 2020.

# The Illusion of Delusion: The Murder of Viola Drath and the Strange Case of General Albrecht Gero Muth

◈ ◈ ◈ ◈ ◈

If it wasn't for the sight of a ninety-one-year-old woman lying dead and nearly naked in her bathroom with her neck and ribs broken and head bruised, the whole saga would have been an amusing and colorful tale of Washington society and power grabs run amok. The media loved her death. They loved her accused killer even more.

The headlines were short and pithy. "Georgetown Socialite Murdered!" "Who killed Viola Drath?" Was she the victim of a nefarious intelligence service out to kill her mysterious husband—one time Count, soldier in the French Foreign Legion, South American mercenary, and current General in the Iraqi Army? Or was the murder something more craven than that? The *New York Times Magazine* published an article with a title that supposedly captured the couple's May–December relationship as "The Worst Marriage in Georgetown."

Surely a made-for-TV movie was in store, maybe even the Hollywood big screen.

But there was nothing entertaining about Viola Drath's death. It was a horrific end to a good woman's life that left behind a grieving family and many friends. Its resolution had nothing to do with fancy Georgetown parties that featured hobnobbing with Supreme Court justices, vice presidents, diplomats, and elite journalists. Its aftermath played out in the gritty maw that is the criminal justice system.

Although, in the end, it was just another murder case with a police investigation, forensic autopsy, grand jury investigation, mental health experts opining with certitude completely contrasting viewpoints, and prosecutors and defense lawyers sparring over the law and evidence, there was a mystery at its core. Just who was the accused, one Albrecht Gero Muth, anyway?

## The Murder of Viola Drath

As the case came into the Superior Court, the basic facts were outlined in a detective's affidavit, signed on August 16, 2011, seeking an arrest warrant for Muth. On Friday, August 12, 2011, at 7:59 in the morning, forty-seven-year-old Albrecht Muth called 911, and in a calm and matter-of-fact voice, stated his wife was dead in an upstairs bathroom in their home at 3206 Q Street, Northwest.

The police arrived at 8:18 a.m. and found ninety-one-year-old Viola Drath unconscious and lying on the floor in an upstairs bathroom. An ambulance technician found no vital signs. As such, the police left Ms. Drath's body on the scene and called for a detective, generally called "a natural," whose job is to confirm that a death was not caused by foul play.

When the detective arrived, he took precautionary measures and summoned the police crime scene search division to photograph the body. He also asked a forensic investigator from the Office of the Chief Medical Examiner's to inspect the body.

The forensic investigator, Latoya Jamieson, arrived at 11:20 a.m. and carefully examined the body. It was obvious to her that the injuries suffered by Ms. Drath appeared to be inflicted and not the result of an accidental fall. She recommended that the body be sent for an autopsy. She also called Homicide Detective Gus Giannakoulias and alerted him to her suspicions.

A physician's assistant arrived on the scene and pronounced Ms. Drath dead at 12:22 a.m. Her remains were sent to the Office of the Chief Medical Examiner for an autopsy.

Later that night Albrecht Muth emailed an obituary to the *Washington Post* stating that his wife died after "sustaining a head injury from a fall."

The next day, Saturday, August 13, 2011, the doctor conducting the autopsy, called the Medical Examiner, or ME in police slang, found several injuries including a fractured anterior neck cartilage, hemorrhages in both eyes, fractured ribs, bruises to the scalp, and a torn right thumbnail. The injuries were completely inconsistent with an accidental fall in the bathroom, even for a fragile ninety-one-year-old woman. The ME concluded Ms. Drath's death was caused by strangulation and blunt force injuries. The ME ruled the death a homicide. The ME also determined that Ms. Drath likely died within twelve hours of 11:20 a.m., the time the body was first examined by the forensic investigator on the scene.

Homicide Detectives Giannakoulias and James E. Wilson attended the autopsy. The detectives also reviewed the photographs of Ms. Drath at the scene.

The placement of the body appeared staged to look like Ms. Drath accidentally fell and died of natural causes. It looked like someone had dragged her body into the bathroom. Two area rugs, which presumably would be lying flat on the floor, were scrunched up beneath Ms. Drath's back.

Even more telling, the body was lying face up and completely straight from head to toe on the bathroom floor. It's possible, of course, that someone could faint, hit their head on a sink and fall to the ground. But what are the chances the body would fall and simply lie straight like she was in a coffin?

There was no sign of forced entry in the Georgetown two-level row house with a basement. There were four entrances to the house: a front door on the first level, a front door leading to the basement, and two doors in the rear basement. All the doors and windows to the basement were locked with cast iron security bars, which were also locked.

There appeared to be no damage to the front door on the first level. Two windows next to the front door were locked. There were three unlocked windows in the rear of the first level; one was surrounded by cobwebs, suggesting the window had not been disturbed for a significant period of time; one window was surrounded by thick vegetation that made an entrance almost impossible; and one window had nothing to block an entry but was eleven feet from the ground. No ladder was located or observed in the vicinity of the house.

That same day Homicide Detectives Giannakoulias and Wilson asked Muth to come to the Metropolitan Police Department Homicide Branch for a voluntary interview. He was not under arrest and told he could leave at any time. The interview was recorded on video.

Muth said he and his wife had been married for more than twenty years and were the only people to occupy the house on Q Street. When asked about the forty-four years difference in age with Viola Drath, he responded that theirs was "a marriage of convenience." He stated that he did not have a job but was provided a monthly allowance of $2,000. His wife, however, had recently cut his allowance to $1,800 per month. He did not say why.

He went on. His wife did not have any enemies or problems with anyone, himself included.

When asked about his whereabouts in the hours leading up to her death, Muth stated that he had been with his wife on Thursday, August 11, 2011, until about 4:00 p.m., when he went to meet a friend, declining to name that person. He returned around 9:45 p.m., through the basement door to the house. Without seeing his wife, he went to his upstairs study, next to the bathroom, to check his emails. When finished, he went outside for his evening walk for about an hour, and returned to the basement, where he went to sleep. He claimed he slept there because it was cooler and his wife did not like air conditioning.

Awaking at 4:00 a.m., on Friday, August 12, Muth said he returned to the second floor study to check his emails, had no contact with his wife, and went down the stairs to the basement. At 7:00 a.m., he went outside for his morning walk and returned around 7:50 a.m. Having not seen or heard his wife that morning, he went upstairs to check on her. He found her unconscious on the bathroom floor and dialed 911 at 8:00 a.m. He did not perform CPR on his wife because there was no need to. There was no need to touch the body on the floor either. She was obviously dead.

The detectives had set their trap and were ready to pounce. They informed Muth that the ME's office had declared his wife's death a homicide. He wanted to know the cause of death. The detectives refused to tell him. He then wanted to know the time of death. The detectives told him roughly eight hours from when the ME forensic investigator examined the body at 11:20 a.m., or about 3:00 to 3:30 a.m. Friday morning. In fact, the ME had stated that the cause of death was about twelve hours from the discovery of the body, or around 11:20 p.m. Thursday evening.

Muth denied killing his wife. In the dry, police-speak words of the affidavit: "The defendant maintained he had no involvement in the demise of the decedent."

The detectives then tried to give him an "out"—a way to explain the death without knowingly confessing to murder. The "out" is a classic method of homicide investigations. They told him they knew of prior incidents of domestic violence between he and his wife. Maybe this was all an accident, they helpfully suggested.

Muth didn't bite. "It was no accident," he said firmly.

Who else could be responsible for her death other than him they asked?

"It must have been an intruder," he said.

The detectives told him there were no signs of forced entry, as all the doors and windows were locked.

He replied quickly that some of the widows were unlocked.

They explained that all the screens were intact and nothing was disturbed.

Muth agreed there was no possible way for someone to enter the house. But it must have been an intruder if his wife was murdered, he countered.

"How could they come in?" the detectives asked.

"It's your job to investigate, not mine," he replied contemptuously.

Nothing was stolen or missing, except maybe for Ms. Drath's hat.

"Who would have a motive to come in to harm your wife?"

"I don't think anybody," he replied.

Claiming that he had been at a friend's house until 9:00 p.m., Muth again insisted that he wanted to know the time of death. "I hope it is before 9:00 o'clock," he said.

The detectives left the interview room for a break, all the while observing Muth on video.

Muth rubbed his face and repeatedly saying to himself, "She has ruled it a murder."

When the detectives returned to the interview room, Muth asked, "The next question; is anything linking me to it in your mind?"

The detectives did not respond. They let him go on.

Muth stated, "It doesn't look good for me, though."

The detectives asked him if he was willing to give a DNA sample. He initially agreed but then refused.

Later that Saturday evening the police secured the house on Q Street, not allowing anyone, including Muth, entry. The next day, Sunday, August 14, 2011, the detectives obtained a search warrant from a judge on the Superior Court for the Q Street house and for authority to collect pulled hair and cheek swabs from Muth for DNA comparison purposes. The warrant also authorized the police to photograph any injuries to Muth's body.

While the police were searching the house the next day, Sunday, Muth approached the detectives. It was later learned that he had slept in a Georgetown park the night before. He was told of the search warrant for the house and to collect his DNA. He wanted to see the search warrant and it was provided to him. He agreed to voluntarily comply with the warrant. Muth was allowed to sit in the living room while waiting for the technicians to arrive to start collecting evidence.

He asked again what evidence the detectives had to connect him to the murder. The detectives said that they had found touch DNA on the decedent. That wasn't true, but the police are allowed to lie to a subject so long as they don't coerce him into making a statement. Muth asked, "What is touch DNA?" The detectives explained that a person can transfer skin cells to another individual merely by touching. Immediately he became visibly nervous and stated that he had kissed his wife the evening before he found her. Muth asked the detectives if there was DNA that linked him to his wife's murder. The detectives said, "Yes." Again, a lie. He repeated that he had kissed her the night before he found her and added that he had touched his wife's hand when he found her dead in the bathroom. The detectives confronted him with his statement from the day before when he said that he had never touched his wife's body in the bathroom. He had said there was no need to touch the body because she was obviously dead. Muth did not try and explain away this discrepancy.

The evidence technicians arrived on the scene and took photographs of Muth. They observed several small scratches to the right side of his forehead and a small scratch to the left side of his forehead. Muth asked to see the photographs of the scratches. It was apparent to the detectives that Muth had not been aware of the scratches until just then.

Once again he became visibly shaken and then volunteered that he sustained the scratches when he ran into the kitchen door in the basement the past Thursday night. Detective Giannakoulias didn't respond to Muth, but he had stated in his affidavit to secure the search warrant that, in his opinion, the scratches were more consistent with another individual scratching Muth than his walking into a door.

The affidavit also recounted information from three witnesses. In order to maintain confidentiality for the time being, the witnesses were only identified by number and general relationship to the case. The gender of each witness was referred to as "IT."

W-1 reported that after Viola Drath's body was taken to the ME's office, Muth produced a letter dated April 11, 2011, to members of her family, purportedly signed by his wife, saying that if anything should happen to her, the family should pay him $150,000. W-1 stated that Ms. Drath's signature was well known to IT and that the signature on the letter was not hers. According to W-1's report, the letter also instructed Ms. Drath's estate to pay Muth an additional $50,000 in the event the liquid assets of the estate exceeded $600,000. W-1 also reported that Muth also asked if he could continue receiving his monthly allowance of $2,000.

W-1 and a second witness, W-2, interviewed separately, both reported that in the twenty years of marriage to Muth, Ms. Drath had been the victim of multiple incidents of domestic violence. W-2 recalled one specific incident when IT was called to the house and Ms. Drath said Muth had assaulted her. Broken furniture and dishes were scattered on the floor and soup ran through Ms. Drath's hair. W-2 reported that Ms. Drath said Muth had thrown what he was eating at her and then assaulted her.

Muth's known criminal history began in 1992 when he pled guilty in the Superior Court to Simple Assault of Ms. Drath. His official record also showed that on January 12, 2008, Muth was arrested and charged with Assault with a Dangerous Weapon, a felony, arising out of an incident where he had assaulted Ms. Drath with a wooden chair. The case was later dismissed, however, when Ms. Drath refused to go forward with the prosecution.

Finally, W-3, a next-door neighbor, came forward to the police and reported that "IT" is a light sleeper and woke up around 3:30 a.m. on Friday morning. Sometime between 3:30 a.m. and 6:30 a.m., IT heard what appeared to be a faint cry followed by a sinister laugh. IT couldn't tell if the sound was coming from the Muth/Drath house or the house of her other neighbor, who had a baby in the home. The next morning after learning of Ms. Drath's death, IT asked the neighbor with the baby if the child had awoken during the night. The neighbor said the baby had slept through the night. W-3 felt that it was important to report what IT had heard to the police.

On Tuesday, August 16, the police obtained an arrest warrant for Muth and he was taken into custody and charged with murder.

## The Delusional General Muth

The legal saga of Albrecht Gero Muth was just beginning to unfold as the burial arrangements for his wife were being made.

By all accounts from her children, friends, and co-workers, Viola Drath was an accomplished woman who was often wrongly caricatured by the press as a frivolous Georgetown socialite. Born in Dusseldorf, Germany in 1920, Ms. Drath had a varied career as a playwright and journalist for a number of German and Austrian newspapers and magazines. One of her plays, *Farewell Isabell*, was performed in Munich after World War II. Other plays were developed into movie scripts.

She met and married her first husband, Lt. Colonel Francis S. Drath, in Europe, and moved with him to his hometown of Lincoln, Nebraska. She studied literature and philosophy while raising two daughters. One contemporaneous article pictured a striking blond woman who was called the "modern career woman" managing a household while writing plays, movie scripts, and radio shows. Later, she was a political correspondent for the *National Observer*, commentator on a local radio show, and writer of style for the German magazine *Madame*.

Colonel Drath's work took him to Washington, D.C., where they settled in the home on Q Street in Georgetown. Ms. Drath wrote for *Washington Dossier* on various topics and became involved in American and German relations, authoring "The Reemergence of the German Question" for the National Committee on American Foreign Policy, and "The German State in Historical Perspective" in *World Politics*. She authored textbooks and taught at a number of American universities. Later, she served as a foreign policy advisor for President George H.W. Bush's presidential campaign.

Somewhere along the way she met a German national who was serving as an unpaid political intern on Capitol Hill,

Albrecht Gero Muth. Colonel Drath died of cancer in 1986. They had been married for forty years. Muth started calling upon Ms. Drath thereafter and filled her lonely days and nights. They married in 1990. She was seventy years old; he was twenty-six.

When a newly arrested person comes into the court system, he is interviewed by court staff to determine if he has the ability to hire his own counsel or, if indigent, whether the court should appoint an attorney at public expense. Other than saying that he was married, with no children, and not employed, Muth declined to provide any financial information at his interview. He was also interviewed by an independent body, the Pretrial Services Agency, which is charged with providing biographical information for the court to consider as to whether an accused should be released or held in jail pending trial.

The ensuing report was sparse. Muth said he was born in Cologne, Germany, on May 10, 1964. He asserted he had a Bachelor's degree but declined to name the school. Rather than saying he was unemployed, he claimed to be a Brigadier General in the Iraqi Army.

Appearing on paper to be indigent, he was appointed excellent lawyers from the Public Defender Service. After his first court appearance, Muth was held in the D.C. Jail for a preliminary hearing in ten days to determine whether he would be released pending a grand jury investigation and possible trial.

At the hearing before another Superior Court judge, the prosecution called witnesses to support its argument for continued detention. The defense cross-examined the witnesses and attempted to show the evidence against Muth was purely circumstantial, arguing that the judge should dismiss the case and release him.

In a sign of things to come, Muth did not defer to his lawyers. He stated in open court that he was a serving officer in the Iraqi Army and entitled to wear his uniform in the courtroom. Claiming privileges under the Geneva Conventions, he denied the jurisdiction of the court. "I'm an officer in a foreign army, and I have rights as an officer," he said.

He also stated that before leaving the jail to come to court, he had refused correctional officers' requests to wear underwear under his jail-issued orange jumpsuit. Referring to his status as a General, Muth said, "We don't wear underwear."

The judge found there was probable cause to believe that Muth killed his wife and was both a danger to the community and a risk of flight to avoid prosecution. Muth was ordered detained pending further proceedings. The case was referred to a grand jury to investigate and consider whether to issue an indictment against Muth, or anyone else for that matter. The court also ordered the prosecution to respond in writing to Muth's claims under the Geneva Conventions.

The government's response on September 30, 2011, was a bombshell. It reported that hanging in Muth's study in Georgetown was a framed certificate announcing his appointment as a Brigadier General in the Iraqi army. The certificate was signed by the Prime Minister of Iraq, Nouri al-Maliki and dated April 9, 2011, Baghdad. The certificate went on to extol Muth's "exceptional professionalism, personal initiative, diligence, loyalty and devotion to Iraq." In the house on Q Street, however, police also found a receipt from a Maryland print shop showing that Muth himself ordered the certificate. The detectives checked out the print shop and secured a work order, which showed that Muth composed the certificate and had it delivered to his home on Q Street in April of 2011.

The prosecution also verified with the State Department that Muth had no affiliation with the Iraqi Embassy. It was also brought to the court's attention that after his arrest, Muth told the detectives that his Iraqi Army uniforms were custom made by a private tailor in South Carolina.

The response also indicated that Muth had assumed a number of identities with no relation to reality: East German spy, Soviet spy, CIA operative, South American mercenary, Albanian Count, and Arab Sheikh, in addition to his masquerade as an Iraqi general.

The lead prosecutor in the case, Glenn Kirschner, stated, "The sad truth is that the defendant is a long-term con man who changes his persona as it suits his purposes."

Shortly thereafter the case was transferred to my docket. I reviewed the complete file. To say the least, Muth's profile promised trouble ahead for me to manage in court. Although rare, there have been cases where a defendant assumes a character or takes a position in an attempt to derail a prosecution. Every now and then a defendant claimed to be a "sovereign citizen" and thus outside the reach of the laws of the United States. Asserting that the courts are illegitimate, a sovereign citizen would often proclaim his independence, fire his lawyer, and go on to represent himself. Much of this was posturing and when crunch time came and a trial and possible imprisonment became a reality, he would bring counsel back into the case. Occasionally he would act as his own lawyer, but usually played it straight to try and win the case.

Perhaps the government's complete unmasking of Muth's myth would stop what appeared to be a charade and he would get down to the business of working with his lawyers to develop a defense. I set a status hearing for November 18, 2011, to schedule various dates that would lead up to a trial.

At the hearing, I saw Albrecht Gero Muth for the first time. He was about six feet tall and approximately 175 to 185 pounds. He wore a brownish-gray goatee and stood erect and proper in his bright orange jail jumpsuit. The courtroom was packed. I could see members of the press, as well as a number

Reprinted by permission, William Hennessey,
see http://courtroomart.com/index.html

of people sitting next to the prosecution's victims' rights advocate. I assumed they were members of the Drath family. I didn't know who the others were, but a case that makes the news always draws curious onlookers.

I was advised by Muth's lawyers, Dana Page and Craig Hickein, early in the hearing that he wanted to represent himself. Counsel also stated their client wanted to address the court of various matters.

Reading from a prepared paper, Muth complained in a strong, authoritative voice, only slightly tinged with a German accent, that there were fleas and stagnant water in his jail cell; there was no heat, and he was not afforded adequate time to bathe. He stated that he was in protective custody in jail—kept separate and apart from other prisoners—and only allowed out of his cell a brief period of time each day, because he had received death threats.

Muth insisted he was a General in the Iraqi Army and wanted to wear his uniform in court. I told him that we would discuss appropriate attire when we were closer to trial.

In a quick, staccato voice, he said, "It is my judgment that my wife's murder was a hit by Iranian agents." He went on to explain that his wife was assassinated by agents from Iran's secret service and that he was actually the intended target. It had something to do with a plot against the ambassador of Saudi Arabia.

I let him ramble and wondered to myself if he was mentally ill with some type of delusional disorder, or simply enjoying the spotlight and showboating for the press.

Muth then demanded the courtroom be closed so that he could discuss clandestine intelligence operations. I denied his request, saying he was welcome to put in writing any evidence he had that would warrant the very rare closure of a criminal courtroom from the press and public.

He nodded his head and clicked his heels.

It was time to move on and determine if Muth was competent to represent himself in court. His conspiracy-laden outburst did not bode well to prove that he was capable of doing so without going off into flights of fancy. But the Constitution permits a defendant to act as his own lawyer as long as he understands the risks and knowingly, voluntarily, and intelligently waives his right to counsel. It's almost never a good idea for a defendant to take on this responsibility, but it is a valued right and would be error for a trial judge to deny without a very good reason. As I do in every case, I told him that it is generally not wise for someone to represent himself, especially in a murder case where there was likely to be a lot of complex scientific evidence. I told him it was my duty to ask him a series of questions to make sure he understood his rights and was willing to give them up.

> *Q. You have a right under the Constitution to represent yourself, and I am required to ask you certain questions to satisfy myself that you understand your rights and are willing to waive them.*

*How old are you sir?*

*A. Forty-eight.*

*Q. How far have you gone in school?*

*A. Bachelor's and Master's almost finished.*

*Q. Have you taken any medication in the last forty-eight hours that would affect your ability to understand what's going on here today?*

*A. No.*

*Q. Have you ever been treated for a mental illness?*

*A. No.*

His denial of mental illness, or at least being treated for a mental illness, was telling. Although there are, of course, exceptions, one would expect most people with a serious mental illness would have had some treatment by the time they were forty-eight years old. Because of the stigma attached to mental illness, however, it is also quite common for a person with a mental disorder to deny it.

We went through a litany of required questions and answers and he answered each one in a measured and rational way. He understood what he was charged with and the possible penalty of life imprisonment without the possibility of release. He understood that he had a right to hire his own counsel and if he could not afford one, the court would appoint qualified lawyers. He knew about a trial by either a judge or jury and that it was his decision alone to either plead guilty or go to trial; that he was presumed innocent and that the government had the burden to prove him guilty beyond a reasonable doubt was well known to him.

He understood that there were risks to representing himself and that while the court could make some accommodations for him, he would be required to conduct himself under the rules of the court. We went through all of his other Constitutional rights. I also advised him that should he be convicted at trial, he couldn't complain on appeal that he went to trial without a qualified lawyer. He said he understood.

At the conclusion of the questioning, without objection from his lawyers or the prosecution, I ruled that he was competent to act as his own lawyer. As is customary when the court allows a defendant to represent himself, I ordered his present attorneys to remain as attorney-advisors in case Muth wanted to take advantage of their expertise or if he changed his mind in the future and wanted his advisors to resume their role as his lawyers.

February 3, 2012, was set for a possible formal arraignment of charges from the grand jury. I also set a tentative trial date in October of 2012. And with that, the day's business for the case was complete.

But Muth was not done. He informed me that the Archangel Gabriel had commanded him to fast, and he would follow Gabriel's orders beginning the coming Sunday. He also stated that should he die in jail, his remains should be forwarded to the U.S. Army for liaison with the Iraqi Army.

There was really nothing to say to this last remark, so I recessed Court and went back to chambers. My law clerk, Heidi Hansberry, looked at me, her eyes wide in astonishment. Paraphrasing one of my favorite Grateful Dead songs, "Truckin'," I said, "What a long strange trip it's going to be."

It didn't take much longer for the journey to take a detour. On January 12, 2012, Muth addressed a letter to me. It read:

> *Hon. Russell F. Canan*
> *Judge*
> *D.C. Superior Court*
> *Subj: Refusal of Medical Treatment*
>
> *Sir:*
>
> *Greetings and felicitations. May an abundance of Heavenly blessings shine upon you now, as always.*

> *I am on Day 53 of the Fast, announced in Court on 18 Nov 11, and about to enter the even more demanding regimen on 16 Jan 12. I am writing… to advise the Court that under no circumstances whatsoever am I to be given any medical treatment! I petition the Court to enforce my wish and desire to exercise my faith freely under the Constitution of the United States.*
>
> *My wish pertaining my remains, expressed to the Court of 18 Nov 11, remains in effect.*
>
> *I avail myself of this occasion to renew to the Court assurances of my ctd. highest esteem.*
>
> *Very respectfully,*
>
> *Albrecht Muth*

I read the letter again. Perhaps he was truly delusional. Who starves themselves to death on the commands of an angel? Or maybe the answer was staring us in the face. Muth may have come to the conclusion that his case was hopeless in court and that he didn't want to spend the rest of his life in a federal prison. Suicide might seem to be a rational alternative. A competent person is allowed under the law to refuse medical treatment, even if it results in his death. But was he competent? Would I be asked by the government to impose forced medication and hydration on a recalcitrant Muth?

The prosecution had a great interest in taking the case to trial to bring justice and closure to the family and the public. Muth's death at his own hands would ring hollow to the family and deprive them of a sense of retribution. There would be no accounting for this monstrous crime. There would be no justice.

From my perspective, Muth was legally presumed innocent of the murder, had been found competent to represent himself in court, maybe delusional, maybe a con artist, maybe hyper-religious, or maybe suicidal. I considered taking proactive measures to assure myself of his safety and his competence to stand trial. Since there were excellent lawyers on both sides who would strongly advocate their positions, I decided to wait for a time for developments to come officially to the court.

It didn't take long. At the February 3, 2012, hearing, Muth was not present. Jail authorities represented to me at the bench, outside the hearing of the audience in the courtroom, that Muth was hospitalized and being treated for medical complications resulting from his fast. We needed more information, and I instructed the hospital to submit Muth's medical records privately to me to consider at a future hearing on February 9, 2012. The defense objected to the collection of Muth's private medical records. A defendant's medical history is ordinarily private and none of the court's business. However, when a defendant consciously jeopardizes his own health to avoid coming to court, it is the court's business. I overruled the objection.

In this procedure, which is called filing records under seal, documents are officially filed in the court, but not available to the public and the prosecutor. At the next hearing, I would disclose the information to the parties at the bench and hear arguments from Muth's attorney-advisors and the government as to whether his medical records should be made public. I would have to balance Muth's right to privacy with the public's right under the First Amendment to have access to criminal court proceedings.

On February 9, 2012, Muth was, again, not present. Jail authorities told me at the bench that Muth's fast had rendered him too ill to come to court. Although a defendant's right to represent himself is very important and should not be taken away lightly, I ruled that his voluntary refusal to eat and drink rendered him unable to represent himself in court. To put it plainly, if a lawyer went on a hunger strike to make herself too ill to come to court, that lawyer would be fired by the client or removed by the judge. Muth essentially fired himself. I suspended his right to represent himself and reappointed his attorney-advisors as official counsel of record and set the case down for a further hearing in five days. I made it clear that Muth could resume his role as his own lawyer if he stopped his fast, got well, and was able to return to court.

On February 14, 2012, Muth was still hospitalized due to his refusal to eat and drink. After listening to defense counsel's argument seeking to protect Muth's privacy by prohibiting the release of his medical records, it was my view that since Muth had followed through on his November promise to fast, his conduct had caused his absence from court and the public had the right to know why. The openness of an American criminal court is a hallmark of a free society and the very integrity of the judicial process requires that court proceedings be open for all to see. The court records were then unsealed.

But what to do next? In light of the gravity of the fast commanded by Archangel Gabriel and Muth's possibly delusional belief that he was an Iraqi General, the government asked that he be declared incompetent to stand trial and sent to a mental hospital for a full evaluation. A court declaration of competency requires two distinct findings. An accused must be able to understand the charges against him and have a basic knowledge of the legal proceedings. Further, the accused must be able to rationally assist his lawyers in preparing a defense. Failure to satisfy either standard meant the accused was not competent to go forward to trial and he would be returned to a mental hospital with the hope that mental health treatment would help restore him to competency.

Other than saying he was fasting on Gabriel's orders, Muth was not communicating in any reasonable way with his lawyers. My sense was the prosecutors didn't believe for a minute that Muth was incompetent; I thought they were concerned about how the record looked on paper. In the event the case went to trial and Muth was convicted of murder, his lawyers could easily point out to an appellate court that all the red flags showed an apparent mental illness prevented their incompetent client from having a fair trial. I was pretty sure the prosecutors were thinking: "have him shrunk, get this over with, and let's go to trial."

Muth's lawyers were in a bind. They were ethically charged with following the dictates of their client, but he was not communicating with them in any meaningful fashion. They undoubtedly understood the prosecutor's true motives in having Muth evaluated. The chess game between the prosecution and the defense had begun in full swing. Defense counsel's job was, to some degree, to muck up the works. The more legal errors committed by me before trial, the better chance their client would win an appeal if he was convicted at trial. They objected to an evaluation, stating the evidence was insufficient to send their client to a mental hospital.

I found that the very nature of Muth's conduct was such that he was possibly incompetent, and we needed an objective evaluation from mental health experts in a hospital setting. The next leg of this long, strange trip, therefore led to D.C.'s mental hospital.

Originally called "The Government Hospital for the Insane," the hospital opened in January of 1855. Its creation was in part inspired by Dorothea Dix, one of the progressive forces for the treatment of the mentally ill in the nineteenth century. Its name changed in 1916 to Saint Elizabeths, with its peculiar spelling, after the piece of land it was founded upon. The institution went through much development over the years in structure, mission, and reputation. The deinstitutionalization movement in the 1960s and 1970s for more compassionate care of the mentally ill caused a drastic reduction of its population, which in turn resulted in more resources and modern treatment techniques.

Initially a series of colossal Gothic-style buildings that at one time housed almost 8,000 patients, St. E's, as it is commonly called, fell under court supervision in the 1990s for lack of proper care to its patients. By the time Albrecht Muth entered St. E's in 2012, it was a brand new facility that had just opened two years before and was limited to about 300 patients. Its reputation had largely been restored, and judges generally believed that St. E's could be relied upon to provide professional care for the patients and accurate reports to the court about their diagnosis and prognosis.

Muth was admitted to St. E's on February 15, 2012. While he was being evaluated, the Grand Jury returned an indictment on March 6, 2012, charging him with First Degree Murder. If convicted, Muth faced a mandatory thirty years in prison. In addition, the indictment also charged two special aggravating factors—that the murder was "especially heinous, atrocious, or cruel" and that Ms. Drath was "especially vulnerable due to age." If convicted of First Degree Murder, the jury would be asked to consider whether aggravating factors applied in the case. If they found either one, Muth's sentence could be increased to life imprisonment without the possibility of release. He would die in prison.

If competent, he would be formally arraigned or charged on the next court date of March 14, 2012, and a trial date would be set. If incompetent, the arraignment would have to be put off because a judge cannot arraign a defendant who, by law, does not understand the charges against him, or can't assist his counsel.

Meanwhile, on March 13, 2012, St. E's submitted a two-and-a-half page report. A team of psychologists and a psychiatrist participated in Muth's evaluation. Reading the report in chambers, I was struck as to what it did not contain: there was no mention of the Archangel Gabriel's command and Muth's fast, which had precipitated his hospitalization. I had to assume he had resumed eating or else a continued fast would have been at the center of his stay at St. E's, if only for the obvious medical challenges it would pose to the hospital.

The report stated that Muth had a "factual understanding of the court proceedings." He clearly comprehended what he was charged with, the potential penalties, his plea options, the key actors in the case—judge, prosecutor, defense counsel, and witnesses, the purpose of a trial, and his right to testify in his own defense. He was well aware of proper decorum and behavior in the courtroom.

In discussing his case and possible defenses, however, Muth still insisted his wife's death was a "hit by the Iranian Army" because of his status as a General in the Iraqi Army. Muth ordered that his attorneys secure witnesses and obtain information from the "High Command of the U.S. National Command Authority and the Captain of Iraqi Air Force from the National Command Authority of Iraq." Since his attorneys refused to follow his demands, he did not have a working relationship with them.

The report further noted that Muth "again expressed a desire to represent himself so that 'I can find the criminal who did this.'"

As a result, the hospital concluded that Muth lacked the ability to consult with his attorneys "to a reasonable degree of rational understanding." He was considered incompetent, but the hospital stated there was a "substantial probability" that he would regain competence in the foreseeable future.

St. E's then qualified its conclusions. "Many of the thoughts that Mr. Muth has expressed could be the result of several factors to include genuine psychosis or feigned psychological processes in order to avoid prosecution." He was diagnosed with Psychotic Disorder Not Otherwise Specified. The diagnosis was not defined, but I generally understood it from other cases to mean that he had some type of psychosis, such as delusions or hallucinations, though there was not enough data or information to be sure, or that contradictory symptoms made a detailed opinion impossible at the time.

The report stated he was receiving medication, presumably anti-psychotics, but the exact kind was not noted. Psychological testing would be conducted to aid in "diagnostic clarification, but also to explore the possibility of feigned psychological problems as part of his clinical presentation." St. E's recommended Muth remain hospitalized until the next hearing.

The hearing on March 14, 2012, was perfunctory. Neither the government nor the defense objected to St. E's report. There was nothing to do but set another hearing and wait for another report. Muth was present, looking frailer than before, but also somewhat forlorn or possibly drowsy. Perhaps it was his circumstances or maybe the effect of the medicine he was taking. He said nothing at the hearing, and the case was adjourned to April 25, 2012.

The next two reports from St. E's, dated April 23, 2012, and June 19, 2012, also found Muth incompetent. Both reports indicated that Muth had undergone an extensive battery of psychological tests that supported a diagnosis of Delusional Disorder, Persecutory Type and Schizotypal Personality Disorder, a mental illness that is characterized by disarrayed thoughts, unconventional beliefs, paranoia, and breaks with reality. The tests also found no support for a malingering diagnosis. It appeared that four months into his hospitalization at St. Elizabeths, Muth was becoming more mentally ill, not recovering, and much further away to ever having a trial.

When Muth was informed at the hospital that his doctors concluded he was delusional, he strongly denied it.

"If you take away my memories, you take away my life," he said.

Of some interest to the clinicians, but mentioned almost in passing, was that Muth had inquired of hospital staff about the possibility of his never becoming competent. What happens then? He was informed that in such a case the government would have the opportunity to try and have him civilly committed, and have a court declare that he was mentally ill and a danger to himself or others. In such a scenario, he would be committed to the hospital, but in time could be placed back in the community. He was also informed, however, that in light of the gravity of his charges, the focus would be to help restore him to competency.

At the next hearing on June 22, 2012, Muth greeted me politely, but otherwise said nothing. Neither the prosecutor nor the defense opposed the St. E's report. Neither side had any basis to object; it was the only evidence of Muth's mental competence.

It appeared the case was at a standstill, and the question of whether Albrecht Muth killed his wife would never be tested in the courtroom. Then the government requested something unusual; they wanted to hire a psychiatrist and psychologist, independent of St. Elizabeths, to separately evaluate and report on Muth. Ordinarily the government relies on the St. E's doctors, as they are generally considered reliable and conservative in their methodology and conclusions regarding forensic issues. For the prosecution to seek outside consultants was very rare and showed to me they had significant doubts about the St. E's report. The defense had no cause to object to the government's request, and I granted it. The defense reserved the right to hire their own experts in the event the prosecution's experts contradicted St. E's diagnosis. We set another hearing to await further reports from St. E's and the government's experts.

## The Talented Mr. Muth

A few weeks later on a Monday in July, I was at lunch with colleagues in the judges' dining room. One of my friends asked, "Hey, Russ, did you see the article about General Muth in yesterday's *New York Times Magazine*?"

"I didn't see it."

"Do you want me to talk about it?" he said.

Judges are very careful about unnecessarily reading or seeing publicity about their cases because judicial decisions are supposed to be based solely on the record in court and not on outside, and often unreliable, sources. I was appreciative that he didn't tell me anything I shouldn't know. Sometimes while in the midst of a jury trial, I will track publicity in case inflammatory or inadmissible evidence is mentioned that might poison the jury's deliberations. But we were very far from a jury trial.

"I'd love to read it, but I better not," I said. "Please hold on to it in case the time comes."

It didn't take too long. On July 24, 2012, two days before their next report was due, St. E's requested an extension in order to "receive additional documentation to include conducting collateral interviews with family members, a review of records including Mr. Muth's employment history, journal entries, and copies of reports generated by other experts involved in Mr. Muth's case."

St. E's request came on the heels of the *New York Times* article. *Was there a connection*, I wondered? Many of our cases are in the local press; it's very rare that the *New York Times* would cover what otherwise appeared to be a D.C. domestic violence murder. I had sound reasons for not reading the article; St. E's did not. I had to take St. E's at their word for their reasons requesting the extension of time, but the timing was suspicious.

At the hearing on July 26, 2012, Muth again politely greeted me and again said nothing. Prosecutor Kirschner reported that the government's experts had evaluated Muth and found him competent, contradicting the St. E's diagnosis. Their reports would be filed shortly. He also indicated that members of Ms. Drath's family would be meeting with the doctors at St. E's. Given these developments, it was clear our tentative trial date in October was out the window, and we were probably heading for an extended and contested hearing as to whether Muth was competent to stand trial. A further hearing was set for September 6, 2012.

On August 21, 2012, St. E's reported that Muth resumed his fast and had abstained from food and drink. He had been sent to the emergency room at a different hospital three separate times and was monitored and given intravenous hydration. After returning to St. E's, he resumed his fast and was "weak and unable to engage in activities for any substantial length of time." St. E's asked for and was given additional time to file its next report.

In the next few weeks reports were filed by St. E's, and the psychiatrist and psychologist who had been hired by the government. All the reports were thorough and relied on a great deal of collateral information from court records, outside documentation, interviews with the Drath family, and others. They all found Muth competent to stand trial and concluded that his "delusion" that he was an Iraqi General was simply a continuation of various personas that he had employed over the years for manipulative purposes. St. E's concluded Muth had the ability to work with his lawyers and apply information in a rational way if he chose to and that "his current beliefs appear to be rooted in his maladaptive personality structure and are under his volitional control." St. E's now changed Muth's diagnosis to "Factitious Disorder Not Otherwise Specified (NOS), Personality Disorder (NOS), with Narcissistic, Antisocial and Schizotypal Traits, and alcohol abuse." I understood factitious disorder to mean a disorder, rather than a mental illness, where a patient acts as if he has a mental illness, but has in reality assumed the symptoms of illness to gain sympathy, attention, or for some other personal reason. Basically, the consensus was that Muth was malingering.

One of the reports referred to and attached the *New York Times Magazine* article written by Franklin Foer. Apparently when the story was presented to Muth at the hospital "he expressed delight in the change in title from the internet version, 'The Worst Marriage in Georgetown' to the hard copy in the paper, 'The Talented Mr. Muth.' Muth described the article as 'amusing' and a 'nice puff piece that makes for a good movie.' When asked who would play his part in the film, he replied, 'DiCaprio.'"

The article was now part of the record. I read it. I did not find it amusing. Viola Drath was portrayed as a name-dropping socialite—"When I speak German to Henry Kissinger, he starts talking like a little boy"—who bragged at hosting Norman Mailer in her home while he was researching his book about the CIA. Recognizing she was very lonely after the death of her husband of forty years, she rejected more appropriate suitors for Muth because she was "attracted for his lust for power... and he was young and interesting."

Foer painted a picture of Muth as a serial fabulist who was a master of building a "social Ponzi scheme." Muth well understood "Washington's susceptibility to fakery," as he exploited his wife's contacts and reputation to hide in plain sight with a succession of personas designed to feed his own ego by appealing to the vanity and anxieties of the power elites. Calling himself at various times Count Albi, a member of the French Foreign Legion, and an Iraqi General, he arranged fancy dinner parties at their Georgetown home with guests such as Supreme Court Justice Antonin Scalia, Vice President Dick Cheney, President Barack Obama's Ambassador to Egypt, and prominent journalists from *Newsweek* and the *Washington Post.*

He somehow secured funding from the George Soros Foundation to create a non-governmental organization called the Eminent Persons Group (EPG), whose aim was to bring together international experts to advise the U.N. Secretary General on the issue of the expansion of small-arms sales. The trick, of course, was to corral "eminent" persons willing to work with Muth, who created the post of Executive

Director for himself. Using fancy stationery signed by Count Albi, Muth hit upon the key to most of his recruits: they were "formers." Former Prime Minister of France Michel Rocard, former Defense Secretary Robert McNamara, former Canadian Ambassador to the United Nations Peggy Mason; all signed on. Rocard admitted that he had never heard of Muth but "liked the group's mission and his political career needed new purpose." Once Rocard agreed to serve as Chairman, and his name put on an elaborate letterhead, others quickly followed. Mason was quoted as saying: "Of course, I figured if these other eminent persons were already in...."

In an email to his wife, Muth cynically summed up his strategy: "You meet someone of import, check him out, determine if he can be of use. You make him yours. At some point you must decide whether to run him as a useful idiot, he not catching on as to who you are and what you do."

I could just imagine the doctors at St. E's reading the article. Had they been played by Muth for half a year as useful idiots? Or was the article itself simply a wild and entertaining satire? As a judge, I certainly could not give it credence but, if true, it seemed that Muth might have conned the doctors as his newest gullible victims.

The article went on to track the highlights of Muth's machinations. The EPG actually published a few documents and had a public relations statement issued on what appeared to be United Nations stationery. But the organization collapsed within a few years after its members came to suspect Muth was a fraud. Rocard quit and was quoted as saying, "I no longer wish to work with Albrecht Gero Muth... some obscurities of his past irritate some of our interlocutors more than ourselves, and this also has its price." The Soros money dried up and the EPG was no more.

In 2006, Muth was arrested for assaulting his wife again. He fled to Miami where for most of the next two years employment records showed he worked as a desk clerk at a hotel. While in Miami he wrote emails claiming to be in Villa Zarathustra, Sadr City, Iraq, and working with rebel leader Muqtada al-Sadr in an effort to bring together the warring factions and end the conflict.

During this time he called and emailed Viola Drath and convinced her to take him back. Apparently she did so even though on phone calls he claimed to be in Iraq while caller ID said he was in Miami. She was quoted as saying, "When I talk to Albrecht, I'm not sure if he's in Iraq or next door." She ultimately refused to cooperate with the police and the case was dropped.

A friend of Ms. Drath explained her willingness to reunite with Muth despite his acts of violence against her, "He was her weakness, her obsession, her addiction." She took him back also knowing that he was gay. Foer reported that at one time before he left for Miami, Muth moved in with a boyfriend. Muth described his relationships in an email that "he was the boy, she was the wife. You have one for one set of reasons, the other another, the lives were fully integrated."

The *pièce de résistance* was still to come. Upon his return home, Muth would walk the streets of Georgetown smoking a cigar while wearing what purported to be an Iraqi uniform. He took to identifying himself as a Staff Brigadier General of Iraq. With his wife's influence he had a role in creating Iraq Liberation Day in conjunction with Gold Star Mothers, a nonprofit organization of American mothers who lost sons or daughters in the military. In April of 2010, members of American and Iraqi military, as well as families of soldiers killed in Iraq, participated in a wreath-laying ceremony at Arlington National Cemetery. The keynote address was delivered by the son of the Iraqi President. Muth was photographed at the ceremony standing stiffly in his Iraqi uniform, a photograph that after Ms. Drath's death would be widely circulated in the press and on the internet.

The ball was now in the defense court. Muth had the option of accepting the new diagnosis of competency and preparing for trial, or hiring his own experts to contest it. Contested competency hearings are rare, as in most cases the status of a defendant's mental status is pretty clear cut. Given St. E's shifting diagnoses, however, it would not be surprising that notwithstanding Muth's stated desire to be found competent to tell his side of the story and prove that he was in fact a General in the Iraqi Army, his lawyers might think he would be much better off remaining incompetent.

Although they never said so, I knew the lawyers were in another bind. They were ethically charged with generally following the dictates of their client. Because he was legally incompetent, however, and theoretically not able to understand the proceedings or assist counsel in his defense, his wishes would not be given priority. They would make the call as to whether to challenge the competency finding or not.

Of course, this could be a shell game being played out by Muth, with him using his lawyers to purportedly go against his will to further his real goal.

One of the St. E's reports indicated that he had asked staff about the scenario where he was never found competent; in that case he was told, there would be no trial and punishment. The Government would undoubtedly pursue civil commitment, which would require a court to find that he was mentally ill and a danger to himself or others. He would then be confined at St. E's until such time he was no longer mentally ill or a danger.

The key is that if a patient demonstrates recovery, he can eventually be outplaced in the community, a far cry from the harshness of a life sentence in a federal prison. Although saying he wanted to be found competent and go to trial, his "delusions," would in effect force his lawyers to go against his will, challenge his competency, and if successful, ultimately get him civilly committed—the result he actually wanted.

I didn't know. From my perspective, I had to wait and let the case develop and not get ahead of myself. As in all cases, I had to be careful and not prejudge the outcome as there was certainly enough confusion about Muth's life and mental makeup to envision any number of possible outcomes. It was likely that the defense would produce opposing evidence from well-qualified experts. As of September 2012, Muth had been declared legally incompetent; but three new reports had now been filed saying he was competent. The defense team would have to make a hard decision and time would tell how the drama would unfold.

At a status hearing on September 6, 2012, I received a phone call from St. E's saying that Muth had been taken to an emergency room the night before after claiming to suffer chest pains. We were also advised that he had again been intermittently fasting. His lawyers announced that they had retained independent experts and expected to contest the finding of competency. Our tentative trial date of December 3, 2012, was converted to a competency hearing, where the experts and other witnesses from both sides would testify as to Muth's ability to go to trial.

Based on St. E's deeming Muth competent to stand trial, prosecutor Kirschner asked that Muth be transferred back to the D.C. Jail. Referring to Muth's recent fast, Kirschner said, "It's a pattern that makes it more and more obvious that he is gaming the system."

I denied the government's request. Muth was still incompetent in the eyes of the law until a hearing could be held to prove otherwise. Muth would remain at St. Elizabeths.

Over the next few months the reports from the defense psychiatrist and psychologist opined that notwithstanding the new reports from St. E's and the government experts, Muth was still incompetent. A neuropsychologist conducted tests and diagnosed Muth with a cognitive disorder. Importantly, all defense experts believed that Muth was not malingering or faking his symptoms.

Reading all the conflicting reports from St. E's, the prosecution, and defense experts, I had a wry smile. Over the past ten years or so there has been a sea change in how the law assesses different types of "hard science" forensic evidence, especially what's called pattern evidence, such as hair and fiber comparisons, ballistics, blood splatters, arson evidence, and even fingerprints. The National Academy of Science indicated that some of the so-called sciences were really not science at all since they did not have a sufficiently based scientific methodology to be considered reliable evidence in court. The term "junk science" entered the court lexicon and many cases were reviewed and convictions overturned because "experts" had overstated the validity or accuracy of their conclusions.

This revolution in considering forensic evidence was for what had been considered "hard sciences." Psychology and psychiatry were always considered "soft sciences." From a judge's perspective, so much depended on the competence and integrity of the examiner to provide opinions that could be reliably counted on in a field where any conclusion would, by nature, have a very subjective component. The notion that you can pay your way to the expert opinion of your choice is all too often true. On the surface, I had no reason to question the honesty or capability of any of the witnesses. The more likely scenario is that the experts, all in good faith, saw Muth's competence through a different prism. That was going to make my job tough. Muth's story thus far was so fantastic that anything could be true.

And so the battle of the experts began.

## The Illusion of Delusion

Starting on December 3, 2012, I heard eight days of testimony and received reports from six mental health professionals and one lay witness to determine whether Muth was competent to stand trial for First Degree Murder in the future.

St. E's had the most explaining to do. The hospital had submitted three previous reports to the Court saying Muth was incompetent. Now it changed its diagnosis to the contrary and had to explain its reasons for so doing. The report and testimony indicated that interviews with the Drath family, access to collateral records, and Muth's recent conduct at the hospital basically tracked the *New York Times Magazine* article. Muth had a "history of becoming various personas that would assist him with developing elite social relationships or alliances with key political people... the involved individuals would believe Mr. Muth's narrative of his background, credentials, and notoriety for various periods of time before eventually realizing that what he represented was unfounded and they would subsequently break ties with him."

St. E's reinterpretation of the psychological data "revealed that the diagnosis of Schizotypal Personality Disorder was limited as it did not fully encompass his full personality structure, particularly the grandiosity and deceitfulness that appear to be focal parts of his personality."

The St. E's doctor also stated the hospital now had the benefit of the reports filed by the psychiatrist and psychologist hired by the government. St. E's concurred with their opinions. I had to wonder what the folks at the hospital were thinking now because the independent experts hammered St. E's handling of the case in no uncertain terms.

The reports and testimony from the independent psychiatrist and psychologist hired by the government corroborated much of Mr. Muth's fabulist history and then added some context that had not been part of the record. Muth had apparently also claimed to have been a Senior Political Advisor to the Foreign Minister of Estonia, Military Aide to King Hussein of Jordan, and Special Representative of the President of Mali. Muth's serial personas were long-standing and pre-dated his marriage to Ms. Drath. At one point he wore an eye patch, claiming that he had lost an eye in an assassination attempt while serving as a mercenary soldier in Uruguay. After some time passed, his eye miraculously recovered, no eye patch needed, and he was on to another character.

Muth had posted his resume on a website describing himself as "Secret Agent, Diplomat and Militia Leader, replete with his motto: *'Tou est bien fini. Je ne regrette rien.'* (Everything is well finished. I regret nothing) and epitaph: *'Pro DEO et FIDE et utiliate HOMINUM.'* (For God's sake and for the benefit of the people of faith.)"

Recent psychological tests indicated a high range of intellectual function with an IQ of 110, a personality that was "primarily hedonistic, self-centered and quite insensitive to the needs of others, manipulating them for his own ends and feeling no guilt about it." One recognized test reflected "a grandiose, adventurous, risk taking and impulsive personality style with indications of a strong need for interpersonal control and dominance coupled with cold detachment."

He was diagnosed with a Narcissistic Personality Disorder.

The psychiatrist cited a test that measured psychopathy and "classified him as being in the moderate to high range of psychopathy." The psychologist went further and wrote in bold: "**Mr. Muth is a psychopath, in the high range of psychopathy**."

The psychiatrist concluded: "Mr. Muth is a masterful manipulator.... Mr. Muth has mastered the art of lying. His lies are so well formulated, and his belief in and execution of his lies are so good, that to others, his beliefs may appear to be delusional. To the contrary, in my clinical opinion, there is no evidence to support a diagnosis that he is delusional."

There was reference to a social worker and a recovery assistant that had both spent many hours with Muth on varying tasks, far more than the doctors. They both stated they never saw any psychosis or signs of mental illness in Muth. Their views had never been recorded in St. E's earlier reports to the court. Oftentimes people on the ground have great insight into a patient's mental status. I wondered why they were not consulted, or if they had been, why their views were not reflected in the past reports because they so obviously contradicted St. E's doctors' prior opinions.

New evidence from Muth himself came to light. Muth made a number of damning statements to the doctor when questioned about his varying characters and costumes.

"As the Queen Mother always said, 'You want to play the act, if you want to play the part, dress the part.'"

"Most of my life has been a camouflage."

Most surprising of all, a young man, whom I will call JC, was a border/intern for Muth and Viola Drath and lived for a time in the Georgetown house with them. At some point he felt it necessary to secretly record a conversation with Muth while he waxed poetic on his scams. JC turned over the tape to the prosecution and it was supplied to the experts and the defense. JC reluctantly testified in court. Some highlights from the tape and testimony:

- *Great People, ambitious people, of whom I shall readily admit that I am one of them, always attach themselves to great minds who can be helpful, who can be my greatest teachers.*
- *I create the persona of Count Albi; Count Albi is a complete invention and fabrication.... No such person exists.*
- *So you come up with cover story, Count Albi is created, and of course ninety percent of the people are none the wiser.*
- *The Eminent Persons Group. The objective is always to find the "has been" of the highest caliber—heads of state and the people in between—so that you always have the hook in some ambitious person's ambition—who is really vulnerable to you.*
- *The world always loves a Count. Especially somebody who behaves like one. A man I've never met writes back, "Dear Count Albi, it is not just my honor to join the EPG, it is my duty. I am at your full disposal."*
- *My first victim. You have one, you catch them all. The list goes on.*
- *If you want to play the part, dress the part... Put on a show quite well. It's always posture, disposition, demeanor, etc.*
- *Always have a guest book, get your menu cards signed. You have the signatures.*
- *Every once in a while the actor needs a new script, the gambler to a new game.*

Hearing Muth's voice brag about his exploits was powerful evidence. I had to wonder if JC was a main source for Foer's *New York Times Magazine* article.

But there was more. Muth supplied the psychologist with a 250-page hand-written memoir titled "Judgment at Washington, Triumph of Illusion: A Journal of Life in D.C. Jail by Staff Brigadier General A.G. Muth, Iraqi Army." "The Triumph of Illusion" was a detailed outline of the evidence against him, a critique of police and prosecution misconduct, an outline of inconsistencies, such as varying times of death for his wife in the police records, and discussion of possible traditional defenses such as alibi and the fact that an intruder, Iranian or not, could have entered his home through an unsecured window, killed his wife, and escaped undetected. Although still hewing to the Iranian hit job conspiracy theory, it was an intelligent, focused, and nuanced understanding of the case.

The prosecution also played the videotapes of the police interrogations of Muth, before and after his arrest. Although I had read police affidavits summarizing the interviews, seeing them on video is different. The detectives and Muth sparred with each other in the moment, each trying to outwit and trap the other. Muth more than held his own, dismissively treating his interlocutors as mere plebeian policemen. He adamantly denied killing his wife and set forth an alibi.

Midway through the interrogation, the detectives left the interview room, ostensibly to take a break, but in reality to spy on Muth's reactions to his predicament. Muth did not disappoint; he muttered to himself, bemoaning the fact that the Medical Examiner opined that his wife's death was a homicide, laying to rest his claim that a very old woman accidentally cracked her head in a common fall. One could almost see him pondering his next chess move in the cat and mouse game he was playing with the detectives. There was no Iraqi general then; no Iranian hit squad; no Count Albi. That would come later.

The government also produced powerful evidence of Muth's motive in maintaining his latest masquerade as an Iraqi general in contrast to all documented evidence. Records showed Muth was focused on the likelihood that he would never be found competent and thus would be civilly committed with the possibility of ultimately being released to the community on an outpatient basis. He stated bluntly to a social worker, "I will be civilly committed outpatient." He knew the exact date of his diagnosis of Delusional Disorder, which would trigger his potential eligibility for Social Security Income after he was civilly committed and eventually released to live free outside the hospital.

The prosecution's psychiatrist and psychologist strongly disagreed with prior St. E's testing which showed Muth's delusional symptoms were not the product of malingering. The psychiatrist concluded that Muth's intermittent fasting, purportedly done at the behest of the Archangel Gabriel for ritual purification, was the "intentional production of symptoms (psychological or physical) solely for the purpose of assuming the role of a sick person." In the end, Muth's fasting "behaviors are more consistent with the manifestations of malingering."

The psychologist summed up the prosecution's position:

"Succinctly, Mr. Muth is an accomplished con artist. Mr. Muth's long history of moving comfortably and effectively within national and international military, political, and media elites suggests that Mr. Muth has a rational basis for confidence in his strategies, which are usually played out on many levels at once. For example, Mr. Muth's professed priority of establishing his generalship while dismissing completely any concern for the trial, if believed, advances his goal of being found mentally ill, incompetent and civilly committed as an outpatient....

"Mr. Muth flaunts his talents as a con artist with the title of 'Triumph of Illusion.' Delusions shape and control the individual whereas the individual uses illusions to shape and control events. Mr. Muth knowingly traffics in illusions not delusions; since incarceration at the D.C. jail, he has been steadily trying to con everyone by creating the illusion of a delusion. . . .

"Mr. Muth appears to have been running the con and scam of his life in the wake of being charged with the alleged First Degree Murder of his wife of two decades, Mrs. Viola Herms Drath Muth."

The prosecution put on a powerful case but the defense fought back hard.

Defense counsel challenged the credentials of the psychiatrist; (How come he never passed his Boards?); the honesty of the psychologist; (Wasn't he being investigated by APA—the American Psychological Association?); the competence of St. Elizabeths; (How can you trust the hospital after their inconsistent reports? Isn't the hospital simply caving to pressure?); and the motives of JC; (Wasn't he in it for the money and fame?). They made valid points and severely put the witnesses to the test. I admired their fight; they were under a lot of pressure and no doubt had a very difficult client to contend with.

The defense also presented three witnesses.

A neuropsychologist from the prestigious Johns Hopkins Hospital conducted another battery of tests, concluding that Muth had a cognitive disorder that caused severe impairments of learning, memory, and executive functioning. The source of this disorder was not known but the neuropsychologist hypothesized that the likely cause was "residual effects of previous traumatic brain injury, the presence of a psychotic disorder, or both." The report specifically stated, "I do not think Mr. Muth tried to exaggerate or feign cognitive dysfunction."

The defense psychiatrist had the benefit of the full record, including the recent government expert reports, independent interviews with the Drath family, and the transcript of JC's secret audio of Muth. He performed screenings, which not only confirmed the neuropsychologist's findings of cognitive disorder, and added that Muth "demonstrated frontal and temporal lobe dysfunction." He concluded that "there was evidence of a thought disorder, involving grandiose and persecutory delusions, which significantly interfere with his ability to relate to his attorneys."

As for the possibility that Muth was simply faking his symptoms, the psychiatrist wrote, "I considered the possibility that Mr. Muth malingered his impairments, but in my opinion, he did not. Given the consistency in presentation across examiners and time, the detailed nature of his delusional thought processes, his delusional beliefs of being an intelligence officer and Staff Brigadier General long pre-dating this alleged crime, his denial of mental illness and steadfast belief in his competency to stand trial, his expressed desires to move forward and go to trial, the consistency in his deficits on my neurocognitive screenings and neuropsychological testing administered, and his correctly answering simple questions to detect overt malingering, I do not believe Mr. Muth is malingering."

"It is my opinion to a reasonable degree of medical certainty, that Mr. Muth is incompetent to stand trial."

I knew and respected the psychologist who reported and testified. He had appeared before me in other cases and I always thought of him as independent and a straight shooter. He sharply criticized the government's psychologist's report, accusing him of ignoring tests that showed delusion and overstating tests that showed malingering. Acknowledging, without criticizing, the government's psychiatrist's conclusion of malingering and competence, he noted in detail the defense psychiatrist's contrary conclusion.

The psychologist conducted his own test, concluding that Muth was not malingering. He acknowledged that Muth "readily admits that he manipulated others and fabricated information (including his title as Count) in an effort to advance both his and his wife's social standing." He concluded, nonetheless, that the weight of Muth's psychological profile showed that "there is no evidence that his belief in being a general is such a fabrication."

He summed up: "Currently, Mr. Muth has a good factual understanding of his case and the judicial system. However, there appears to be significant deficits in his rational understanding of his case and the judicial system, as well as his ability to assist his attorneys. These deficits arise from the presence of long-held beliefs of a delusional level of distortion and cognitive rigidity, as well as concerns about whether Mr. Muth is not attempting to preserve himself and he may be actively attempting suicide. Because of these issues, in this examiner's opinion Mr. Muth does not appear competent to stand trial."

After eight days of testimony, including aggressive cross-examinations by all lawyers, numerous exhibits, videotapes, and argument of counsel, the hearing was over. It was by far the longest competency trial I had ever participated in as a lawyer or judge and, as far as I know, the longest in D.C. Superior Court history.

A lot was riding on my decision. Although keenly aware of the repercussions of my judgment, I understood those considerations could not drive the decision. A finding of competence would lead to a trial where once and for all his guilt or innocence for the killing of his wife would be revealed in a pubic courtroom for all to see. Hopefully, justice would emerge, however you define it.

A finding that Muth was incompetent, however, could very well lead to his being civilly committed and ultimately released. A different kind of justice would dictate that Muth never stand trial because the law cannot countenance putting on trial a mentally ill defendant who doesn't understand why he is in court or can't help his lawyers prepare a defense. Our system provides the alternative of civil commitment so that the safety of the community can be addressed while the defendant can be treated for his mental illness in a hospital, and maybe even in the community.

Undoubtedly the government, the public, and Ms. Drath's family would feel that a cold-blooded killer got away with murder and was never held accountable. But that could not be my concern. I was called upon to resolve a complicated dispute and nothing more.

Under the law, a defendant is presumed to be competent for trial. The party seeking to find him incompetent, usually the defense, has the burden of proving the defendant is incompetent. Once a defendant has been found incompetent by the court, however, it is the government's obligation to prove him competent.

Did the government prove to my satisfaction that Muth was competent or not? I recessed court and asked the parties to return the next day. I wanted to study the record and carefully review my notes.

The defense relied heavily on the psychological testing that showed that Muth was not faking his symptoms. If he was not malingering, so went the argument, his claims to be an Iraqi general had to be delusional. I certainly believe such testing has its place and can be an aid in figuring out the complexities of the human condition. But it seemed to me Muth's own words and actions spoke the real truth. In the end, the image of Albrecht Muth playacting his multiple personas in plain sight to advance his own goals, all the while counting on the human foibles of his victims to follow along out of vanity, ignorance, or hubris, stuck out. The philosophical principle of Occam's Razor—that in order to solve a complex problem that offers multiple explanations, the simple answer is more often the correct answer—also stuck out.

On December 20, 2012, the courtroom was packed as I delivered my ruling. I could see members of the Drath family as well as a large press contingent. After a brief introduction of the issues before the court and the legal standards that applied, I quickly got to the point.

> *There are a number of nuances and permutations as to how to look at this case.*
>
> *One, the defendant is telling the truth and is in fact, an Iraqi general.*
>
> *There's not a shred of evidence proving this to be true. In fact, there's a great deal of evidence refuting this claim—custom-ordered Iraqi-style uniforms made in the United States, fabricated appointment certificates, emails from Florida saying he was on the Iraqi battlefield when he was a hotel clerk in Miami, no pay slips or other verification from any Iraqi source and, finally, the cease and desist notifications from the Iraqi embassy.*
>
> *Second, the defendant is simply, as has been discussed, in the common notion, a con man, who lies to achieve his own ends, whatever they may be.*
>
> *Three, the defendant is now and has been in the past delusional and not consciously lying about being an East German intelligence agent, Iraqi general, Uruguayan mercenary, wearing an eye patch, having a stigmata, being a Pasha, being Sheik Ali or Count Albi and is, therefore, presently incompetent.*
>
> *Four, the defendant is not, in fact, delusional about being an Iraqi general and not consciously lying, but still able to work with his lawyers and craft a vigorous defense.*
>
> *A more complicated alternative is five, that he is a classic narcissistic personality who lies and fabricates personas to advance his own goals.*

*Or, perhaps, six, an individual suffering from a delusional disorder who also lies and fabricates personas to advance his own goals.*

*If he is a simple con man or narcissistic personality, the defendant is gaming the criminal justice system in an attempt to avoid trial.*

*If he is truly delusional, he is unable to assist his excellent counsel and may well be on the road to civil commitment.*

*The parties have presented a wealth of evidence over these past days of trial—including mental health experts, three on each side, psychological testing, medical records, grand jury evidence, defendant's video statements to the police, collateral interviews, contemporaneous biographical and historical information of Mr. Muth through emails, records, letters, and a secretly recorded interview with a tenant and so-called assistant or protégé.*

*Well-credentialed and respected experts have reached diametrically opposed conclusions as to the question of defendant's competence.*

*The Court concludes that the government has proven by a preponderance of the evidence that the defendant is competent to stand trial.*

*To put it bluntly, defendant's actions in his life and during the course of this case speak louder than words.*

In a lengthy recitation of facts, I concluded Muth was simply attempting to avoid trial with the goal of being civilly committed. Words from his own mouth or pen—to JC in the secretly recorded meeting; in videotaped interviews with the detectives; emails to various people, including his wife; statements to doctors and social workers; and fittingly, his own memoir, "The Triumph of Illusion," highlighted the findings of the competence by government's experts, including the revised St. E's diagnosis of a Narcissistic Personality Disorder. I agreed with the psychologist who stated that Muth's conduct has been to create "the illusion of a delusion."

I concluded that Muth's intermittent bouts of fasting at the behest of the Archangel Gabriel were a sham to achieve his goal of derailing the court proceedings.

To the extent that various psychological tests showed a cognitive disorder, poor executive functioning, memory deficits, and neurological impairment, it was my view that such testing "simply does not match Mr. Muth's actions over his lifetime and to this day."

*Although there may be, in fact, some elements of impairment, defendant's actions and other evidence substantially outweigh the defense psychiatric and psychological evidence.*

Muth showed no emotion, remaining impassive throughout my ruling. I turned and specially addressed him, locking eyes, and said,

> *The Court recognizes the proffer from experienced counsel that Mr. Muth is rigid and fixed on proving that he is an Iraqi general to the exclusion of other defenses.*
>
> *And the Court well appreciates counsel is in a very difficult posture. But the Court concludes it is one of Mr. Muth's own making. Whether he assists his lawyers or not, the Court concludes it is within his own control. It's Mr. Muth's choice to cooperate with his excellent lawyers in his defense or not to. But in any event, this case is going to go forward.*

Defense counsel then stated that her client wanted to represent himself again. Because he had just been found competent to stand trial, he was entitled to be his own lawyer as long as he understood the risks and consequences of doing so and waived his constitutional right to court-appointed counsel. Although we had already been through the laborious Q&A that the law required when I first allowed him to represent himself over a year ago in November of 2011, it was necessary go through it again so the record was up to date.

Throughout the litany of questions, he played coy, blithely announcing that he would not make a single objection at jury selection or at trial and would "leave it to General Petraeus to relay my defense." General David Petraeus had been the Commanding General of the Multi-National Force—Iraq. In response to my question as to whether anyone had promised him something to give up his right to counsel, he mysteriously stated he had received such a promise, but was not at liberty to state what the promise was or who made it. It appeared to me that Muth was transferring his considerable skill at playing mind games from the detectives, to his lawyers, to his doctors, and now to me as the presiding judge of his case. I had the distinct feeling that Muth was crafty enough to know how to set up an issue for appeal in case he was convicted. After further questioning, I was satisfied he understood that he could not raise this so-called promise by the unknown promisor as a basis for any future appeal.

Finally, I advised him that I was keeping his lawyers Page and Hickein on the case as his "attorney-advisors" in the event he wished to take advantage of their expertise. I also informed him that he could change his mind at any time and allow his now "attorney-advisors" to resume their role as his counsel, but that such a change of heart would not be a basis for changing his trial date in March. I wasn't going to allow him to play the "switch back to my lawyer game" as a reason to postpone the March trial.

He looked me straight in the eye, bowed officiously in an old-world way, and said in a clipped tone, "There will be no trial in March."

More games and mystery from Muth.

"Well," I said, "you understand the case is set for trial. Do you understand that?"

"Yes," he said. "But it's an irrelevant date."

I considered engaging him further, advise him that his charade was now over and there would be a trial, no matter what he said. But I didn't. There had been more than enough melodrama in the case already and I didn't want to provoke a confrontation. Although he didn't appear angry, I thought he might realize that if he ever wanted his freedom again, his best bet would be to cooperate with his lawyers and put on his best defense.

I didn't say it in court, but the irony to me was that if he dealt with the real facts and eschewed the Iranian hit man defense, he had a good chance to win at trial. The government's case appeared strong, but, so far as I knew at the time, it was not overwhelming. Although for some it might seem straightforward, and maybe obvious, that he killed his wife and then tried to cover it up, it was a case based solely on circumstantial evidence and had some flaws.

There were no eyewitnesses to the murder; he had not confessed to the police, far from it; he adamantly denied killing his wife; there was no scientific evidence tying him to the crime; no fingerprints, blood, or DNA pointing right at him as the killer. During his video-recorded interview, the detectives told him that there was a DNA connection but that was a ruse meant to shake him up and get him to confess. He was too crafty for that.

Moreover, although the house appeared to be secure, there were the three unlocked windows in the rear of the first floor. The detectives had rational explanations as to why there was no entry in each one, but they could not definitely rule out that someone else had gained entry. While the Iranian-spy-service-conspiracy-hit-job-theory was pure poppycock, Muth's lawyers could undoubtedly try and create uncertainty in the prosecution's case in the old-fashioned way. Maybe someone else used a ladder, opened the window, killed Ms. Drath in a common robbery and took the ladder with him?

Forensic pathology is more of an art than a science and the time of death could be subject to different expert opinions. Maybe Ms. Drath died before 9:00 p.m. on Friday, August 11. If so, Muth had a solid alibi with people who had no reason to lie for him. Such are the questions the defense could use to raise a reasonable doubt with the jury. Such is the stuff of not guilty verdicts. It wasn't by any means a slam dunk case for the prosecution.

But, at least for now, Muth wanted to play his new role—defense lawyer at the bar.

I advised him that he would be returning to the D.C. Jail that day.

He had effectively delayed his trial for the year 2012 with his side trip to St. Elizabeths.

I had said we were going to trial in March of 2013.

He had said there would be no trial in March of 2013.

He was right.

## He Is on His Way to Jesus

On February 4, 2013, I received an email from Rainey Brandt, the Attorney Advisor to the Court's Criminal Division. She was in constant contact with authorities from the D.C. Jail regarding issues with Superior Court prisoners. The email was short and to the point. Muth resumed his fasting on December 20, 2012, the day he returned to the jail.

"He is gaunt, pale and weak. He states he is on his way to Jesus and his brother… His vital signs are abnormal… but he continues to refuse to eat or drink. He is in the United Medical Center Hospital since January 20, 2013. He cannot sit up, let alone walk. He cannot be transported to Court in his condition… He is refusing care and has executed a Do Not

Resuscitate (DNR) in the hospital. Staff are trying to make him as comfortable as possible and persuade him to end his fast and refusal of care."

I determined that a hearing should be set to address Muth's current status. On February 6, 2013, all counsel were present, and we patched Muth in by speaker phone at the hospital. It was hard to hear on both ends, and in the courtroom the lawyers and I huddled around the phone on the bench to raise our voices as we communicated with Muth.

The head physician at the D.C. Jail was present and stated that Muth was in "very, very poor health." Such extreme fasting causes hypotension, hypoglycemia, and dehydration.

She stated he was bed bound to the extent that hospital staff could not even lift him to be weighed. I advised Muth that I was considering suspending his right to represent himself. I informed him that any lawyer who could not physically come to court on his own accord would either be fired by the client or be removed by the judge. Muth's case was no different. Before I did that though, I wanted to allow him to state his case.

He objected. The fast was commanded by Archangel Gabriel for ritual purification.

"I don't see how my fast should interfere with my ability to represent myself," he said.

I disagreed. I suspended his role as counsel and reappointed his attorney-advisors as the lawyers of record. I told him I was willing to reinstate him as counsel but he had to stop his fast, regain his health, and be able to come to court. I told him we were still planning to go to trial on March 25 as scheduled.

I set a status hearing for February 21, 2013, to monitor developments. If Muth was hell-bent to kill himself, there was probably nothing to be done. The government hadn't raised the issue of forcibly feeding him and my guess was his fragile health was so poor that the time for such an extreme measure had come and gone.

But a series of court hearings showed that suicide was apparently not Muth's high-risk game. He would intermittently eat and drink enough to keep himself alive, while remaining near death and unable to come to court.

*How does one master that art?* I wondered.

But where did his fast leave the trial? It cannot be that a defendant accused of a crime, the crime of First Degree Murder no less, gets to decide when, and if, he goes to court. Like all things Muth, his method to avoid trial was unusual and extreme, but in the end, it could not be allowed to succeed.

It's not common, but every once in a while a defendant carries on and creates such a disturbance in the courtroom that the trial cannot go forward in his presence. The remedy for such conduct is not difficult. A judge should warn the defendant that he had the right to be present at the trial, but that if he continued to disrupt the proceedings, he would be waiving his right to be present, escorted out of the courtroom, and the trial would go on without him. If he was willing to behave appropriately, he would be allowed back in the courtroom at any time.

I had a case where a temperamental defendant completely lost it in front of the jury and started yelling, screaming, and cursing at the eyewitness who had just identified him in the courtroom. He wouldn't stop shouting and carrying on. I excused the jury from the courtroom and warned him that if he kept it up I was going to order the marshals to put him in the cell block and the trial would go on in his absence. He then started yelling and screaming at me. It was around 3:00 in the afternoon, and though I hated to recess court early, I told the defendant that he should sleep on it and we'd try again the next day. The choice was his; carry on and sit in the cell block while the trial continued, or behave appropriately and be present at his own trial. The next day he had calmed down and was allowed back in the courtroom. The trial proceeded without incident to its conclusion.

The days of gagging a defendant in the courtroom have long past.

I couldn't help but think of the circus that became the trial of the so-called "Chicago 8," radicals and activists, including Abbie Hoffman, Tom Hayden, and Jerry Rubin, who were charged by the government with conspiracy to incite riots during the Democratic National Convention in Chicago in 1968. During the trial, Bobby Seale, a member of the Black Panthers, claimed he was forced to go to trial without the lawyer of his choice, denied the right to represent himself, and that Judge Julius Hoffman was lawless and racist. He yelled and screamed at Judge Hoffman in front of the jury. Judge Hoffman lost control of his emotions and bound, gagged, and chained Bobby Seale to his chair in front of the jury while he struggled to get free and attempted to cry out in protest. After several days of trial in this surreal atmosphere, William Kuntsler, one of the attorneys for another defendant was quoted as saying: "This is no longer a court of order, Your Honor, this is a medieval torture chamber." Judge Hoffman ultimately withdrew Seale from the trial, and sentenced him to four years in prison for contempt of court. Seale's conviction and imprisonment were later reversed on appeal.

Muth's case was, of course, different as he had not even made it into the courtroom, but to me the principle of warning him and giving him a choice to attend or not was basically the same. Once again, we all would have to wait and see what came next.

On March 14, 2013, two weeks before the scheduled trial, with Muth still at the hospital and listening by speaker phone, his attending physician testified that his "self-induced starvation and dehydration had placed him at imminent risk of death." When Muth first entered the jail in August of 2011, he weighed 173 pounds; he weighed 138 pounds in January of 2012; now, in March of 2012, his last measured weight was 105 pounds. The physician went so far as to state that the act of standing or even sitting could lead to sudden death. He also testified that transporting Muth to court in a supine bed would constitute a grave risk to his health and place a great burden on the court's medical staff.

The doctor noted that if Muth resumed eating and drinking in a supervised setting he would get better in a matter of days and be able to attend court in a few weeks. There was no reason to question Muth's mental acuity. Had he been incompetent there was no way the hospital would have allowed him to sign a DNR.

It was time to look at all options. I had researched the possibility of forcible feeding in case it came up. I noted that some rare cases supported forcible feeding of inmates who are trying to starve themselves to death in order to preserve their life. But the medical proffer confirmed what I suspected. Forcible feeding was not a possibility because it would require intubation and the invasive procedure itself would be life threatening.

I decided to start the process of warning Muth of the risks and consequences if he continued his fast.

"You have the right to be physically present in the courtroom for all stages of the proceedings and you also have the right to face your accusers by physically being in the courtroom." I asked him if he understood.

"Yes, I hear what you're saying," he replied.

"I encourage you to cease your fast, so that you will be able to physically be in the courtroom.

"But if you continue your fast and if you're not physically able to be in the courtroom, the Court will consider that you have knowingly and voluntarily and intelligently waived your right to be physically present in the courtroom."

I asked him if he understood.

He replied:

"Frankly, given the choice of throwing my lot in with a bunch of secularites or the heavenly host, in all due respect,

I opt for God.... I follow orders. You follow orders.... It's a secular world. It's a religious world. You live in one. I live in another."

Muth had succeeded in scuttling the March trial date.

Even if he resumed eating immediately, it was too short a time for him to be physically able to come to court.

Round 1 to Muth.

I set a date in April as a status hearing to see if Muth had changed his tune. In the event his status remained the same, I asked counsel to be prepared to state their positions and the legal considerations in proceeding to trial in his absence.

The more we researched the law, the more convinced I became that even though most of the cases, both locally and nationally, dealt with disruptive defendants in the courtroom itself or defendants free on bond who later absconded after the trial had begun, the basic principles should apply to a case where a defendant, by his own actions, makes himself unavailable to go to trial.

I assumed the defense would raise the argument that the rule governing a defendant's right to be present in the courtroom only applies when the defendant was there at the start of trial, and then, either by disruptive actions in the courtroom or fleeing during the course of the trial, made himself unavailable. There were no local cases that covered Muth's scenario where he would not be present to begin the trial. I assumed the prosecution would argue otherwise; that whether the defendant was initially present at trial was a distinction without a difference.

I was wrong.

At our next hearing on April 25, 2013, the attending physician once again testified that Muth was still in "a state of chronic starvation" and could not be brought safely into the courtroom. It was reported that Muth "intermittently eats quite a bit and then chooses not to eat for periods of time." For example after fasting for several days, on April 16, 2013, he consumed nine cups of ice cream, four yogurts, two puddings, one sandwich (lunch), two cups of hot tea, six ounces of tomato soup, one brownie, a grilled cheese sandwich (dinner), coleslaw, and crackers. In other words, nothing had changed.

I indicated that consistent with what I had stated at the last hearing, I was inclined to go on to trial, but I wanted to hear each side's arguments.

"We are in this category of a disruptive defendant who has chosen of his own volition to absent himself from court," I said. Muth understands the consequence of his actions and concluded that "if he chooses not to participate, that's his choice and that we go forward." I indicated that we could mitigate the prejudice to Muth with a video feed so that in reality he could see and hear everything in the courtroom. If he chose to testify in his own defense, he could be video-conferenced in as well.

Defense counsel objected and made the expected technical argument that the local rule did not permit such a trial and pointed out that a trial in absentia had never been convened in the Superior Court.

Prosecutor Kirschner then dropped a bombshell. Somewhat sheepishly, he stated in essence that the appellate division of the U.S. Attorney's Office had concluded that there were not sufficient legal grounds to proceed under this scenario.

I was stunned. I read the law completely differently.

Kirschner was the U.S. Attorney's top homicide prosecutor, and I had a great deal of respect for him and his opinion. But I had a hard time believing that he personally thought my hands were tied.

I communicated to the parties that I wasn't prepared to go to trial if the government is not going to support the decision on appeal. But what happens next? How do we go to trial? Just wait until Mr. Muth decides, if ever, that he's ready? I made it clear that I strongly disagreed with the government's legal position.

Kirschner said, "The trial team is here to speak with one voice regarding the government's position." He went on to indicate that if the Court ordered the government to go to trial, it would be ready. Well, I had my answer. Kirschner didn't agree with his own appellate division. But he had his marching orders.

I still thought I was right, but if the government disagreed, it would be lunacy to go to trial if it would not defend my decision on appeal in case Muth was convicted. It would be a free trial for Muth. Win and he goes home; lose and the government concedes I was wrong and a new trial would be ordered. No point to any of that. It looked like Muth had prevailed after all.

Round 2 to Muth.

The law can be convoluted, counterintuitive, and sometimes inflexibly rooted in a past that no longer exists for modern times. I don't think of myself as stubborn, but I was convinced that justice would not be served by allowing an accused murderer control when, and if, a trial would begin.

I needed to be convinced that I was wrong, and needed to see it in black and white. I ordered the parties to put their positions in writing. If I was wrong, so be it. I certainly wasn't going to force the parties to go to trial only to face a certain reversal on appeal.

In what now seemed an unlikely event, I maintained our previously scheduled trial date of December 2, 2013. In order to give us maximum flexibility in case further curveballs came up, a backup date of January 6, 2014, was also set.

In the midst of this surreal level of uncertainty as to how this case would ever go forward, I received a letter from the Consul General of the Embassy of the Federal Republic of Germany. The Consul General stated that the Embassy had been providing consular assistance to Muth and was "extremely concerned about Mr. Muth's state of health and the potential health consequences of his fasting." The Consul General inquired if "Your Honor sees a possibility within your powers to ensure that Mr. Muth's health can be stabilized and his fasting does not leave him in grave danger."

I had more than enough of my plate than to worry about the concerns of the German Embassy, but knew it was appropriate to keep them informed.

I wrote back indicating that since Muth was competent in the eyes of the law to make decisions regarding his own health, the Court was "not in a position to order the Department of Corrections, or any hospital, to stabilize Mr. Muth's health."

The briefs from the prosecution and the defense came in over the summer. The government completely reversed its position and agreed with me that "in refusing to eat, Muth is disrupting the trial proceedings no less than a defendant who yells in the courtroom. The courtroom door stands open to Muth, who, if he chooses, can regain his health through regular nourishment. Muth should not be permitted by his disruptive conduct indefinitely to avoid being tried on the charges brought against him."

Why did the government change its position? The brief didn't say. From my perspective it did not matter, but I speculated that Kirschner convinced his appellate folks that they had completely missed the mark. I also thought that requiring the appellate division to put its position in writing forced them into more rigorous research and analysis.

The defense opposition's first argument was worthy of serious consideration. The defense maintained its argument that the Constitution and the local rule did not cover Muth's situation. Only a disruptive defendant in the courtroom or one who flees after trial had started may be tried in absentia.

The second argument was creative; it asserted that Muth's fasting was a ritual purification and protected by his First Amendment right to the free exercise of his religion. The defense argued that "The government may not condition Mr.

Muth's right to be present at trial upon his relinquishing his right to the free exercise of his religion."

On August 28, 2013, the day after his lawyers had filed its opposition, Muth addressed a letter to me. He identified himself as Staff Brig. Gen A.G. Muth, Iraqi Army. He stated in part:

> *Greetings and felicitations. I hope you had a fine summer and trust this submission finds you well and in good spirits. I avail myself of this occasion to assure you, and through you, D.C. Superior Court of my highest esteem and consideration…*
>
> *I AFFIRM, I wish to be present for my trial and to represent myself. I am willing, able, and ready. Assertions to the contrary are misrepresentations of fact….*
>
> *Sure, it may be held that fasting is somewhat weakening me, physically, but what I am losing in the flesh I am gaining in the Holy Spirit, who resides in me, and protects and guides me.*

He then later proclaimed that General David Petraeus would confirm his status as a General in the Iraqi Army and prove his claim that his wife's murder was a hit by renegade agents of the Iranian Revolutionary Guard Corps.

I suspected that the "Petraeus card" would have to be played out in the future, but first I needed to get the parties together and decide once and for all that we were going to actually have a trial.

On October 31, 2013, Muth was still in the hospital and was on the speakerphone. His attending physician testified that Muth's health was progressively worsening; that he sometimes ate, but he weighed a mere 92 pounds and was losing weight. He again reiterated that should Muth stop his fast he would be able to come to court in two to three weeks.

Muth interjected. He said that breaking his fast was not an option and that it was unbecoming for the court to interfere with his religious life. He accused me of being biased against him and moved that I recuse myself from his case.

I essentially told him that the game was up. I ruled that he had waived his right to be present in his own case and we were going to trial with or without him. I instructed him that he had more than enough time to regain his health and come to court. Once he came to court, I would reconsider and probably allow him to represent himself again. I warned him again of the consequences of his actions. The motion to recuse was frivolous and denied.

Status hearings were held in November and December, with testimony from the attending physician that revealed more of the same. Muth was still fasting but keeping himself alive by intermittently eating. I warned him again. For the convenience of all, I set the trial for January 6, 2014.

Muth had successfully tied up the criminal justice system for two years.

The year 2012 was lost due to Muth's mental health excursion to St. Elizabeths Hospital.

The year 2013 was lost due to Muth's self-starvation excursion to United Medical Center.

We were now set to go to trial in 2014. As with all things Muth, we came to expect the unexpected. Time would tell.

## Cheap Tickets to Iceland

Before trial, in writing and later in open court, Muth, through his lawyers, sought court permission to subpoena General David Petraeus to trial. He asserted Petraeus could provide relevant testimony as to his occupation at the time of his wife's death and the nature and circumstances of his relationship with his wife. Defense counsel also stated that "It is Mr. Muth's belief that General Petraeus, if he were under oath and offering testimony, would testify that; one, Mr. Muth is an Iraqi general; and two, that General Petraeus learned from the Iranian government that Mr. Muth did not kill Ms. Drath and that the Iranians did."

Any person, no matter how high up in the government, is required to come to court and testify if he has important testimony for the jury to consider. The Court, however, has to be careful not to subject present and former senior government officials to harassment, abuse, and frivolous claims on their time. But at the end of the day, no person is above the law, and a defendant has a right to call witnesses at trial on his behalf.

The government opposed the subpoena and stated that the prosecutors personally spoke to Petraeus, and he informed them that he had never met Muth, nor heard of him, and knew nothing about him other that what he had read in the newspaper. Petraeus also stated that he had absolutely no information regarding Muth's occupation or his relationship to Viola Drath. Petraeus did say that it was possible that he was photographed with Viola Drath, but he had no specific recollection of ever meeting her.

In a Jason Bourne movie high-level government conspiracy is common and it certainly has happened in real life. Perhaps Petraeus was lying; or maybe the prosecutors were lying as well. As it should, the law bends over backward to allow an accused the right to call witnesses in support of his defense. But such leniency has its limits and the rule of reason must be applied. Had there been a sliver of corroboration of Muth's Iraqi General claim, it might have been a different story. Every verified fact, however—phony uniform, phony certificate of appointment, phony past impersonations, disclaimers of Muth by the Iraqi Embassy and the Department of State—all showed that General Muth was a fraud.

I denied the subpoena. General Petraeus was out of the case. If Muth were smart, he would now devote his efforts to winning his trial. He had a chance. He had top-flight lawyers and the government's case had its weaknesses.

On January 2, 2014, we had a status hearing to determine Muth's medical status, prepare for jury selection, and resolve any pending legal issues. Not surprisingly, Muth's health remained the same; sometimes eating; sometimes fasting; he was medically unfit to come to court but remained mentally competent. There was no point in warning him anymore; even if he pledged to resume eating, it would be too late. The trial was going forward.

We tested the technical aspects of the audio-video feed. It all worked without a hitch. But an unexpected problem arose. Although Muth would be able to see and hear everything in the courtroom, the defense asked that the jury be able to see him as well. I asked technician Alvin Melvin to put Muth up on a screen in the courtroom so we all could see how he looked. In a few minutes we saw an emaciated Muth lying in bed, on his side in a fetal position, staring into the camera.

The prosecution objected, claiming that Muth's pitiful appearance would gain him sympathy from the jury. There were a number of dimensions to this issue. The Constitution states that a defendant has a right to be physically in the courtroom to face his accusers. On the other hand, a number of cases around the country held that a defendant who voluntarily absented himself from his trial had no right to have a video feed into the courtroom. In some of those states, the court simply did not have the technological capacity to arrange such a feed.

Although the Superior Court had such a capability, I ruled in favor of the government. Muth shouldn't be allowed to profit from orchestrating his own absence. I further ruled, however, that should Muth elect to testify during the trial, I would allow the camera to show him, reasoning that he would be subject to cross-examination by the prosecutors and could explain to the jury why he was in a hospital. He would have to explain that I had encouraged him numerous times to stop his fast, and warned him if he did not the trial would go on in his absence. The jury would then have all the facts and could make their own independent evaluation of Muth's situation.

The hardest part was to explain Muth's absence from the trial to the citizens of the District of Columbia who were randomly selected to take part in jury selection. Muth was presumed innocent and despite the extreme measures he took to avoid the day of reckoning, I had to make sure that he, and the government, had a fair trial. It wasn't going to be easy. The jury was bound to wonder just what the heck was going on? Was this defendant so dangerous he could not be brought into the courtroom? Was the prosecution so overbearing and unfair that they are trying a defendant who was unable to come to court? The key was to craft language to mitigate as much as possible the prejudice to Muth, without also putting the government in a bad light. It wouldn't be perfect, but the situation was of Muth's own making.

After getting input from the lawyers, I prepared my remarks and questions for the jury panel. We resolved the remaining legal issues and were good to go.

On January 6, 2014, I enter the courtroom to see approximately 100 citizens in the audience to begin jury selection. After introducing myself to the panel, I invite the lawyers, one at a time, to face the panel as a matter of courtesy and to find out if any panel member knows counsel in a professional or personal capacity. No one knows any counsel.

*So far so good*, I think.

Ordinarily, I would now introduce the defendant and have him face the panel for the same reasons.

*Okay, here we go*, I think, *into the unknown.*

> *Ladies and Gentlemen, as you see, the defendant at trial, Mr. Muth, is not present here in the courtroom, and will not be present during the course of this trial. As the judge presiding in this case, I have decided that it is lawful and proper to try the case in his absence. Mr. Muth is in the custody of the Department of Corrections, and by videoconference he is able to see and hear everything that goes on in the courtroom.*
>
> *I am now instructing you as a principle of law that the fact that Mr. Muth will not be present in court during the trial is not a matter you should take into account in any way. In other words, you should not hold it against Mr. Muth or the government whatsoever the fact that Mr. Muth is not present during the course of the trial. Indeed, it should play no role in your consideration of the evidence in the case.*
>
> *So the question to the panel is whether or not there's any member of the panel who believes that he or she is either unable or unwilling to follow that instruction which I just gave.*

Under the law, jurors are presumed to understand and follow the judge's instructions. Is that always true? Of course not. But I don't think it's a bunch of legal mumbo jumbo. I believe in the jury system and the intelligence and commitment of total strangers coming together to do justice as a jury. In many respects, the jury panel's response to this question will be the most important part of the trial. If either Muth or the government are going to be significantly prejudiced from the get go, this whole trial will be a failure.

No one responds to my question. I am satisfied and believe we will have a fair trial on the evidence.

It takes the balance of the day, but the rest of jury selection goes without incident, and we have a jury. As I do in every case, especially a case in which there has been publicity, I instruct the jury to refrain from exposure to any press reports on TV, radio, or the newspapers. If by accident they see or hear something about the case, I ask them to turn off the TV or radio, and not read any articles about the trial.

It's been a long and arduous day, but we get through it.

The next day, January 7, 2014, the trial begins. Prosecutor Kirschner makes his opening statement before the jury. Much of what he says is familiar to me but some is quite surprising. He outlines the theory of the government's case saying that only Muth had the motive, means, and opportunity to kill his wife. The history of the domestic violence is brutal.

> *He struck her in the head inflicting blunt force trauma injuries to her head. He broke her ribs up and down both sides. Her thumbnail was nearly ripped off in the struggle… and he ultimately choked the life out of her, strangling her to death.*
>
> *And you will hear, Ladies and Gentlemen, that unfortunately, this domestic violence homicide, this murder, was a very long time coming.*

He also adds some facts about the time of death and Muth's actions immediately after that I had not heard before. Perhaps the government's case is stronger than I thought.

Defense counsel Hickein gives a strong opening statement for his client:

> *Albrecht Muth is not guilty. He did not kill his wife. He did not strangle his wife. He did not strike his wife. He's an innocent man charged with a very serious offense that he did not commit.*

Counsel points out all the strong points for the defense. There are no eyewitnesses to the murder, no forensic evidence tying Muth to the crime. He called the police and reported his wife's death; even after it was obvious that he was a suspect, he did not flee the area. He did not act like a guilty man. He even consented to be interviewed by the police.

Counsel accuses the government of *making assumptions about what they think happened. They looked at Mr. Muth as their only suspect from the very beginning, and they worked backward from there. Instead of trying to figure out who killed Viola Drath, they tried to figure out how to prove that it was Albrecht Muth who did it. And there won't be evidence to help you figure it out.*

We settle into the rhythm of a trial. The government calls witnesses that show Muth's history of assaulting his wife. In March of 1992, shortly after they were married, Ms. Drath came home after a long flight abroad and called out for Muth. When she didn't receive a reply, she called out for him again, but apparently interrupted him while he was on the phone. She laid down in bed to rest. Muth walked into the bedroom and punched her in the face a number of times as she lay in her bed.

A friend from church, "CT," testifies that "She came to church one Sunday with bruises on her face. She had glasses on, dark glasses, but you could see the bruising." CT identifies brutal black-and-white photographs of Viola Drath's battered face. The photos are displayed before the jury. The jury is solemn as they look at Viola Drath's beat-up face. She looks like a frail old lady and the photos were taken twenty-two years ago. CT testifies that after learning of the murder, she contacted a police hotline and volunteered her information. After first denying hitting his wife, Muth pleaded guilty in court and was placed on probation.

A police officer testifies that in another incident in July of 1992, he investigated a report of a domestic violence incident. At the Georgetown home, the officer personally heard Muth threaten to kill his wife.

A former boyfriend, "DD," a legislative director for a trade association, testifies that in the early 2000s Muth confided to him in earnest that while he and Ms. Drath were on a trip to the Middle East they were on a cave tour "in these tunnels and they're deep, you know, underground that his intent was to, you know, knock her down and push her down and kill her. And, you know, and then leave her there, but then these American tourists came through on a tour group and there was nothing he could do, so they left."

The defense tries to show that Muth was either drunk when he made the statement or didn't really mean it. After all, DD never reported the incident to the police.

DD makes it clear that the last thing he wants in life is to be in a public courtroom talking about Albrecht Muth. *Poor guy*, I think, to have to be dragged into this melodrama.

Ms. Drath's grandson says he was called at his clothing store in Georgetown by his eighty-six-year-old grandmother to the house on Q Street. She had noodle soup in her hair and told him Muth hit her with a chair and threw a bowl of soup at her. He saw the broken chair and broken dishes. Muth fled the District to Florida after a warrant was issued for his arrest. He claimed in emails and phone calls to be on the Iraqi battlefield, but records show he worked as a hotel clerk in Miami.

Ms. Drath files for divorce; she takes him back; she refuses to prosecute. The case is dismissed in 2008.

In January of 2011, a computer repairman entered the home. Ms. Drath interrupted Muth while he was talking to the repairman. Muth became enraged and cursed her out and pushed her in the chest with two hands causing her to fall backward, only to catch herself in the doorway. The prosecutor asks the witness to demonstrate the push by reenacting it on him in front of the jury. It's an effective strategy. Kirschner is about six feet two inches tall and sturdy. The witness pushes him hard and the prosecutor stumbles backward three steps.

The computer repairman confronted Muth: "Why would you do that to your mother?" He says Muth ignored him.

The defense attacks him by pointing out that he only came forward when he saw that the police placed a reward poster for $25,000 for anyone with knowledge about the death of Viola Drath. Although he never asked for a reward, his credibility has been called into question.

The former deputy chief of staff to Vice President Cheney, a lawyer, testifies that in April of 2011, he worked with Ms. Drath and Muth regarding the Blue Star Mothers organization. He says Muth asked him to lunch one day with the main goal of seeking advice on how to void or revise his prenuptial agreement. The lawyer says he refused to get involved.

Later, he attended a luncheon relating to the Blue Star Mothers where Muth humiliated his wife in front of everyone for a perceived breach of protocol. Muth later forwarded him an email with a train of comments from himself and his wife.

> *VD: You berate me in public... night and day.*
>
> *AM: May au contraire, it must remain my objective to get you ready for a high-visibility role in Baghdad. I'm not certain if you are up to it because you cannot follow even the simplest—or, smallest scale protocol.*
>
> *VD: You never have said a kind word to me in 14 years.*
>
> *AM: I HAVE CREATED THE POST-JOURNALISM PERSONA OF THE HONORABLE VIOLA HERMS DRATH; THAT'S AMPLE PAYBACK FOR WHATEVER YOU MAY THINK TO HAVE DONE FOR ME. LOOK TO THE DOWNSTAIRS PICTURE WALLS OF THE OLD JOURNALIST VERSUS THE WALL OF THE GRANDMOTHER OF THE NATION. I AM GERMAN; NOT GIVEN TO IDLE*

*COMPLIMENTS. I LEAVE THAT SUPERFICIALITY TO AMERICANS.*

*VD: I think I have been good to you during the last 20 years. I can and will no longer take it. I have been useful to you and you have enlivened my life to some degree.*

*AM: I HAVE HELPED MAKE YOU.*

*VD: But now I am at the point where I can no longer take your constant abuses culminating in never-ending references to my age as if I were an old fool.*

*AM: JUST NOT WILLING TO LIVE UP TO THE TASK HANDED YOU IN PUBLIC LIFE, AND YOU NEED NOT BE; I MUST.*

*VD: Anyway, this old fool who has run her life and household all these years is sick and tired of this painful and most degrading situation. I am finally ready to find a resolution of this untenable mode of being in a civil way. I wish you well.*

The lawyer testifies that the next day she contacted him and asked for help to get a divorce, but she never followed through. Four months later to the day, she is murdered.

One of Viola Drath's daughters, "FD," who works in commercial real estate, testifies that her mom at ninety-one was in very good health, active in many causes, walked up and down two flights of stairs without a cane in the Georgetown home numerous times a day. She says that when Muth drank he became "belligerent, more persistent in arguing, louder, and hostile." He would call her mother to her face, "old and past her time."

The day of the murder, Muth left a message on her phone and, in a staccato voice without emotion, said her "mother was dead and the police were at the house and please come down immediately."

FD walked to the Georgetown home and had to identify a photograph of her dead mother. A short time later, she says Muth encountered her and handed her what appeared to be a codicil, or addition, to her mother's will. As far as she knows, her mother executed a will that left her whole estate to her two daughters. Muth was specifically disinherited. A lawyer later testifies that Ms. Drath and Muth signed a prenuptial agreement where he gave up all claims to her estate. The codicil, however, granted Muth $150,000, and an additional amount of $50,000, if the liquid amount of her assets exceeded $600,000. The codicil, which has a signature that purports to be that of Viola Drath, has no witnesses. She also testifies that Muth asked for his allowance of $1,800.00, which was overdue.

The prosecution has scored some points with the jury. Aside from love and hate, money comes next as a motive for murder.

The defense fights back.

Defense counsel Page cross-examines FD and points out that the family tried to discourage her mother from marrying Muth, saying something to the effect "you can live with him, but you shouldn't marry him, you don't need a piece of paper." FD admits on cross she was concerned that when her mother married Muth, he would run off with all of her money. FD admits that she dislikes Muth, and that her mother at times elevated him over her as the center of her life.

The prosecution shores up the money motive. An Army Judge Advocate General (JAG) officer testifies that months before her murder, Ms. Drath went to have her will drafted. She showed him the same so-called codicil that Muth presented to FD the morning of the murder. Ms. Drath said Muth wanted this codicil in the will; Drath said that not only did she not want the codicil but she wanted to disinherit Muth. Her new will left her entire estate to her two daughters. Muth got nothing.

The defense is handcuffed in cross-examining the JAG officer. He also has documents from Ms. Drath showing that she was afraid that Muth was going to hurt her. The government, recognizing the documents were inadmissible in trial, did not try and get them before the jury. Cross-examination by the defense as to what Ms. Drath wanted in her will, however, could possibly open the door to the admission of this damning evidence. It is a tightrope the defense wisely chooses not to walk.

The stage has been set. The prosecution now turns to the murder of Viola Drath. "AA," a friend of Muth, is called to the stand. If DD was embarrassed, AA is mortified. You get the feeling that he knows all too well his lot in life is about to change and he will be on the front page of the *Washington Post* for all the wrong reasons.

AA is twenty-seven years old and comes from Pakistan. He's a mathematician and works for the government. AA testifies that he met Muth through Craigslist on August 8, 2011. AA tells the jury that he was only seeking a mentor, nothing else. Confronted on cross-examination by the defense that he emailed Muth a photo of himself with a bare chest, he stubbornly clings to the mentor motivation. Sexually explicit emails back and forth clearly show that Muth was intent on starting an intimate relationship. Muth writes that AA can be "the General's boy."

Everyone in the courtroom is uncomfortable listening to his testimony. I see some of the jurors drop their heads in embarrassment. AA finally admits that in addition to help with his career, he was looking for a sexual relationship.

Muth offered to help pay AA for his own apartment. Muth also offered to help with his career. He was planning a future together. They had briefly met on August 9 at the Tabard Inn, a high-end bar and restaurant.

They next made plans to meet on the evening of August 11, 2011.

That evening they went to downtown swanky bars, first the W Hotel, and then on to the Hay-Adams. Muth started drinking, "rum with a fruity juice." Muth bragged about his contacts at the White House and the Department of Defense. AA doesn't drink. They hopped in a cab and arrived around 6:30 p.m. at the Georgetown home of "TT," a former ambassador and acquaintance of Muth. Muth started drinking hard liquor heavily, becoming aggressive, obnoxious, and domineering. They left "around 9:30 p.m., give or take," and walked the ten to fifteen minutes to Muth's home. AA says Muth was so drunk he stumbled, could barely stand, and slurred his words. AA helped Muth stay upright.

Muth invited AA into his home. AA refused.

The prosecutor asks:

Q: "And why—why didn't you want to go into the house with him?"

A: "Because, personally, I don't like to be with people who are piss drunk."

The last time AA saw Muth he was walking into his house. The next day, with Viola Drath dead in the bathroom, they emailed back and forth. AA does not know that she is dead. Muth does. Muth insisted in his email that he didn't remember what happened the night before and hoped that "he was a gentleman." AA confronted him with his drunken and loutish behavior and Muth apologized. They planned to get together again soon.

As much as Muth's friends dreaded their day in court, TT, the former ambassador, loves being onstage with a captive audience. Asked a simple question about how he knows Viola Drath, he carries on in a loud and enthusiastic voice.

"When you retire from government you either move to Kansas City and play golf or you stay in Washington and become a consultant. And you trip over them if you walk down K Street. There are more consultants than taxi drivers, I would guess. I'm a consultant. And I work on things I know a lot about and I work on things I know nothing about."

Some of the jurors smile.

*This guy is a trip*, I think.

TT says Muth contacted him and wanted to set up a meeting and implied a mysterious person from Pakistan might be useful to know for his international consulting.

Q: "Did Mr. Muth tell you anything more about the gentleman from Pakistan that he wanted you to meet?"

A: "No. And when I finally met him he was monumentally uninteresting and didn't say boo. And so, if he was a famous spy or interesting person, that was monumentally unimpressive."

More smiles from the jury, even some mild chuckles. *That's okay*, I think. Some comic relief from all the tension in the courtroom is not bad as long as it does not get out of hand. I glance over to the Drath family. They seem fine but I think they must be furious.

TT waxes on, loving the spotlight. Muth and AA came over around 6:00 p.m. He knows this he says because he doesn't drink all day long anymore and 6:00 is the cocktail hour. He knows he shouldn't say it because we're "on the record," but he served Muth illegal Cuban rum, because it is so much better than Bacardi. Muth drank three or four rums and animatedly discussed with TT the Treaty of Westphalia. What does that mean, he's asked?

A: "We have a phrase in the State Department: Foggy Bottom mumble. That means, somebody's talking at you and you say afterwards, 'What the hell did he say?' Listen to the Secretary of State periodically and then ask yourself 'what did he say?' There'll be a quiz on that."

Everyone laughs. I turn my chair away from the jury, trying to stifle my laugh. But it's too late.

Even with his carrying on, on cross-examination defense counsel scores many points. TT says he had seen Muth and his wife on quite a few occasions and all had been fine. He didn't see any hostility between them.

TT testifies that on the evening of August 11, 2011, Muth had been drinking but was not aggressive, or obnoxious, certainly not physical in any way. Maybe Muth was somewhat animated, but that's Muth. Muth was not "piss drunk" and did not stumble while walking, nor slur his words. Everything was fine. Yes, TT had his three Irish whiskeys, but he's a "good Irishman" and can hold his liquor. Everyone was in a good mood when Muth and AA left.

Q: "And you found this evening enjoyable as well, right? I mean, it went on too long, I understand that—"

A: "It went on too long, but I found it enjoyable. I like to talk about those things. He was saying he was a socialist, and he's worked for the Iraqis in a military uniform. And, you know, what the hell is he?"

For all his eccentricity, TT contradicts much of AA's testimony.

The comic relief does not last long.

The next witness, "SJ," lives in the adjoining row house to the Drath/Muth home. Their homes share a common wall. SJ appears to be in her late thirties, or early forties, and is dressed very conservatively with well-coiffed hair. She speaks very precisely, with a deep Southern accent.

She knows her next-door neighbors only to say hello to; casual conversation on the street, and small talk with Ms. Drath about her garden. She has seen Muth walk around Georgetown in his military uniform.

She describes the layout of her home. Her daughter's bedroom upstairs aligns with Ms. Drath's bedroom.

She is a very light sleeper and in the early morning hours of August 12, 2011, around 3:20 a.m., her husband's snoring machine kept her up. She went to her daughter's empty bedroom and tried to fall back asleep. She heard what she first thought was the sound of a father and a baby playing.

She woke up in the morning to see the police at the Drath/Muth home and learned of Ms. Drath's death. Through the media she found out that Muth was a suspect. She checked with her other next-door neighbor, who indeed has a baby. No, he told her, we weren't up in the middle of the night.

SJ tells the jury that she realizes what she really heard was a whine, and then a cackle. Prosecutor Kirschner asks her if she can replicate what she heard. She says she can.

All of a sudden this prim and proper woman emits a long whining noise, followed shortly with what seems to be an almost satanic cackle.

The courtroom is stunned. I'm stunned. I didn't know the government had such powerful evidence. There is a pin drop silence as Kirschner lets the moment sink in. He asks for permission to describe her imitation so that the record can reflect what happened. He asks:

Q: "For the record, the witness first made sort of a—a higher-pitch distressed, staccato sort of whining sound—if that's an accurate description—followed by a louder, robust laugh, louder and sort of lower-pitched. Is that a pretty fair description?"

A: "Very, very accurate."

There are times in a trial when a piece of evidence is so powerful and has such an impact that you remember it forever. The imitation whine and the cackle from SJ is that kind of evidence.

The defense tries its best to shake her, but she is not shaken. Cross-examination tries to shift the focus to what she originally thought she heard, a sweet sound, but it is tough going. SJ says she couldn't imagine she was hearing a murder taking place. She now knows what she heard and when she heard it.

She finishes her testimony and quietly leaves the witness stand. Everyone in the courtroom—the jurors, lawyers, and spectators—are still in a state of shocked silence. It is lunchtime, and I recess court to the afternoon.

The government calls the other next-door neighbor to verify that he and his baby slept through the night of August 12, 2011.

You never really know in a trial, but I've got a sense that the tide may have turned in the government's favor. A case based on circumstantial evidence may have pivoted on a witness who actually heard the dying breaths of Viola Drath. Why would she lie about what she said she heard?

The government is not done with surprises though. Although by law the defense would have been made aware before trial of any proposed expert testimony, I had no reason to know it in advance, and hear the testimony along with the jury.

The next day the prosecution calls an expert witness in forensic computer evidence. He gives a long, rambling explanation in computer speak that nobody really understands about how he downloaded Muth's Toshiba laptop computer to uncover its secrets. One juror actually falls asleep. I don't blame her, and we take an early fifteen-minute recess to let everybody stretch their legs.

The computer expert testifies about emails from Muth in 2006 claiming to be on the Iraqi battlefield when really he's a hotel clerk in Miami. Nothing new there; we had already heard that before.

But then he testifies about Muth's history of Google browsing. The prosecution blows up spreadsheets and projects them onto an overhead screen for the jury's easy viewing. We're about to go into Muth's inner digital life. Nobody is asleep now.

There is Muth in May of 2010, searching Google for Iraqi military uniforms.

There is Muth on July 19, 2011, three weeks before the murder, questioning Google how to challenge a pre-nuptial agreement.

There is Muth in the early morning hours of August 12, 2011, again searching Google for answers. SJ testified that she heard the dying whine of Viola Drath and the satanic cackle of her killer at around 3:20 a.m. Muth is on the computer at 5:15 a.m., browsing the internet, laying his digital footprint on various sites seeking "cheap flights to Iceland"; ten minutes later, at 5:25 a.m.; he's checking out "extradition from the Mexico border"; and finally, also at 5:25 a.m., he's seeking out tips about "driving across the U.S. border into Canada."

The defense has no questions of the expert.

You don't have to be Sherlock Holmes to figure out what Muth was up to and why.

The videotaped interview with Muth and the homicide detectives the day after the murder plays before the jury. Usually the prosecution chooses not to show an interview with a defendant who denies the murder. Why allow a defendant to put on his defense without having to testify and face aggressive cross-examination by a skilled prosecutor?

The detectives, however, set him up in the interview. They locked Muth in by getting him to agree there was no forced entry, just a husband and his wife in the house after 9:45 p.m. No possible intruder, nothing stolen. No one has a motive to kill her. He thinks he's saying all the right words, and he is if she fell and hit her head and died. His disdain for the common policemen comes through. Although I've seen the video before, the most striking part occurs when the detectives inform him that the ME ruled his wife's death a homicide. Not only a homicide, but the time of death was within the time he just admitted to being solely at home with Viola Drath. Muth's accidental death theory just went down in flames.

The detectives take a break, but what they really want to do is observe him alone on the video. He doesn't disappoint. He hangs his head down and says to himself over and over: "She's ruled it a murder. She's ruled it a murder." He realizes he's trapped and he's got to come up with something else. He looks like a guilty man.

The trial starts winding down. An evidence technician testifies about photos and measurements taken at the crime scene. The doors were locked and there were no signs of a forced entry. The windows were either locked, realistically incapable of being opened, or so high off the ground that a burglar would need an extension ladder to gain access. No property was missing. The forensic investigator from the Medical Examiner also went to the crime scene and raised red flags about the position of Viola Drath's body and signs of injury inconsistent with an accidental fall.

The assistant medical examiner testifies about the autopsy she performed and the extensive injuries to Ms. Drath's body. Many of the photographed injuries are placed on the overhead screen. Some jurors are looking down, sometimes sneaking a peak at the photos. Others are transfixed. It's a hell of a thing to see photographs of a dead body at an autopsy. Maybe we've been oversensitized by TV and the movies, but in real time the power of a life ended by violence is hard to take.

The doctor testifies there were multiple rib fractures on both sides, ten in all; multiple abrasions and bruises or contusions to the face, neck, scalp, abdomen, upper arms, and lip; there was a fractured thyroid cartilage and hyoid bone, the bone that sits between the thyroid cartilage and the tongue. There were hemorrhages to the eyes and epiglottis, cartilage by the root of the tongue by the entrance to the larynx. The right thumbnail was almost entirely torn off. All the injuries, she says, appear to have occurred at the same time, in one incident. The ME rules that the cause of death was strangulation and blunt force injuries. She rules the manner of death a homicide.

The doctor discusses rigor mortis, lividity, and blanching, and roughly sets the time of death to be within twelve hours from the forensic investigator's examination of Ms. Drath on the scene at 11:20 a.m., on the morning of August 12, 2012.

The defense does its best to challenge the ME, but there is little that they can do in face of the number of injuries to Ms. Drath.

The government then rests its case.

It is now time for the defense case.

The defense calls a DNA expert who testifies that DNA in various items of evidence—fingernail clippings of Viola Drath, blood on the bathroom floor, and a nail polish bottle found on the scene—all match Viola Drath's DNA. Muth's DNA is not found on any of the items.

Defense counsel asks to approach the bench. They advise me that their client has chosen not to take the stand in his own defense.

I recess the jury, as there will be a discussion that needs to take place in their absence.

It is now crunch time for Muth, for it is his time to decide whether or not he wants to testify. In a bizarre way he has almost been an afterthought during the trial. We check each day to be sure the videoconference is working. He occasionally calls his lawyer in the courtroom, but otherwise he has been totally silent during the trial. If the past was prologue, I was expecting some type of shenanigans, or some type of legitimate medical emergency. I didn't expect silence.

I am required to personally ask him if he wants to take the stand because the right to testify is his personal right alone and he can testify against his lawyer's advice. I am also trying to protect the record against any later claim by him, should he be convicted, that he wanted to testify at his trial but his lawyers prevented him from doing so.

As the jury is in recess outside the courtroom, I ask that Muth's image now be shown on the screen. Everyone in the packed courtroom gazes at him with intense interest. I see members of the press scribbling in their notebooks. He appears as he did before, weak and frail. He stares at me with apparent contempt.

*Q: Mr. Muth, can you hear me? And if you can, try to speak as loudly as you can. Do you understand that you have the right to testify and tell your side of the story in this case? Do you understand?*

*A: Yes.*

*Q: Have you consulted with your lawyers as to whether or not you wish to testify?*

*A: Yes.*

*Q: And do you understand that you can testify even if your lawyer recommends that you don't testify? Do you understand that?*

*A: Yes.*

*Q: Do you have any questions about your right to testify?*

*A: No.*

*Q: All right. Then, Mr. Muth, I'm going to find that you have knowingly, intelligently, and voluntarily waived your right to testify. Thank you, sir.*

*A: Thank you.*

I ask that his image be taken down from the screen as the jury will be brought back into the courtroom to allow the defense to rest its case on the record. Closing arguments by the lawyers will take place the next day along with my instructions on the law. After that, the two alternate jurors, juror #7 and juror #13, will be excused from service. The remaining twelve person jury will then retire and begin its deliberations.

Prosecutor Laura Bach, Kirschner's co-counsel, gives a strong and tough argument to the jury. She highlights all the key points—the history of domestic violence, the numerous and brutal injuries to Ms. Drath, the financial and personal motives, the aggression while drunk, Muth's unknowing confession to the detectives, and his reaction to the news that the ME ruled his wife's death a homicide. Alone in his thoughts, "You can see the wheels spinning," she says. She highlights

SJ's hearing the whine and cackle around 3:20 a.m., undoubtedly Viola Drath's dying utterances, followed by Muth's sadistic pleasure. And then there are the Google searches shortly thereafter: cheap flights to Iceland, extradition to Mexico, and border crossings into Canada.

Bach concludes with a tell-it-like-it-is style:

> *Viola Drath was a ninety-one-year-old mother, grandmother, and great-grandmother. She's a woman who wasn't going to let her age stop her. She's still going strong at ninety-one. She's supporting causes for mothers of kids killed in combat. She's doing everything she can. She's living her life.*
>
> *She was not going to let anything stop her, but something—not something, someone—did stop her, and that's Albrecht Muth. He stopped her because she wouldn't give him what he wanted. So, back on August 12th, he was angry. He wanted that money. He wanted to go on and live his life the way he wanted it. He did not want to be bound to this old lady anymore and he was mad, so he strangled her initially. He chokes her into unconsciousness. He took that woman into that bathroom and he just got out twenty years of rage. He beat her head repeatedly on that floor and he strangled her. He put all of that force on her. He looked that woman in the eye for minutes as he took that life away from her.*
>
> *That's what this case is about. When you go in the back and you think about what this case is about, we know you're going to hold Mr. Muth responsible because it's time that he's held accountable for what he did to Viola Drath.*
>
> *Thank you.*

Defense counsel Page fights back strong. Although I have instructed the jury as to the law, counsel hits the highlights, which are all in her client's favor. Muth is presumed to be innocent and he remains innocent unless and until the government can prove him guilty beyond a reasonable doubt. The burden is totally on the government, the defense does not have to prove a thing. If the jury has a doubt based in reason, the jury is required by law to acquit. She takes one out of the defense lawyer's toolbox and in stark, but accurate, terms, explains what reasonable doubt is not:

> *It means because the burden is so high that if you think maybe Mr. Muth did this, you have to find him not guilty. You have to acquit him because that's not proof beyond a reasonable doubt.*
>
> *If you think more likely than not Mr. Muth did this, you have to acquit him because that's not proof beyond a reasonable doubt.*
>
> *If you think probably he did this, you have to acquit him. That is not proof beyond a reasonable doubt.*

Counsel attacks AA as obviously lying about seeking a mentor and not a lover; he wanted a sugar daddy; to be the General's boy. She attacks him again when he said Muth was piss drunk and stumbling when he left TT's home; TT saw no such thing.

Counsel attacks the government's theory of dual motives; he had all the money he needed; his gay lifestyle was well known to his wife; he didn't need to kill her to have an affair with AA.

Yes, he assaulted her some twenty years ago, but that was the only documented showing of domestic violence. The rest came from family members who despised Muth or from a few oddballs who had their own financial motives for coming forward.

The staged murder theory was just that, a theory, something out of TV. There was no proof Muth staged the killing.

He didn't flee the area after her death; he had nothing to hide; a guilty man would have taken off. An innocent man does not. He knew he would probably be a suspect so looking up options was not the act of a guilty man. The fact is he didn't flee and was not afraid of whatever might come because he knew he didn't kill his wife.

There is no eyewitness, no forensic evidence, and no confession. Just a theory; they assumed he was guilty and worked backward by putting a sinister spin on every event to prove a faulty theory.

Same thing with SJ's testimony. She originally heard a sweet sound—father and baby playing. Now she is spinning it as a dying woman's last breath followed by her killer's satisfaction. Now she is spinning it as something creepy. How neat! How can you not doubt her testimony? And most of the civilian witnesses acted like they didn't want to be in court. Not SJ, she seemed to dig it.

Counsel Page is passionate and finishes strong:

> *I've talked to you about the failure of their motive theories; the failure of their financial motive theory, the failure of the domestic violence theory, the failure of their theory of this staged murder, the failure of their theory of lack of flight or proof of consciousness of guilt, the failure of it all together.*
>
> *Ladies and Gentlemen, when you consider the failure of all of those theories, the failure of the actual evidence to prove to you beyond a reasonable doubt what the Government is asking you to do, you know that they haven't met their burden and when they get back up here and they say to you there's no evidence*

*that he did it because we couldn't have evidence because he did it when nobody was there, so it must have been him, that's not proof beyond a reasonable doubt. It must have been him is not proof beyond a reasonable doubt.*

*Ladies and Gentlemen, Mr. Muth is not guilty.*

*Thank you.*

The government has the right to a rebuttal argument. Prosecutor Kirschner takes on defense counsel's argument point by point and is indignant that it was suggested the police and prosecution made up a theory and then tried to justify it:

*But folks, we didn't make it up. We're not in the business of making stuff up. We're in the business of presenting the witnesses and the testimony and making reasonable arguments, particularly when the evidence is so overwhelming that this man committed this murder.*

*You could have seen it coming a mile away.*

*You could have seen it coming two decades away. Nothing was made up. No argument was made without evidentiary support.*

Kirschner has the last words:

*That killing a ninety-one-year-old woman by a forty-seven-year-old man is cruel, atrocious, and heinous, and she wasn't a vulnerable person in her life, but she was a vulnerable victim in connection with the murder committed by Mr. Muth, and for those reasons we respectfully ask that you hold him accountable by convicting him of first degree murder and you find the two aggravating circumstances that the Judge has instructed on.*

*We thank you all very much for your time and attention.*

The courtroom is still. Everyone knows the public drama of the trial will now shift to the privacy of the deliberations in the jury room. It's now 3:30 p.m. I excuse the alternate jurors and briefly instruct the jury to select a foreperson and take their time in their important work.

Deputy Clerk Greg Ellis escorts the jury to the jury room. Court policy requires us to recess no later than 4:45 p.m., but I'm sure the jury is anxious to at least get started.

I go back to chambers and try to decompress. Murder trials are played for high stakes with profound consequences to the defendant, the victim's family, and the entire community. Luckily, I had excellent lawyers before me who generally respected each other, but they were appropriately aggressive with legal objections, motions, and general sparring coming at me to resolve at light speed. The trial has been stressful, and I'm tired.

Despite all the extreme attempts Muth made to avoid this day, I tried to give him a fair trial to the best of my ability. I wait in chambers for the jury's verdict, nervous, as I am in all tough cases. The inherent drama of allowing random citizens make such monumental decisions is truly a crowning hallmark of our legal system. Do they always get it right? No. But would judges always get it right? Also no. Will justice be done?

I'm too exhausted to start working on another case. I shoot the breeze with my law clerk, Heidi Hansberry, and administrative assistant, Mary Davey. We usually try and predict the jury's verdict. The government's case came in strong, particularly with SJ's testimony and the cheap flights to Iceland and other Google searches. Of course he killed her they may think! A quick guilty verdict was certainly possible.

But it was a circumstantial case, after all, and juries sometimes are very leery of convicting a defendant without more direct proof. Any break in a link in the circumstantial chain can cause doubt and sow confusion, and the defense team has certainly stirred up a lot of commotion. Key prosecution witnesses all had some question marks and explaining to do. Question marks can translate to a reasonable doubt and a not guilty verdict.

Then again, the possibility of a hung jury also looms large. The law requires a unanimous verdict of all twelve jurors. Just one stubborn, hard-headed, even irrational juror can muck up the works, whether for guilty or not guilty.

I'm a great believer in the jury system and think the jury generally gets it right. But trials are very human endeavors with all the human errors and frailties that come along with an inexact search for the truth.

The true answer to anyone's ability to predict a jury verdict? You just don't really know. Every trial lawyer and judge has walked out of a courtroom dumbfounded at a jury's verdict at one point or another. We will have to just wait and see.

We hear nothing for the next hour and fifteen minutes. I bring the jury back and instruct them to avoid any publicity. I also tell them that while it is tempting to want to talk about the case with the people they usually share their most important decisions, the law specifically prohibits them from doing just that. I tell them many counties in other states do not recess a jury's deliberations; instead they have the jury continue deliberating through the night, bringing in dinner if necessary, in order to avoid exposure to publicity and the problem of family and friends wanting to weigh in on a murder case.

I instruct them that we realize the inconvenience to the jury, and the court staff, of such a practice, so we really need them to be vigilant in this very important part of the trial. I ask them to return at 9:30 a.m. the next morning to resume their deliberations.

The next day a juror is delayed so the jury resumes its deliberation at 10:34 a.m. I allow counsel to return to their offices to await the verdict. The time passes slowly; I do some light reading for a future case. I shoot the breeze again with Heidi and Mary. I return some emails I have neglected the past few days.

Shortly after noon, Deputy Clerk Greg Ellis comes into chambers and hands me a note from the jury.

It says: "We have reached a verdict."

"I'll call the lawyers and make sure the video is up and let you know when we're ready," he says.

An hour and fifteen minutes of deliberations yesterday, and an hour and half today; two hours and forty-five minutes total, to reach a verdict in a murder case. Not very long.

I pull out my "cheat sheet," a form I use whenever I take a verdict, though I know it by heart and rarely use it. It's there as a crutch—in case I forget something. The only tricky part of the process is the polling of the jury after the foreperson announces the verdict. I have to be sure each juror agrees with the verdict and there are exact words I use when taking a poll. The polling of the jury is high drama because the solemnity of the verdict is just sinking in, and the losing party is throwing a "Hail Mary" pass in a last ditch effort to stave off defeat. Although it's very rare, occasionally a juror actually balks during the poll, changing his or her mind, and refuses to join in the verdict. In that case, I don't accept the verdict and send the jury back to continue their deliberations.

An hour later I walk into a packed courtroom. I see Drath family members, the press, lawyers from the U.S. Attorney's Office, the Public Defender Service, and curious onlookers. It is very quiet, and the atmosphere is tense.

The case is called: "The United States versus Albrecht Muth." The lawyers identify themselves for the record. I verify that the videoconferencing is up and running.

"Counsel," I say, "I have received a note from the jury at 12:03 p.m. It says, 'We have reached a verdict.'

"Are we ready for the jury?"

Both sides say they are ready.

Mr. Ellis goes back to the jury room. Everybody in the courtroom waits in total silence. I see a few reporters quietly scribbling in their notebooks. Several very long minutes pass. We're all lost in our thoughts. The back door leading to the jury room swings open and the jury files into the courtroom looking grim. No one says a word.

I turn to the jury and nod my head. I'm not using the cheat sheet.

*The Court: "Would the foreperson please rise?*

*"Ladies and gentlemen of the jury, speaking through your foreperson I have received a note which says:*

*'We have reached a verdict.'*

*"Is that correct, sir?"*

*The Foreperson: "Yes, sir."*

*The Court: "Ladies and gentlemen of the jury, again, speaking through your foreperson as to Count 1, the charge of first degree premeditated murder, how does the jury find Albrecht Muth, guilty or not guilty?"*

*The Foreperson: "Guilty."*

*The Court: "As to Count 1A, as to whether or not the murder was especially heinous, atrocious, or cruel, is the answer yes or no?"*

*The Foreperson: "Yes."*

*The Court: "As to Count 1B, that Ms. Drath was especially vulnerable due to age?"*

*The Foreperson: "Yes."*

*The Court: "Thank you, sir. You may have a seat."*

Mr. Ellis walks into the well of the court and receives the verdict form from the foreperson. He hands it me and I review it.

*The Court: "The jury verdict form conforms to the verdict announced in open court.*

*"Defense Counsel, is there a request for a poll of the jury?"*

*Defense Counsel: "There is, Your Honor. Thank you."*

*The Court: "Ladies and gentlemen, there has been a request for a poll of the jury. As I explained to you during the instructions, polling a jury is a simple procedure which allows the parties to be sure that your verdict is, in fact, unanimous. Polling means that now that the foreperson has stated your verdict I will ask each of you individually whether your verdict agrees with that announced by your foreperson. Your job in this regard is easy. If you agree with the verdict announced by your foreperson, you should simply say yes when I call you by your juror seat number. If you disagree with the verdict announced by your foreperson, you should simply say no.*

Everyone in the courtroom stares at the jury thinking the same thing: Will they be unanimous? Will one juror say no? Will the guilty verdict stand?

I take a deep breath.

*I'm going to start with the juror sitting in seat number 1. Juror number 1, do you agree with the verdict announced by your foreperson?*

*The Juror: Yes.*

*The Court: Juror number 2, do you agree with the verdict announced by your foreperson?*

*The Juror: Yes.*

*The Court: Juror number 3, do you agree with the verdict announced by your foreperson?*

*The Juror: Yes.*

*The Court: Juror number 4, do you agree with the verdict announced by your foreperson?*

*The Juror: Yes.*

*The Court: Juror number 5, do you agree with the verdict announced by your foreperson?*

*The Juror: Yes.*

*The Court: Juror number 6, do you agree with the verdict announced by your foreperson?*

*The Juror: Yes.*

*The Court: Juror number 8, do you agree with the verdict announced by your foreperson?*

*The Juror: Yes.*

*The Court: Juror number 10, do you agree with the verdict announced by your foreperson?*

*The Juror: Yes.*

*The Court: Juror number 11, do you agree with the verdict announced by your foreperson?*

*The Juror: Yes.*

*The Court: Juror number 12, do you agree with the verdict announced by your foreperson?*

*The Juror: Yes.*

*The Court: Juror number 14, do you agree with the verdict announced by your foreperson?*

*The Juror: Yes.*

*The Court: Juror number 15, do you agree with the verdict announced by your foreperson?*

*The Juror: Yes.*

*The Court: The jury has been polled, and the jury is, in fact, unanimous, and therefore, the jury's verdict shall be recorded in the court files.*

*Ladies and gentlemen, with the return of your verdict you have completed your service in this case. And before I excuse you I did want to say just a few brief things. First, now that you have completed your verdict you are permitted to talk about the case with anyone you care to, including the attorneys, who occasionally like to talk to jurors after a case is over, or members of the press or the public for that matter. There's nothing wrong or illegal or inappropriate about that at all. However, it's your right of privacy at stake, so if you want to talk about the case with anyone, you're permitted to do so; but if you don't want to talk to anyone about the case, your privacy will be respected.*

*Ladies and gentlemen, I stated at the beginning of the case that in my view, sitting on a jury is more than a right that we all share and enjoy as citizens. I believe that sitting on a jury is civic duty and an obligation. Indeed, I believe it's a high honor to serve as a juror.*

*On behalf of the court and community I want to thank you very much for your service to your court and to your community in participating and resolving this particular case. The next step in the process is I will ask for a report regarding Mr. Muth, and when I receive that report, in due course, I'll set a date for sentencing, and then I'll impose sentence, and that will conclude this particular case.*

*Ladies and gentlemen, with my thanks and appreciation, you are now excused. Thank you.*

The jury quietly leaves the courtroom. After a verdict is taken, whether for guilty or not guilty, it is only human nature to watch the defendant's reaction to his fate. Since the video screen is not showing Muth's image, no one, other than Alvin Milton, the video technician at the hospital, can see Muth's response to the verdict. Viola Drath's family members are hugging each other and crying.

I set a date for sentencing. The trial of Albrecht Muth is over.

## A World That Is Unrecognizable to Me

The original sentencing date had to be converted into a status date. Muth had maintained his religious fast/binge eating act and was not medically cleared to come to court. On March 19, 2014, I advised him by videoconference that he had a right to be present at his sentencing but, like the trial, that right could be waived if he did not resume eating on a full-time basis. I set a new sentencing date of April 30, 2014. I warned him if he's not medically cleared, the sentencing would go forward in his absence. A week before the sentencing Muth's status had not changed. The sentencing would proceed without him in the courtroom, but again he could view the court hearing by videoconference.

I settled in to think about my options for sentencing. First Degree Murder carries a mandatory sentence of thirty years' incarceration with a maximum of sixty years. There is no more parole in the District of Columbia. A sentenced defendant serves his entire sentence with one exception. If he behaves while in prison and does not accumulate disciplinary actions, his sentence can be reduced by no more than fifteen percent for "good time."

However, since the jury found the aggravating factors that Ms. Drath's death was heinous, atrocious, or cruel, and that she was a vulnerable victim, Muth could be sentenced to life in prison without the possibility of release. Life without the possibility of release means what it says—Muth would die in prison.

In light of the trial and extensive competency hearings, I knew more about Muth's life, background, and criminal history than I would have in a typical case. I had ordered a presentence report, and though it was thorough, it provided no new information.

The government filed a Sentencing Memorandum seeking life without release. It attached two Victim Impact Statements from Ms. Drath's two daughters, outlining the effect this cruel murder had on them and their family.

One daughter stated in part: "I miss my mother... I miss her wisdom, her advice, her insights.... Singing carols on Christmas Eve... her visits to my home in California."

The other daughter said in part: "That her life would be stopped sometime in the early hours of August 12, 2011, with such violence is something I will never be able to forget or accept. The violence of the attack, the long road to trial, and the unwanted publicity has been an ordeal that has left me feeling the world is cruel and unforgiving, that justice can be manipulated and delayed, and that my family has been exploited and exposed by the press and so-called 'bloggers' for self-serving purposes....

"My wish would have been to protect my family, but I could not... I also dread the day when I will have to tell my grandchildren about their great-grandmother and how she died. I only hope that we can shelter them from the public side of this tragedy....

"My health has suffered and my peace of mind is gone. I am trying to navigate a world that is unrecognizable to me..."

Ordinarily, the defense would have filed its own memorandum setting forth its requested sentence. I was not surprised that none was filed. I assumed Muth was probably uncooperative with defense counsel.

When I was a criminal defense attorney, I often wondered before a client's sentencing the extent to which a judge had completely decided the sentence before he or she entered the courtroom. I've learned on this side of the bench that there's no hard-and-fast rule. I spend a lot of time before a sentencing, weighing all the important factors that should be considered because I am leery of letting the passionate emotions of the victim's or defendant's family have too much sway in the courtroom. On the other hand, sometimes the courtroom dynamics can change my mind. A victim's daughter's pain or a defendant's legitimate remorse can be so much more intense and convincing in person than it is in writing.

I studied all aspects of Muth's case. I felt that I had all the information I needed to impose a just sentence, but would keep an open mind to see what developed in the courtroom.

On April 30, 2014, the courtroom is again crowded. Muth is once again on videoconference. His image is on the screen for all to see.

I announce that I have reviewed all the submitted documents and we are ready to go forward with sentencing. I turn to the government.

Prosecutor Kirschner identifies family members in the audience and says they are content to have their written victim impact statements speak for them. They do not wish to speak today. I honor their wishes.

Kirschner speaks in a passionate voice as he reviews the brutal facts at trial. He is always professional, though I see his personal sympathy for the Drath family and contempt for Muth shine through. He concludes:

> *And that's what's most important here, is the Defendant took Ms. Drath from her friends, from her family, from her three grandchildren, from her then one great-grandchild. There have since been twin great-grandchildren that were born to Ms. Drath's grandson and his wife. And she never had the opportunity to meet them. And then his steadfast, ridiculous orchestrations trying to find a way to get out from under responsibility for what he did. First, trying to be civilly committed in lieu of being criminally tried. When that didn't work, and Your Honor concluded that he was competent to stand trial, the only reasonable conclusion based on the evidence, he stood up and announced 'there will be no trial.' And he did his level best to avoid being present for the commencement of the case.*
>
> *But as the Court told him literally ten times over, you have every right to be present, and all you have to do is stop your starvation campaign. He thought he was going to put up hurdles that the criminal justice system could not surmount. You know, this is a man who doesn't know what it's like to take responsibility for anything he has done in his life. And he has*

> *done little that was not from a platform of fraud and conning people and misperception and misdirection. That's the life he lived.*
>
> *For all of those reasons, the Government asks the Court respectfully to consider life without the possibility of release. And if the Court is not inclined to impose that dramatic sentence, we would ask for a sentence of upwards of fifty years. Something that ensures Mr. Muth will not be out in the community again looking for his next victim of physical abuse or his life as a con man.*

There is a still silence in the courtroom as Kirschner sits down next to co-counsel Bach.

I turn to defense counsel Page. She tells me Muth declines the opportunity to speak for himself. Instead, counsel reads a short letter from him, which states in part:

> *I affirm my innocence of the charge against me. I did not kill my wife. My conviction is a miscarriage of justice. As General Soleimani told General Petraeus, my wife was killed by renegade elements of the Iranian revolutionary guard core who was targeting me.*

Counsel sits down stone-faced. She must know what's coming.

I hear nothing today that changes my mind. I review my notes one more time. I'm ready to impose sentence.

> *In this case, like in any other sentencing, the Court is required to weigh a number of different factors, including the protection of society, deterrence not only of Mr. Muth but for others who may contemplate committing crimes, to afford a sense of retribution that justice is being done and that the punishment fits the crime, as well as the rehabilitation of the offender.*

*In weighing these various factors, the Court always considers what could be mitigating factors or aggravating factors. In this case, the Court finds far from being a miscarriage of justice, as Mr. Muth claims, the evidence of his guilt was overwhelming. For a circumstantial case, it was about as strong a case as I've seen. The Court also finds there are no mitigating circumstances. Mr. Muth didn't accept responsibility for his conduct. He certainly didn't show and hasn't shown any remorse. Nor is there anything in Mr. Muth's background or history that would warrant consideration of a lesser sentence. Indeed, from what I gather, although this is still not quite clear because the source is Mr. Muth, at least from his version of events, he grew up in a very privileged background and went to schools and universities. This is from Mr. Muth.*

*Rather than finding any mitigating circumstances, he has, in essence, continued his charade of creating different personas. The Court heard testimony of him being a South American mercenary, a European count, an Iraqi general. And now, apparently he has taken the pose of being some type of religious zealot in what has been, in my view, a rather transparent attempt to avoid justice in this case.*

*So setting aside his fascination with celebrities and the decorative eye patch and the fancy uniform, the evidence in this case is overwhelming that Mr. Muth is nothing more than a common, serial domestic violence abuser, made worse when he drinks, who subjected Ms. Drath, unfortunately, to years of ever-increasing abuse. Sadly and tragically, like many domestic violence victims, she didn't cut ties, although I think she was planning on cutting ties.*

*From everything I've learned about Ms. Drath, she seemed to have been a wonderful person who was*

> *a very valued member of the community and a family member that was deeply loved and cherished, and she should have passed surrounded by her family. Not beaten to death, and bludgeoned to death, and really in some ways tortured by Mr. Muth in the middle of the night.*
>
> *The jury found aggravating factors that she was of a vulnerable age… This certainly was a heinous, atrocious, and cruel crime. Thus, the Court believes that the predominant factor in sentencing is protection of the community and a sense that justice is being done.*
>
> *So, therefore, it is the judgment of the Court, that defendant be sentenced to fifty years' incarceration.*

I advise Muth that he has the right to appeal his conviction and sentence.

I ask counsel if there is anything further. Both say that there is not.

I recess court and leave the bench.

## The Pursuit of Justice Is Rarely Perfect

Two years later, almost to the day of Muth's sentencing, I received in chambers a Joint Motion for Reduction of Sentence, signed by both the defense and government counsel. The motion indicates the parties have cut a deal in what they say is their mutual interest, as well as the public interest. In exchange for a reduction of his sentence from fifty to thirty years, Muth agrees to waive his right to appeal his conviction and sentence. The motion says that Ms. Drath's daughters "have assented to this resolution of the case."

To say the least, this is an unusual end to a murder case on appeal.

I can well understand why the government and the victim's family would accept such an agreement. Trying Muth by videoconference had never been done in the Superior Court. There's always a chance the Court of Appeals would find my decision unconstitutional, reverse the case, and order a new trial. The deal locks in the conviction and sentence. The case is finally over. And thirty years' incarceration in a federal prison is very hard time, and a very long time, for a forty-eight-year-old man.

But why would Muth accept such a deal? Innocent defendants may make deals to get out of prison early and give up the fight for exoneration. But the best case for him is that he receives every possible day of "good time" and is released in his seventies.

His lawyers must have given him their best advice about his chances for a new trial and concluded it did not look good. And even if he received a new trial, the evidence of his guilt was not going away. There was no reason to believe a second jury would find him not guilty. Maybe the possibility of living as a free man for the remainder of his life was reason enough for him to make the deal.

Some defendants seek forgiveness for their crimes and understand that doing penance is the road to grace. Given the fantastic life he had created and his obstructive conduct leading up to the trial, I had my doubts about Muth's motivation. But I didn't really know. I would like to think that Muth came to terms with his true self, the self he spent a lifetime hiding, and was trying to make amends for his crime and to his victim.

I had the discretion and power to reject the Joint Motion if I believed the negotiated sentence did not comply with the law or the result was not fair to the defendant, the government, or the community. There was no doubt but that the Joint Motion asked for a sentence that is recognized by the law and a defendant can certainly waive or give up his right to appeal. But was the resolution fair to the community? Although the pursuit of justice is rarely perfect, I believed thirty years in prison for Muth in exchange for the final closure of the case was fair and just to all.

I granted the motion.

# Acknowledgments

A special recognition goes to Allen Chaney. Allen's courage, grace, and generosity were the inspiration for this journey.

A shout out to my new friends at Twelve Tables Press, publisher Steve Errick and production editor Sharon D. Ray, for their guidance, patience, and expertise as we worked as a team to complete the book.

My deepest thanks and appreciation to my family, friends, and colleagues who supported and encouraged me in the writing of this book: Julie Blair, Jeb Boasberg, Frank Burgess, John Burgess, Karen Buck Burgess, Elkanah Burns, Rainey Brandt, Ethan Canan, Lukas Canan, Stacy J. Canan, Gabriel Canan-Zucker, Marisa Canan-Zucker, Nathan Canan-Zucker, Lee Coykendall, Mary Davey, Angela Davis, John Dedakis, Dennis Doyle, Martha Doyle, Marc Feldman, Jerry Fisher, Susan Fitzgerald, Gus Giannakoulias, George Greer, Ruth Guyer, Richard Hawks, Susan Schott Hawks, Barbara Horne-Pedersdoff, Glen Kirschner, Gerry Kittner, Ken Kunken, Ralph Lindeman, Ken Long, Kerry Maliwista, Judy Marx, Andrea Carla Michaels, Nicole Miller, Greg Mize, Andrew Norman, Mike Phillips, John Scheibel, Rick Seltzer, David Shneyer, Peter Slevin, Greg Smith, Sydney Smith, Larry

Suffredin, Sara Taber, Heidi Turner, Katie Weidmann, Fred Weisberg, Jessica Westerman, and Jon Zucker.

Grateful acknowledgment to Temple University Press and The New Press for permission to reprint "Burning at the Wire: The Execution of John Evans" and "Rough Justice," respectively.